# Cultures of Ageing

# Cultures of Ageing
## Self, citizen and the body

CHRIS GILLEARD

and

PAUL HIGGS

*An imprint of* **Pearson Education**

Harlow, England · London · New York · Reading, Massachusetts · San Francisco
Toronto · Don Mills, Ontario · Sydney · Tokyo · Singapore · Hong Kong · Seoul
Taipei · Cape Town · Madrid · Mexico City · Amsterdam · Munich · Paris · Milan

**Pearson Education Limited**

Edinburgh Gate
Harlow
Essex CM20 2JE
England

and Associated Companies around the world

*Visit us on the World Wide Web at*
*www.pearsoneduc.com*

---

First edition published in Great Britain in 2000

ISBN 0 582 35641 5

*British Library Cataloguing-in-Publication Data*
A CIP catalogue record for this book can be obtained from the British Library.

*Library of Congress Cataloging-in-Publication Data*
Gilleard, C.J.
   Cultures of ageing : self, citizen, and the body / Chris Gilleard and Paul Higgs.
     p.  cm.
   Includes bibliographical references and index.
   ISBN 0–582–35641–5 (alk. paper)
      1. Aging—Social aspects.  2. Gerontology.  I. Higgs, Paul.  II. Title.
HQ1061.G54   2000
305.26—dc21                                              00–037366

Typeset in $10\frac{1}{2}/14\frac{1}{2}$ pt Sabon by 35
Produced by Pearson Education Malaysia Sdn Bhd
Transferred to digital print on demand, 2008
Printed and bound by CPI Antony Rowe, Eastbourne

# CONTENTS

# PREFACE

Plans to write this book began ten years ago. At that time, ageing was still represented in academic textbooks as either the product of biology or the outcome of social policy. Since then ageing has become more evidently inserted into the cultural world. The emerging interest in the 'third age' and the recategorization of later life as 'post-working' life constitute a significant shift in our approach to later life and the leisure opportunities it presents. Bowed neither by a weakened body nor an empty purse, many retired people now experience an infinitely richer lifestyle than that envisaged in the various old age pension Acts passed by Western governments in the late nineteenth and early twentieth centuries.

Social gerontology remains tied to concerns over lack and need, and still defines much of its subject matter around these themes. Attempts to move it away from this emphasis upon disability and the impoverishments of age are still met with considerable resistance. Attention paid to third-age lifestyles is often seen as misguided, reflecting either an insensitivity to, or an ignorance of, the 'real' needs of pensioners.

While a small minority of ageing individuals have been acclaimed by the academic community as heroic – Maggie Kuhn of the Gray Panthers being archetypal as the politicized pensioner fighting for her rights – those other minorities who mask their age by insisting upon remaining 'beautiful people' are derided or ignored. By insisting upon loss and lack as the necessary criteria for a sociological interest in ageing, social gerontology has structured a discipline of ageing that can see it only in these outmoded terms.

No doubt it is true that the extremes of life are more interesting to portray than the modes. Our aim, however, is not to draw attention to examples such as Sophia Loren and Clint Eastwood as the epitomes of an ageing counter-culture. Rather it is to acknowledge the sheer variety of practices that, for a growing number of people, now make up the experience of later adult life. It is also to understand more of the cultural, social and economic processes that are sustaining and supporting that variety. Our subject, therefore, is the fragmentation of modern culture to which ageing is now a party. If biology has been seen to impose a growing homogeneity in experience with increasing age, there are also cultural processes at work that increasingly challenge such uniformity, a uniformity that had been sustained by some two hundred years of social policy. The outcome that this dialectic will have over the course of the twenty-first century is not yet clear. But what is clear is that Tom Paine's suggestion, back in 1791, to establish a pension of £6 per year for those aged 50 and over will be forever seen as a product of its time, as will any assumption that such 'pensioners' constitute 'the aged in need'.

Times change and ageing too is changed by time. The cultures of ageing outlined in our book will no doubt become more diverse over time and our understanding of ageing more contingent. Nevertheless, the themes of self and identity in later life, the material expression of ageing and the civic representation of post-working life are central dimensions through which that process of differentiation is taking place and, we believe, will continue to do so.

*Chris Gilleard*
*Paul Higgs*

# ACKNOWLEDGEMENTS

The authors would like to thank Martin Hyde, Ian Jones, Carolyn Richardson and Graham Scambler for their helpful comments on earlier versions of the book.

# CHAPTER 1

# Introduction

The argument of this book is straightforward. We believe that since 'old age' has become a predictable expectation of the adult lifespan, ageing has ceased to be understandable in terms of any common or totalizing experience. It is no longer the fixed and homogeneous process of personal and physiological decay by which it has been understood for much of recorded history. Ageing has become more complex, differentiated and ill defined, experienced from a variety of perspectives and expressed in a variety of ways at different moments in people's lives. Now a near-universal experience, ageing is the subject of intense personal reflection and widespread public debate. Central to contemporary fears of finitude and failure, it is the antithesis of a youth culture that is itself growing old.[1] The centrality and universality that ageing has achieved serve only to increase the contradictions it embodies. It is this fragmentation of a highly socialized biological process which makes ageing such a key feature of the times in which we live and which is the subject of our book.

Our argument has many links with those approaches in gerontology which treat ageing as a complex and diverse entity made up of numerous psychological social and biological processes each related yet potentially independent from one another.[2] However, it is not our intention to pin down ageing along any set of foundationalist parameters. Instead, our concern lies with the various social meanings by which the contemporary experience of ageing is structured. These meanings and the structures that express them have become, we argue, less coherent and more contradictory than ever before. As a result, there is a gradual and irreversible fragmentation of ageing as a socialized attribute. Nevertheless, despite, or perhaps because of, this fragmentation, ageing is an attribute that an increasing number of adults must address, whether or not they accept, ignore or reject it. Distilling and analyzing the cultural precipitate from these various encounters with ageing, together with the structural contexts in which these encounters take place, form the main theme of our book. Choosing to adopt this explicitly 'cultural' approach, we also intend a critique of those functional and structural models of ageing that continue to dominate not just social gerontology but the whole gamut of 'ageing studies'.

## Cultural studies and ageing

All cultures have their material bases, which they in turn influence. The cultural and material expressions of 'ageing' are shaped by existing social relationships. The contradictions that make up the emerging cultures of ageing exist within an increasingly reflexive modernity. Their origins can be traced through the social history of the second half of the twentieth century. At the same time these processes must be set in the context of demographic changes of much longer duration. It is this combination of population, social and cultural change that provides the main framework by which we seek to approach and understand 'ageing'. While it is conceivable that the demographic changes will be reversible, it is highly implausible that there will be any return to earlier demographic structures. Likewise the contemporary fragmentation of the cultural texts and practices that make up the lived experience of 'ageing' is unlikely to be a temporary and short-lived affair of merely passing curiosity. Rather it seems probable that ageing will be expressed in increasingly unstable and contested practices and contradictory texts for well into the twenty-first century.

We have called our book *Cultures of Ageing: self, citizen and the body* to give priority to the role of culture in shaping the experience and expression of ageing. By culture we are referring to the various and complex systems of meaning that constitute everyday life. By and large we are following the structural conception of culture outlined by Thompson in his book *Ideology and Modern Culture*, involving:

> the study of symbolic forms – that is meaningful actions, objects, and expressions of various kinds – in relation to the historically specific and socially structured contexts and processes within which and by means of which these symbolic forms are produced transmitted and received.[3]

Our aim is to examine the systems of meaning that 'ageing' takes on, both in individual lives and in social institutions and how those systems of meaning are located in the changing social structures of the twentieth century.

The appearance and consolidation of 'cultural studies' as an academic field of study did much to stimulate a renewed interest in the concept of culture within the social sciences.[4] This 'cultural turn' has taken a long time to penetrate social gerontology. Stimulated to a large extent by the pioneering work of Mike Featherstone and Mike Hepworth there are signs of a growing interest in how 'ageing' is treated in everyday texts, in the media, in advertisements as well as in art.[5] There is also an emerging interest in the everyday experiences of older people that is not preoccupied with their health and potential frailty.[6]

Making sense of the chronology of the lifecourse and the processes of growing up and growing older has been part of human culture for a very long time. The various divisions made within the human lifespan and their characterization may have changed somewhat over the centuries but they all have taken as unchallenged the idea that there clearly exists a singular lifecourse through which all men (and women, though most historical writings have focused upon the male lifecourse) must pass.[7] Only in the late twentieth century has the idea emerged that human agency can be exercised over how ageing will be expressed and experienced. The assumption that individuals can choose the manner in which they wish to mark out their lives is a radical break with the past. It is the erosion of this unitary 'ages of life' culture which is the principal concern of this book.

We have chosen to write about 'ageing' rather than 'old age'. Old age does not figure in the 'plastic' or 'flexible' lifecourse of men and women in current society. Rather, it acts as a kind of reference point around which various cultures of ageing revolve. Old age itself is not a site that is seriously contested or challenged. It remains a period of life that is excluded, marginalized or institutionalized. Whilst the changes that accompany ageing are being reframed and revalued – the 'empty nest', retirement, the menopause, greying, and so on – the changes that tip a person into 'old age' cannot be so easily reframed or transgressed. One may speak of nursing-home cultures, cultures of health care or even cultures of dying, but old age remains an obdurately singular category – a

3

future end that most people choose to avoid however long their lives may be.[8]

It would be disingenuous to completely separate ageing from old age. The various cultures of ageing each have their own representation of old age. We would argue, however, that it is principally by their *resistance to old age* that these cultures are shaped and defined. Whether or not they offer ways to ward off old age, shrink it to a bitter but palatable pill or prepare for it as an eventual resting place, no organizations or institutions seek to portray old age to the individual as either an aspirational commodity to choose or a socially valued process to join. Old age lies sullen and unchanging – represented as the end of the social; a point in life after which further choices are irrelevant.

## 'Postmodernity' and cultural fragmentation

Within those disciplines that make up cultural studies, it is impossible to ignore the concept of postmodernism. As Kellner has observed, 'discussions of postmodernism began in the field of cultural theory'.[9] However, if culture is 'one of the most complicated words in the English language',[10] postmodernism must be a strong competitor for definitional complexity. Almost everything written about postmodernism and postmodernity makes mention of its terminological ambiguity and equally often its insubstantiality. Still, the term has become so widespread that it is difficult to deny its power to represent the 'zeitgeist' of our times. Despite, or perhaps because of, this, it is a term that leads to continual disagreement about its parameters, a tension that has made writing this book a longer, more protracted and possibly more challenging task than was originally conceived. At the risk of oversimplification, there are two general formulations regarding the postmodernity/postmodernism debate. One is supportive of the idea that everything has changed while the other takes a more nuanced, maybe cautious, approach to a world which may have changed but which nevertheless remains amenable to modernist methods of inquiry.

The first perspective argues that postmodernity is a shorthand way of capturing the sense of difference and ambiguity that touches all aspects of life in contemporary society. It is expressed most vividly in the way in which the new century is being greeted. Ideas of a future destined to deliver further steady progress in the improvement of the human condition no longer carry the conviction they did at the beginning of the twentieth century.[11] There is no obvious consensus about what constitutes the good life or how it can be achieved – although there is little disagreement that it should be available to all. There is an excess of information, a 'proliferation' of signs that make all interpretations of social phenomena temporary and equivocal. The more real insights we seem to have of reality, the less convinced we are of its substance. Terms and boundaries are blurred. Experience seems no longer a guide but a goal in itself. While there is more 'information' than before this only makes every statement seem even less significant. Too many 'authoritative voices' are heard for any voice to be authoritative. What can be imagined is much more than previous imaginations; at the same time everything seems less realizable. There is no longer a common trust in any collective means of ensuring an individually satisfying life or even a socially validated one. More weight is placed upon human agency and choice, but the emphasis is on selection rather than action. We are preoccupied with choosing and what the outcomes of our choices might be.

Political concerns are dominated by issues of recognition and representation – of being seen and of being heard. Yet, the numerous attempts to not be ignored make difficult the establishment of any common voice and any common understanding of what social institutions can or should articulate. In postmodernity there is a wish to represent the worth of the individual but less desire to redistribute social wealth. The circuits of capital accumulation seem to act as a directing force, but a force that few believe has a real direction. Global systems of speculation have created a rapidly changing virtual economy more powerful but less predictable than the systems of national capital that forged the modern world. Against a background of an unknowable reality, the known world is changing and, for now at least, postmodernity represents that change.

The alternative view derives from more traditional social theories where the appearance of things is treated separately from their underlying causal reality. From this perspective the distinction between postmodernity and postmodernism is central. In rejecting the idea that we live in postmodernity what is being rejected is the idea that social structures are beyond understanding or indeed that they have any structured nature that can be understood. The epistemological relativism of postmodernism provides no way of studying any issue other than as commentary; postmodern scholarship too easily slides into pose, pretence and pastiche.

Locating the position of humanity within the flux of images created by modern communications in a global commodity market does not invalidate an analysis of the structural regularities that give rise to a postmodern culture. Writers such as Jameson have sought to establish the continuities that link the more ordered realities of modernism with the cultural overload of postmodernism.[12] The subtitle of his book on postmodernism, *The Cultural Logic of Late Capitalism*, provides the beginnings of an argument that locates postmodern culture within the unfolding dynamic of the capitalist mode of production. To this Harvey has added the globalizing dimension of contracting time and space.[13] From less overtly Marxist positions, writers such as Giddens have tried to use the insights provided by postmodernists to describe a state of 'high modernity' or 'reflexive modernization'. This is a preferred periodization as it is seen to capture better the processes of a rationalizing modernity, which disembed individuals from traditions and force them to be agentic and self-directing. The compression of time and space combines with the plethora of sources of information forcing each person to constantly make choices about their lives in an era of 'manufactured uncertainty'.

Rejecting the need for epistemological relativism by stressing the central role of global capitalism in making the world appear chaotic creates the possibility of seeing many of the facets of the modern world as possessing a coherence rather than an unintelligibility. The growth of a global market has commodified many aspects of culture. The distinction between tradition and modernity has collapsed as even tradition is treated as a choice rather than the necessary underpinning of everyday life. If modernizing practices became concrete through government regulation of social life and the technologies of expert control, postmodern culture has turned everything into a matter of personal choice – policed by the technologies of consumer research. No longer directed by a single 'authoritative' voice, each individual must deal with multiple sources of expert advice vying for attention and closure. Predicated on the notion of consumer sovereignty, individuals must increasingly construct themselves and their relationships with the world from a variety of discourses, none of which is capable of providing a totally coherent understanding.

What these differing perspectives share is the recognition that much of the restlessness of late modern/postmodern society stems from the expansion of retail capital and the relentless commodification of everyday life. It is not just the commodification of everyday life that is distinct; it is also its expansion. The cultural space in which people live is broader, more complex, more contradictory and in many ways richer than ever before. The emphasis upon choice that is the hallmark of consumer society raises continuous questions over self and identity – who am I; what do I want; what represents my best interests; what marks my individuality; what meanings am I to give to the shape and direction that my life takes? The expression of individual identity requires an organizing principle and the body increasingly has come to represent that principle. As physical beings we consume – goods, services, experiences – and as physical beings we experience our distinct separateness from others. At the same time what constitutes the appropriate regulation of bodies and identities permeates political thinking. The precise articulation of such policies is a matter of shifting opinion – but its central theme is 'the conduct of conduct', establishing systems of self-government that emphasize personal entitlements linked to personal responsibilities. Described as 'advanced liberalism' the state seeks to govern 'through the regulated choices of individual citizens'[14] linked through complex and multilayered communities of interest. Set in the context of these postmodern concerns over the fragmentation of identity, the body and citizenship, ageing has come centre stage.

## The centrality of ageing

What relevance do these postmodern concerns have to the formation of cultures of ageing? In part, the answer is because the ageing of populations has coincided with the working through of the modernist project, which brought these issues to the fore. At the turn of the twentieth century a marked decline in fertility and infant mortality initiated a period of continuing growth in the size of that segment of the population aged 60 and over. Now, for the very first time, the European population contains as many people over 60 as it does children under 15. By the year 2025, estimates suggest numerical parity across Europe between those under 21 and those over 60 years old.[15] Societies with this kind of age structure have no precedent – as Laslett first emphasized in his book on the third age[16] and as Paul Wallace has more emphatically announced in his recent UK bestseller *Agequake*.[17]

The rise in the numbers of people aged 60 and over has taken place alongside the evolution of the modern state. Increasingly, chronological age has come to occupy an important signifier of social and civic identity. An individual's date of birth provides a key element in virtually every economic and social transaction he or she undertakes in modern society.[18] Not knowing one's age or one's date of birth has become symptomatic of mental impairment – representing as it were the individualized collapse of civilization.[19] Almost every other adult birthday card seems obliged to make some, usually humorous, reference to ageing. Social and cultural distinctions increasingly are made with reference to particular age cohorts – generation Xers; thirty-somethings; baby boomers; the over-fifties; third agers; senior citizens; OAPs; the oldest old; etc. The decade-based dating of modern fashions, cultures and consumer items gives enhanced significance to time and ageing in everyday life.

At first sight, the increase in the numbers of older people might suggest greater opportunities for intragenerational solidarity and a strengthening political representation of and by older people. Precisely the opposite seems to have happened. Age is more a site of contradiction than of community. Instead of thinking of ours as a homogenized 'ageing society', what has emerged is a variety of potentially competing cultures of ageing, none of which is keen to identify itself with the old age that the policies of the 'postmodern' state address. It is increasingly meaningless to consider 'age' as conferring some common social identity or to treat 'older people' as a distinct social group acting out of shared concerns and common interests. The growing disparities of wealth within the retired population and the concomitant rise of lifestyle consumerism mean that more and more 'sites of distinction' are emerging which fragment and render less possible any common cultural position that can be popularly represented as 'ageing'.

These various fragmentary cultures of ageing have come to occupy a central position within postmodernity for a number of reasons. More people are reaching retirement age and those that do experience an ever-larger part of their lives as retired people. The arena of ageing is simply a lot larger than before, with all the variety that larger numbers bring. Secondly, the majority of people reaching retirement age are wealthier and have more disposable income than before. Not only are they better off than previous retired generations but in many cases they are better off in retirement than they were for much of their working lives. In short, people have more resources through which to shape their retirement, enabling a greater engagement with contemporary 'lifestyle culture'. Thirdly the body has become a cultural focus for adults of all ages. Nearly all age groups view health as the most important attribute in life. This widespread concern with improving health and personal well-being is reflected in an ever-widening participation in personal exercise, greater attention to diet and weight, the selective consumption of 'health' foods, vitamins and mineral supplements and the active exploration of self-expression. Fourthly, those who helped shape the post-war 'youth culture' – the baby-boomer generation – are themselves approaching 'retirement' age, confounding ideas of what it means to be 'old'. This 'ageing' of post-war youth culture has established a complex pattern of recycled consumption ensuring that successive generations continue to share in the self-centred preoccupations of consumer society. Finally, the changing nature of the contract between citizen and state that has emerged in recent decades has meant that the financial possibilities of retirement are becoming less determined by the state's pension and welfare provisions. Those who are now retiring derive more of their retirement lifestyle from non-state sources of income and wealth, reflecting their own particular histories of employment, earnings and savings, household consumption patterns and personal expenditure preferences – patterns which are growing ever more diverse as the nature of working life changes.

In sum, ageing has come to occupy such a central position within postmodern culture because there is more 'age' about than ever before, more varied resources to shape its experience, more commonalities across the whole of adulthood established by post-war consumer culture and more sources of 'conflict' around the social regulation and expression of ageing.[20] It is time for a significant and radical rethink within social gerontology to more adequately acknowledge this transformation.

# Notes

1 The concern for social and cultural finitude is evidenced by the popularity of Francis Fukayama's 'Hegelian' essay on the 'End of history' (Fukuyama, F. (1992) *The End of History and the Last Man*, The Free Press, New York). Whether this *fin de siècle* sensibility is qualitatively distinct from that of the last century is arguable; certainly it pervades a much wider range of disciplines and encompasses a much broader social compass.

2 See for example Hayflick's account of the findings of the Baltimore Longitudinal Study of Aging: 'There is no single aging process, . . . there is no general pattern of aging applicable to all of our organs, . . . age changes are highly individualized . . .' (Hayflick, L. (1994) *How and Why We Age*, Ballantine Books, New York, pp. 148–9).

3 Thompson, J.B. (1990) *Ideology and Modern Culture*, Basil Blackwood, Oxford, p. 136.

4 Accounts of the emergence of cultural studies as a social science discipline can be found in Storey, J. (1993) *An Introduction to Cultural Theory and Popular Culture*, Harvester Wheatsheaf, London, in Munns, J. and Rajan, G. (1995) *A Cultural Studies Reader: History, Theory, Practice*, Longman, New York and in Turner, G. (1996) *British Cultural Studies: an Introduction*, Routledge, London.

5 See Featherstone, M. and Hepworth, M. (1989) 'Ageing and old age: reflections on the postmodern lifecourse', in B. Bytheway, T. Keil, P. Allatt and A. Bryman (eds), *Being and Becoming Old: Sociological Approaches to Later Life*, Sage, London; also Featherstone, M. and Hepworth, M. (1993) 'Images of ageing', in J. Bond, P. Coleman and S. Peace (eds), *Ageing in Society: an Introduction to Social Gerontology*, Sage, London; also Featherstone, M. and Hepworth, M. (1998) 'Ageing, the lifecourse and the sociology of embodiment', in G. Scambler and P. Higgs (eds), *Modernity, Medicine and Health,* Routledge, London. See also Blaikie, A. (1999) *Ageing and Popular Culture*, Cambridge University Press, Cambridge.

6 Illustrative of the gap between the foci of gerontological research and the concerns and interests of 'senior citizens' is the directory of one of the main websites for older people – 'Seniors on line'. 'Health and fitness' and 'disabilities' make up just two out of 64 topics that members can gather information about: see *Seniors Internet Resource Center*, http://www.ageofreason.com.

7 The opening chapter of Philippe Aries' book, *Centuries of Childhood*, reviews some of the historical writing on 'the ages of life' (Aries, P. (1973) *Centuries of Childhood*, Penguin Books, Harmondsworth, pp. 13–20). The significance of Aries' account of ages and stages has been questioned. Minois, for example, has argued that: 'the theories of the ages of life which flourished in the Middle Ages were only abstract dissertations, intellectuals' games, which did not correspond with any practical distinctions' (Minois, G. (1989) *A History of Ageing*, Polity Press, London, p. 5). Despite arguing that 'old age was not recognised as such in the texts', Minois nevertheless manages to spend the remaining three hundred pages of his book outlining ancient and mediaeval accounts of that 'unrecognised' period of life called 'old age'.

8 Recent US research has shown that men and women aged 65 and over prefer almost any other term than 'old age' as a descriptor of their own status (Chafetz, P.K., Holmes, H., Lande, K., Childress, E. and Glazer, H.R. (1998) 'Older adults and the news media: utilization, opinions and preferred reference terms', *The Gerontologist*, 38: 481–9).

9 Kellner, D. (1988) 'Postmodernism as social theory: some challenges and problems', *Theory, Culture & Society*, 5, p. 239.

10 Williams, R. (1983) *Keywords*, Fontana, London, p. 87.

11 See the introductory chapter of Jay, M. and Neve, M. (eds) (1900) *A Fin de Siècle Reader*, Penguin, Harmondsworth.

12 Jameson, F. (1991) *Postmodernism, or, The Cultural Logic of Late Capitalism*, Verso, London.

13 Harvey, D. (1989) *The Condition of Post-Modernity: an Enquiry into the origins of Cultural Change*, Basil Blackwell, Oxford. Other writers have addressed the same issue – e.g. Lash, S. and Urry, J. (1994) *Economies of Signs and Space*, Sage, London.

14 Rose, N. (1996) 'Governing "advanced" liberal democracies', in A. Barry, T. Osborne and N. Rose (eds), *Foucault and Political Reason*, UCL Press, London, pp. 37–64.

15 United Nations (1999) *World Population Prospects: the 1998 Revision*, United Nations, New York.

16 Laslett, P. (1989) *A Fresh Map of Life: the Emergence of the Third Age*, Weidenfeld and Nicholson, London.

17 Wallace, P. (1999) *Agequake*, Nicholas Brealey Publishing, London.

18 Hayflick points out that birth certificates only became compulsory in England in 1837 and in the United States they are 'a relatively recent development' of the turn of the last century – the timing differing from state to state. See Hayflick, L. (1994) *How and Why We Age*, Ballantine Books, New York, pp. 195–203.

19 See almost any compendium of mental status tests used in geriatric practice – e.g. Gilleard, C. and Christie, J.E. (1990) 'Behavioural and cognitive problems in the elderly', in D.F. Peck and C.M. Shapiro (eds), *Measuring Human Problems*, Wiley & Sons, Chichester, pp. 241–79.

20 As we shall argue later, the 'centrality' of age may seem, at times, hidden beneath contemporary culture's concerns with youth, health and fitness. Though these traits contrast with their 'other' – age, disease and disability – the desire to retain youth health and fitness *at all ages* provides an increasingly common theme across successive post-war generations.

# CHAPTER 2

# From political economy to the culture of personal identity

Sociology and social theory have undergone a considerable change in recent years. The dominance of grand narrative approaches such as Functionalism and Marxism has been challenged by a number of de-centring influences such as feminism, theories of difference, poststructuralism and postmodernism. The reasons for this have been discussed at length elsewhere.[1] What is most significant about these changes has been the way that issues of agency and identity have come to be regarded as more important than structural determinacy. This shift is equally evident in sociological approaches to ageing and old age. Classical sociology paid little attention to old age and ageing. The study of old age was limited to medical texts and old people made up a small and insignificant fraction of the general population. The first real analysis of the position of those over retirement age was provided by Talcott Parsons himself. He saw retirement as constituting a loss of role and therefore of integration into society. Out of this structural tradition came Cummings' seminal theory of disengagement, which stressed the mutual benefit that older people's disengagement from society brought to themselves and their society. Reacting against this Parsonian functionalism but equally concerned with the bigger picture were those writers who, from a neo-Marxist tradition, stressed the need to see 'old age' from the perspective of political economy. For them, the key feature about old age was its status as a category of redundant labour around which social policies had been constructed. The general destabilization of grand narratives in the social sciences has begun to impact upon these traditional theories in social gerontology. Rejecting social causality for individual narrative and difference, more reflexive approaches to understanding the formation and maintenance of ageing identities now challenge these structural accounts of ageing. In this chapter we explore the shift away from such structural accounts toward approaches that stress the agentic construction of identities. In doing this we want to demonstrate the importance of seeing ageing as a cultural process, moving from the view that ageing is something that happens to people toward recognizing it as something individuals have to engage with.

## The rise and fall of structured dependency theory

Structured dependency theory has dominated most recent thinking within British social gerontology. Its central tenets have been articulated by British writers such as Chris Phillipson, Peter Townsend and Alan Walker in a series of articles and books written during the early 1980s.[2] The work of Carol Estes, Meredith Minkler, John Myles and Laura Olson in the United States has expounded similar views, albeit in the rather different context of American social policy, where it has come to be described as the political economy approach.[3] What both variants share is the idea that the dependent social position of older people is created by social policy. Attention is directed over the lifecourse to pension arrangements; employment practices; and discriminatory health policies. These in turn create environments where older people are excluded, marginalized or rendered powerless. As a consequence it is discriminatory and disadvantaging state policies, not biology, that dominate the lives of older people. The problems that older people face can be overcome therefore by state-determined policy changes, particularly through realizing the full possibilities of social citizenship.

In the UK, many writers from the structured dependency school have sought to show the extent of poverty among older people and in particular among older women. In contrast to the work of earlier twentieth-century reformers, these more recent commentators were writing 25 years *after* the emergence of the British welfare state, which was intended to make such poverty a thing of the past. The establishment of the state retirement pension by the reforming Labour government of 1945 was an attempt to abolish one of Beveridge's 'five Giants', poverty. By the mid-1970s, however, the welfare state was going through a difficult period. Faced with the retrenchment of public expenditure following the oil crisis of the mid-1970s, and the subsequent defeat of social democracy

13

at the polls, these writers reiterated the key role of the state in determining the status and well-being of older people, maintaining that the project should be intensified rather than clawed back if older people were to realize 'the promise' that the Beveridge reforms had introduced.

Coming from a very different policy context, but set against the same background of resurgent neo-Conservatism, Carol Estes' book, *The Aging Enterprise*, sought to show how the American social security system and Medicare programme constituted a multi-billion dollar exercise in regulating the aged so as to make them dependent. Again one of the principle ways that this was achieved was through the reproduction of class, gender, racial and ethnic disparities amongst the older population. From both perspectives the effect of government social policy was to create a structured dependency for older people. Much of the empirical work that social gerontologists have undertaken has been dominated by this paradigm and has concentrated on documenting the nature and extent of disability, dependency and disadvantage within the older population as well as proposing remedies for it.

A particular concern of these writers has been to disconnect ageing and old age from the processes of ill health and physical frailty. The close connection is accepted but the reduction of one to the other is resisted as the 'biomedicalisation of old age'.[4] Since the 1960s, claims Katz, 'gerontological writers, in their critique of negative "ageist" stereotypes and practices, have produced more accurate and positive images that bespeak the vitality, creativity, empowerment and resourcefulness attainable in old age'.[5]

By establishing the dependent and disadvantaged position of older people as their determined status, structured dependency theorists reinforce the very image that they criticize social policy for inducing. Although the 'ageing' process is moved to the social sphere, its weaknesses, vulnerabilities and frailties remain the object of analysis. While the elision of the relationship between physical decline and ageing remains, social gerontologists stress the 'artificial' nature of modern society's treatment of older people as one that can be overcome. However, overcoming 'ageing' is located as a task that should be undertaken by the state, rather than through individual agency. The powerlessness of 'age' is to be reversed by the very structure that it is claimed engineered that powerlessness in the first place.

Furthermore, the structured dependency theorists claim that, by reversing the state-induced dependency of older people, they will regain a status of equality enjoyed by other adult generations. This in turn will undermine those cultural assumptions of generational discontinuity, which it is argued provide the base for an intergenerational conflict.[6] In claiming that older people are not necessarily a homogenous group linked together by a common physical frailty but that they are as diverse as the rest of the population, links are made to the idea of a shared community of interest. The key to 'successful ageing' is limited by the low level of resources available to many older people.

In the UK the finger is pointed at the low rate at which the state retirement pension is paid out when compared with the average wage.[7] The American situation is slightly different given that older people as a group are not under-resourced. Instead the argument goes that inequalities and disadvantages created by the untrammelled ravages of capital during earlier life are reproduced and reinforced by the way the various US health, welfare and social security programmes operate. Thus the state constructs an old age for blacks, hispanics and single older women that sets these groups apart from the affluence enjoyed by other sections of the population.[8]

## Structured dependency theory in the UK

In the UK the key to overcoming the structured dependency has been seen in terms of advocating full citizenship rights for older people. Phillipson has argued that these rights need to be organized so that exclusion from the wage economy does not itself lead older people to occupy an inferior social category.[9] Other rights can vary in scope from anti-age-discriminatory legislation to the creation of generationally representative political structures. Of more significance is the radical reform of pensions policy in order to create greater equality. In *A Manifesto for Old Age* Bornat, Phillipson and Ward proposed that the:

> retirement pension needs to be greatly increased, to a level which provides a 'participation standard' of living for all pensioners. This would probably be higher than the pensioner movement's current goal of one-third the average wage for a single person.[10]

Laczko and Phillipson, aware of the ravages of early retirement as a way of removing older workers from the workforce, wrote about the importance of redirecting pensions policy to abandon the traditional work/retirement dichotomy. Instead they argued for the introduction of a 'decade of retirement' which allowed much greater flexibility for workers wanting to gradually leave employment free of the negative financial effects of lower pensions.[11] The most explicit intervention in the pensions debate was made in a pamphlet authored by Townsend and Walker which made an appeal for both a return to a universalist pensions policy and an uprating of benefit rates.[12] This position became even more determined with the election of a new Labour government in 1997. Many social gerontologists had assumed that the creation of poverty among the old was fundamentally connected to the neo-liberal beliefs of the previous Conservative governments. A Labour government would start from a position much closer to the ideals of the post-war welfare state and want to address this inequality. However, the refusal of the new government to agree to restore the link between the rate at which earnings grew and the level at which pensions were set was only the first shock. The incoming government decided to abandon the idea that the state old age pension should be the principle mechanism through which the security of older citizens would be organized. The then Minister for Welfare Reform, Frank Field, was asked to 'think the unthinkable' and accepted the end of this strategy and the need to shift towards second pensions involving the private and mutual sectors of the pensions industry.[13]

Paradoxically the theoretical focus on financial issues as underpinning the true nature of dependency in later life has often been sidelined by an overwhelming empirical concern with documenting physical and mental dependency. While many writers see the issues around financial security as providing the basis for a reordering of the relationship between older people and the provision of health and social care, it is ironic that much of the research pursues the stereotyping of old age as infirmity. Again, the purported rationale for such research strategies has been to make the needs of older people more socially visible. Charting and monitoring the prevalence and distribution of physical infirmity or chronic illness within the community will enable the state to be better placed to introduce policies that will safeguard the rights and opportunities for older people to live out their lives with the minimum of want and dependency.

At all these various levels what the structured dependency school wants to focus on is the need for the full integration of older people into society rather than an acceptance of their disengagement or separateness. Integrating old age into a concept of a lifecourse shared by all humans would benefit not only older people but also those of different generations. Arber and Ginn point out that the effect of much feminist research on the informal care of older people has been to concentrate on its gendered nature which has produced a division of interest between younger women carers and the older people being cared for.[14] Policies aimed at minimizing these conflicts through the creation and funding of formalized caring options and support would be of mutual benefit and enable a community of interest to exist between the different generations.

As we noted earlier, one major difficulty with the structured dependency approach is that, in trying to overcome the structured dependency of age, many of the proposals end up homogenizing all older people by stressing their need to be made equal. This is not surprising given that the theoretical model of citizenship is one that starts from a welfarist belief in the centrality of mass social benefits. In the earlier formulation of *A Manifesto for Old Age* the recognition that structural inequalities in old age are often the effects of earlier social differences leads to a desire to limit some of the privileges associated with occupational pensions. The reality that there are now considerable wealth differences in the post-retirement population makes implausible the argument that there exists a community of interest to improve the state provision of welfare and pensions.

This development has not escaped the notice of government who feel increasingly confident in abandoning the idea of the universal state pension as a means of improving the social situation of older people. The acceptance of this change has proved difficult for many researchers wedded to the structured dependency approach. Many of the studies examining income differences in old age treat the poverty of older people as defining their 'aged' status while effectively ignoring the 'agedness' of the more affluent sections of the population. Even when it is acknowledged that this group exists and is likely to increase in the future, the full implications are often not considered. However, as the century ended some of the key advocates of structured dependency had to agree that something has changed.

Chris Phillipson's new book *Reconstructing Old Age* examines how ageing has been transformed by the changes in both social policy and the social world.[15] He points to the importance of what he calls 'a crisis of identity' that has occurred to older people. In doing so, he dichotomizes the recent history of old age. From the 1950s to the 1970s the welfare state and retirement played the central role in developing what he calls a secure old age. The crisis of the welfare state which has been documented by many writers as occurring in the mid-1970s and 1980s changed this sense of optimism as the welfare state went into decline and many policy makers questioned the assumptions about future spending on welfare. By the 1990s many of the institutions of the welfare state had been radically transformed. The idea of retirement as central to old age had been usurped by the experiences of redundancy and early retirement as well as changes in the composition of the population.

Phillipson himself makes the point that there has been a major change in the nature of who older people are:

> Writing in the 1970s one had a relatively clear sense of who older people were: mainly poor, probably with similar outlooks (and indeed appearance), and with limited aspirations for future lifestyles. This may have been an unsatisfactory stereotype then; it certainly must be considered as such now. Despite the trends and similarities to be identified in this study, there are huge variations among old people and this diversity has undoubtedly been a feature of social change in the 1990s.[16]

Faced with the challenge of this diversity and transformation of the meaning of old age Phillipson now calls for the development of what he and others have described as a 'critical gerontology'. He argues that such a critical gerontology still continues the interest in political economy but also adds a biographical and narrative perspective:

> the critical elements in this gerontology centre around three main areas: first, from political economy, there is an awareness of the structural pressures and constraints affecting older people, with divisions associated with class, gender and ethnicity being emphasised . . . second, from both the humanistic as well as biographically orientated gerontology, there is a concern over the

absence of meaning in the lives of older people, and the sense of doubt and uncertainty which is seen to pervade the daily routines and relationships . . . third, from all three perspectives, comes a focus on the issue of empowerment, whether through the transformation of society (for example, through the redistribution of income and wealth), or the development of new rituals and symbols to facilitate changes through the life course.[17]

## Ageing in America

The study and teaching of ageing in the USA have considerably deeper roots than in the UK. Gerontology programmes feature in both undergraduate and postgraduate courses and there are a large number of research institutes and specialist publications. However, the policy context regarding the retired is very different to the one encountered in the UK. Instead of age being associated with poverty in a relatively unproblematic way, often it is the reverse in the US. Fred Pampel argues that there are two images of older people in America; one is that they are vulnerable and deserving while the other is that they are affluent and favoured.[18] Interestingly this difference is temporal as well as social in that the former image fits the 1950s and 1960s while the latter better fits the 1970s and 1980s. Furthermore, Pampel argues that this situation has changed because of the effect of public programmes in raising the incomes of many older people.

This position, which seems to be in direct contradiction to the arguments of the structured dependency school, argues that the operation of the US social security system has been very successful in moving considerable numbers of older people out of poverty. Organized through a variety of schemes covering old age, disability and health insurance, social security has ensured that compared with children and the total population 'the elderly [have] experienced the largest decline in poverty rates and the largest improvement in economic well-being'.[19] What is interesting is that not only have social security benefits improved but so has the coverage of the elderly population so that by 1981 95 per cent were eligible. However, while social security has been a success a minority fall through the gaps in what is in essence a contributory system. Those with certain kinds of health problem, dementia or low contributions records can easily end living up to the image of the old as vulnerable.

In the context of ageing being seen as a period of relative affluence, social gerontologists in the USA have focused their attention on two areas: the inequalities that exist within the older population and the intergenerational crisis. In particular they have become interested in the differences brought about by race, ethnicity and gender as well as the effects of poor health. As in Britain this has resulted in a considerable body of empirical research into the prevalence of disability and levels of unmet need. The net effect has been to find ways for social policy to include those who are disadvantaged; in effect a gerontology of the disadvantaged and disempowered.

The second main area resulting from affluence is the threat posed by an imputed intergenerational jealousy regarding the resources being allocated to the retired. Relatively underdeveloped as a theme in the UK, the idea that the old receive a disproportionate amount of the wealth produced by society is one that has had widespread media coverage in America. This led to the creation of the now defunct Americans for Generational Equity, a political pressure group that campaigned for a reduction in the pension and welfare entitlements of older people and a redistribution toward education and child welfare.[20] Although few academic gerontologists have formally supported the idea of a redistribution of resources away from older people, the theme of intergenerational equity has become a much-discussed concern.[21]

What both these themes have done is to concentrate the minds of American writers of the political economy school to revise their ideas much in the way that their co-thinkers on the other side of the Atlantic have done. The need to justify the continuing position of 'age' as a deserving subject of social policy in circumstances where the 'elderly' can no longer be equated with poverty and exclusion has led to a re-orientation of the explanatory paradigm toward issues of meaning and identity.

## From political economy to moral economy

The difficulties faced by advocates of the political economy approach have led many of the most influential writers of English-speaking social gerontology to seek to integrate their work with what they describe as moral economy. What is being attempted is a shift toward understanding ageing as culture. A key point of reference is the humanistic traditions of interpretative historiography exemplified by E.P. Thompson's *Making of the English Working Class*. Using Thompson's discussion of the 'moral economy' of the price of bread in the eighteenth century, Minkler and Cole argue that similar ideas can be extended to the issues surrounding old age and in particular the reciprocal obligations that all societies hold towards their older members.[22] The shift in focus is away from economic rationality and toward moral well-being. This approach continues to challenge more fiscally oriented views that have seen the demographic transition towards a 'greyer' population as a potential crisis to be averted by a variety of restrictive measures to restore generational 'justice'. Proponents of the moral economy of ageing see the discourse surrounding social policy as a conflict between different assumptions concerning ageing and social responsibility. For these social gerontologists the modernist project that treats as central the goal of ensuring economic well-being has foundered. As Cole writes:

> We must acknowledge that our great progress in the material and physical conditions of life has been achieved at a high spiritual and ethical price. Social security has not enhanced ontological security or dignity in old age. The elderly continue to occupy an inferior status in the moral economy – marginalized by an economy and culture committed to the scientific management of growth without limit.
>
> Only recently have economic and political conditions turned this apparently academic question into an urgent political issue. In rebuilding a moral economy of an extended life course, we must not only attend to questions of justice within and between different stages of life, we must also forge a new sense of the meanings and purposes of the last half of life.[23]

Cole has long argued that the cultural meaning of ageing is central to gerontology and that historically there has always been a dualism between 'good' and 'bad' notions of ageing and old age. This failure to integrate the dualism of ageing has led to a one-sided emphasis upon social policy as the means of emancipating older people, which 'has hindered our culture's ability to sustain morally compelling social practices and existentially vital ideals of aging'.[24]

Important as ethical and moral issues are in the area of health and social care, they do not provide the dominant structures through which later life is to be understood. Later life is not lived out as a series of moral dilemmas or ethical considerations. Nor, it could be argued, is any stage of life. These concerns for a deliberative moral consensus reflect the influence of Habermas and his approach to critical theory. In particular they represent the Americanization of Habermas' idea of the 'colonization of the lifeworld'. The dominant norms and values about ageing are viewed as those expressed by the discourse of science and biomedicine. Recovery of the life-world – i.e. the recovery of the moral meaning of old age – requires a conscious public choice which should be arrived at through informed debate.[25]

Here is not the place to assess the adequacy of the Habermasian project.[26] We would argue, however, that this view of ageing constructed out of moral discourse and dependent ultimately upon discourse ethics is too limited. The idea of a communitarian consensus being reached, effectively determining how ageing and old age are to be understood, fails to acknowledge the numerous and diverse cultural and structural dimensions present within 'postmodern' society that are already shaping and influencing identity in later life. Like the earlier political economy approach, the position of moral economy ultimately fails because it ends up offering a one-dimensional account of a multidimensional process.

## The cultural turn

The shift toward culture is nevertheless important, if not quite in the way that the writings of the 'moral economists' might suggest. It is significant for two reasons. Firstly, it questions the state as the central focus for understanding old age. What is important is not whether or not the state is best placed to provide pensions and security in retirement or at what level, but rather the multiplicity of sources that provide the texts and shape the practices by which older people are expected to construct their lives. Instead of having little or no expectations of ageing or assuming it will be incorporated into a mass system of entitlements, the need to plan a post-working life establishes a set of new and very different perspectives.

From these differing perspectives we are beginning to see a variety of 'cultures of ageing' emerge, seeking to establish 'meaning' in ageing. But it is a personal not a moral meaning that is sought. Central to the issue of meaning is the identity that the individual constructs to express and interpret their own ageing. Within consumer society the construction of identity is made up of a large number of choices. In the past, retirement has been an enforced choice connected to a decline of productivity or the need to remove older cohorts from the workforce. The circumstances in which retirement occurs now are more fluid and much more connected to lifestyle or, for some, redundancy.

The cultural shift also serves to draw attention to the neglect of how middle-aged and older people spend their lives. Orthodox social gerontology has treated later life as if it were constituted by inventories of social need and social exclusion. This is not how older people live and experience their lives. The growth of retirement as a third age – a potential crown of life – has been constructed primarily in terms of leisure and self-fulfilment. While these practices may be most fully enacted by a relatively small section of the population of older people, culturally this group represents the aspirations of many whether or not they are able to realize such a lifestyle.

Linked to this changing definition of retirement is the shift in the nature of the state to a form of governance described as 'advanced liberalism'.[27] The key feature of this shift is that the state no longer seeks to provide a uniform level of services to the whole population. Targeting and risk assessment replace the institutions of the collective welfare state. Much is made of the process of 'govermentality': the idea that individuals must organize their own lives and that the appropriate role for the state is to be concerned with the 'conduct of conduct'. In such a polity the idea of being a consumer fits much better than the idea of being a citizen.

Looked at from this perspective, the state and the creation of mass welfare are historically located moments connected to the development of particular types of industrial capitalism. Once the level of consumption of commodities has got beyond the basic need satisfiers, the role of the state radically alters. Political approaches such as 'the Third Way'[28] stress the role of individuals in providing for themselves – not as a way of rejecting the social bonds of community, but rather as a way of enhancing personal choice and satisfaction. It is argued that in a post-scarcity society it is not appropriate for individuals to make themselves deliberately dependent on an all-embracing state. Echoing some of the themes of the 'new right' discourse, Giddens speaks of the need for the individual to be agentic not for purely selfish reasons but in order for both the individual and the community to thrive.[29]

For most of human history identity has been regarded as synonymous with the culture a person was socialized into. Identity was ascribed rather than chosen and the means for its reproduction were embedded in the stable practices and relations of everyday life. This idea of culture as forming the basis of social integration has dominated much of the academic discipline of anthropology as well as the functionalist accounts in sociology running from Durkheim to Parsons (and some would say Bourdieu). The notion of social integration and stable identities arising from commonly-held norms and values has been radically challenged by modernity which turns 'all that is solid into air'. Change becomes an intrinsic feature of modern industrial society. Durkheim foresaw the potential conflicts that would emerge in any society that moved to a more diffuse cultural existence. Not only would there be less integration of society's members but also conflict about just what set of values were to be adhered to or what constituted an appropriate understanding of social processes.[30] The final two decades of the twentieth century have seen this confusion accelerate towards a situation where not only are there large numbers of competing cultural messages but also a significant expansion in the way that they can be transmitted.

Moving from mass industrial to 'post-industrial' society, the processes leading to cultural fragmentation have made identity and culture into commodities, part of what Baudrillard in his early writings referred to as the realm of symbolic exchange.[31] Faced with a surplus of commodities and images the modern consumer does not exist within a coherent structure of values and is constantly obliged to make choices. This growing reflexivity lies at the heart of the 'postmodern' turn in contemporary social theory. No longer located within the social categories of production and no longer confined by the boundaries of the nation-state, cultures proliferate across widening social contexts. These new and more deliberate cultures appear to be woven from a myriad of seemingly disconnected sources. Their very openness demands constant reconstruction while, at the same time, offering the individual the opportunity of choosing a variation from which to promote their uniqueness.

The key to modern culture is the reflexivity that derives from this cultural abundance. It is the necessary starting point for the modern world. Everyone is involved in negotiating an identity within a changing environment that is overloaded with information and unintended consequences. To deny this agency is no longer a choice because that very denial will be treated as if it is a choice with contingent consequences. Post-traditional culture extends equally to life after retirement as well as before. Ageing has become a much more reflexive project. It exists within cultural forms that are established from, contested by and integrated with other cultural agendas. It is impossible to study ageing without being simultaneously aware that it occupies a central, though problematic, position within an increasingly large number of cultural practices and structures that make it not the backwater of social science but one of the main tributaries of postmodernist culture.

If the twentieth century tried to create a stable lifecourse with recognizable stages, the period leading up to the new century has thrown much of this into confusion. Consumer society is as much a culture as was the mass society of industrialism, but even more so. The affluence of large parts of the population has fuelled the idea that identity can be constructed and consumed. Increasingly what marks individuals out is the way that they consume rather than any intrinsic quality that they may be ascribed with. That applies as much to age and ageing as it does to any other socialized attribute.

## Notes

1 See for example the work of Steven Seidman: Seidman, S. and Wagner, D. (1991) *Postmodernism and Social Theory*, Blackwell, Oxford; Seidman, S. (1994) *Contested Knowledge: Social Theory in the Postmodern Era*, Blackwell, Oxford; and of Scott Lash: Lash, S. (1990) *Sociology of Postmodernity*, Routledge, London.
2 See Phillipson, C. (1982) *Capitalism and the Construction of Old Age*, Macmillan, London; Townsend, P. (1981) 'The structured dependency of the elderly: the creation of social policy in the twentieth century', *Ageing and Society*, 1: 5–28; Walker, A. (1980) 'The social creation of poverty and dependency in old age', *Journal of Social Policy*, 9: 45–75.
3 See Estes, C. (1979) *The Aging Enterprise*, Jossey Bass, San Francisco, CA; Estes, C. and Minkler, M. (1984) *Readings in the Political Economy of Aging*, Baywood Publishing, New York; Myles, J. (1984) *Old Age in the Welfare State*, Little, Brown & Co, Boston, MA; Olson, L.K. (1982) *The Political Economy of Aging: the State, Private Power and Social Welfare*, Columbia University Press, New York.

4  Estes, C. and Binney, E. (1989) 'The biomedicalization of aging: dangers and dilemmas', *The Gerontologist*, 29: 587–98.
5  Katz, S. (1996) *Disciplining Old Age*, University Press of Virginia, Charlottesville, VA, p. 70.
6  Minkler, M. and Cole, T.R. (1991) 'Political and moral economy: not such strange bedfellows', in M. Minkler and C. Estes (eds), *Critical Perspectives on Aging: the Political and Moral Economy of Growing Old*, Baywood Publishing, New York, pp. 37–49.
7  Cf. Townsend, P. and Walker, A. (1995) *New Directions for Pensions: How to Revitalise National Insurance*, Pamphlet No. 2, European Labour Forum, Nottingham.
8  Pampel, F. (1998) *Aging, Social Inequality and Public Policy,* Pine Forge, Thousand Oaks, CA.
9  Phillipson, C. (1982) *op. cit.*
10 Bornat, J., Phillipson, C. and Ward, S. (1985) *A Manifesto for Old Age*, Pluto Press, London, pp. 78–9.
11 Bornat, J., Phillipson, C. and Ward, S. (1985) *op. cit.*, pp. 78–9.
12 Townsend, P. and Walker, A. (1995) *op. cit.*
13 Field, F. (1998) *Reflections on Welfare Reform*, The Social Market Foundation, London.
14 Arber, S. and Ginn, J. (1991) 'The invisibility of age: gender and class in later life', *Sociological Review*, 39: 260–91.
15 Phillipson, C. (1998) *Reconstructing Old Age*, Sage Publications, London.
16 Phillipson, C., *op. cit.*, p. 10.
17 Phillipson, C., *op. cit.*, p. 14.
18 Pampel, F.C. (1998) *Aging, Social Inequality and Public Policy*, Pine Forge, Thousand Oaks, CA.
19 Pampel, F.C., *op. cit.*, p. 4.
20 See the debate in Johnson, P., Conrad, C. and Thomson, D. (eds) (1990) *Workers versus Pensioners: Intergenerational Justice in an Ageing World,* Manchester University Press, Manchester; Binney, E. and Estes, C.L. (1988) 'The retreat of the state and its transfer of responsibility: the intergenerational war', *International Journal of Health Services*, 18: pp. 83–96.
21 See the collection of essays referred to earlier (Johnson, P., *et al.* (1990) *op. cit.*) and more recently Moody, H. (1998) 'Should age or need be a basis for entitlement?', in *Aging: Concepts and Controversies*, Pine Forge, Thousand Oaks, CA, pp. 215–65.
22 Minkler, M. and Cole, T.R. (1991) *op. cit.*
23 Cole, T.R. (1992) *The Journey of Life: a Cultural History of Aging in America*, Cambridge University Press, Cambridge, p. 237.
24 Cole, T.R., *op. cit.*, p. 230.
25 Moody, H. (1995) 'Ageing, meaning and the allocation of resources', *Ageing and Society,* 15: pp. 163–84, esp. pp. 180–2.
26 But see Jones, I.R. and Higgs, P.F. (2001: in press) 'Habermas, Rationing and Rationality', in G. Scambler (ed.), *Habermas, Critical Theory and Health*, Routledge, London.
27 See Rose, N. (1996) 'Governing "advanced" liberal democracies', in A. Barry, T. Osborne and N. Rose (eds), *Foucault and Political Reason*, University College London Press, London, pp. 37–64.
28 See Giddens, A. (1998) *The Third Way*, Polity Press, Cambridge.

29 Giddens writes: 'Social cohesion cannot be guaranteed by the top down action of the state or by appeal to tradition. We have to make our lives in a more active way than was true for previous generations, and we need more actively to accept responsibilities for the consequences of what we do and the lifestyle habits we adopt' (Giddens, A. (1998) *op. cit.*, p. 37).
30 See Durkheim, E. (1984) *The Division of Labour in Society*, Macmillan, London.
31 Baudrillard, J. (1975) *The Mirror of Production*, Telos Press, St Louis, MO.

# CHAPTER 3

# Retirement, identity and consumer society

It has become a commonplace in discussions of postmodernity to argue that lifestyles fashioned by consumer activity now form the dominant mode by which personal and social identities are expressed. To speak of identities emerging from and expressed by modes of consumption implies a contrast with the 'modern' view that social identities are shaped principally by people's relationship to the forces of production. According to this orthodox Marxist position, 'we create our identity through socially useful labour which is the transformation of nature to fulfil our needs'.[1] From this perspective later life identity should be shaped by the experience of retirement from the labour force and retired persons' identities expressed in terms of the work they once performed. Though retired, they should be forever 'ex' people – ex-miners, ex-teachers, ex-labourers, ex-nurses – irrevocably defined by their former position in the productive process. From such a perspective, retirement should be a major transition during which individuals relinquish all prospects of developing alternative viable social identities, impelled to live the rest of their lives in the shadow of what they once were, their 'aged' identity firmly in the hands of the state.

Postmodern writers have argued that the rise of consumer society and the consequent emphasis upon lifestyle have led to a radical change in the determination of identity. The individual's role within the productive process is no longer central. Increasingly identities are expressed, revised and represented through consumption. Working and non-working people now share similar opportunities to create and re-create themselves through their patterns of consumption. While there are constraints, these are determined primarily by the resources individuals command for that purpose, rather than by the socially useful work they may or may not perform. The means by which those resources are obtained are less significant than the means by which they are deployed to establish and exemplify a particular lifestyle. In this chapter we explore retirement both as a distinct 'post-work' stage within the lifecourse and as an 'expanded' opportunity for consumption and the development of new later life identities. Central to this position, we suggest, is the contemporary claim that a new stage of life is emerging – the third age – representing a distinctive and culturally salient position within an increasingly age-conscious society.

## Social identities and postmodern culture

It has been customary to distinguish between social identities – the social attributes that are available to an individual through the economic and cultural institutions of a society – and personal identities – those attributes that individuals choose to express, elaborate or articulate through their speech, reflections and actions. While social identities draw upon collective practices, attributions and institutions, personal identities are drawn from the idiosyncratic features of individual lives. They are inevitably heterogeneous. Although not always culturally salient, the individual identity of human beings is taken as given. In contrast, social identities have been seen as varying in more limited ways, dependent upon the culture and the social and economic structure of a particular period. The evolution of capitalist economies, the growth of urban industrial society and the expansion of technology are thought to have contributed to the differentiation of social identities during the course of the last 200 years. Changes in the mode of production have been seen as central to the proliferation of social identities arising from the division of labour in industrial society.

Postmodern writers argue that, most recently, further divisions in social identity are taking place, arising out of the expansion of retail capital, the growth of mass markets and the increasing commodification of experience. Within these divisions, the distinction between social and personal identity is less easily made. The realm of the personal has become not only politicized but increasingly a site for establishing a social identity. The establishment and elaboration of such a self-identity – 'the self as reflexively understood by the individual'[2] – has become a

29

key cultural task in 'postmodern' society. Through the medium of the press and television, through chat shows, 'personal' interviews and popular soaps and comedy serials, identities are created from characters derived or created by the entertainment industries. The establishment of lifestyles has become a key element in the formation of self-identity. The progressive social task seems to focus as much upon building a society where individuals possess self-respect and their distinctiveness is 'recognized' as it does upon building a society based on the collective claims of a common citizenship.[3]

Miller credits the French sociologist, Jean Baudrillard, with providing one of the first and most powerful critiques of the Marxist 'privileging' of production as the means by which individuals shape and express their identities. Marx's view of the identity-forming nature of labour, Baudrillard argued, was historically limited, derived from a particular historical moment when economically productive work took place outside the domestic setting, when the working day extended over much of individuals' waking hours and when the lack of paid work threatened the very material basis of existence. Times have changed and so have the material circumstances in which people live. During the course of the twentieth century there has been a steady reduction in hours worked, a shrinking proportion of people's lives that are spent as employees, a growth in leisure opportunities and a widening base of mass culture and entertainment. There has been greater participation of women in the workforce, increased social regulation of workplace relations and a transformation in the nature of productive labour – from a base in blue-collar, male-dominated manufacturing industry to the less gendered white-collar base of service industries.[4] Far more arenas exist both outside and inside work from which people can draw opportunities for self-creation. Work itself has become a less homogenizing experience. The 'white-collar workplace' supports permeable boundaries that allow the expression of difference in a way that is decoupled from class and position. In contrast to the industrial uniform of manual labour, flexible codes of dress and demeanour enable consumption-based identities to be displayed and developed in the workplace itself.[5] The constraints of time and place that the machinery of manufacturing industry imposed are less evident in the open-plan offices where people now work.

Baudrillard recognized that social relations outside the workplace and particularly those arising within the processes of consumption were becoming important sources of identity for all members of 'consumer society'. While Marx and his followers acknowledged that those whose income derived from the profits of capital were able to display their identities through conspicuous consumption, the privileged relationship between capital and consumption was not seen to extend to the labouring classes.[6] Rather, Marx foresaw a progressive emiseration of the non-propertied working classes – at least until the revolution. What has occurred, however, is the increasing fragmentation and cultural incorporation of the proletariat into middle-class lifestyles. Large numbers of workers are now homeowners, owners of shares and other forms of personal investment; there is a growing amount of socialized capital and a much expanded ownership of 'luxury goods'. Marxist class divisions no longer represent points of fundamental rupture out of which individuals are expected to develop their sense of collective social identity. Rather than class coming to serve as a cornerstone in people's sense of self, that role increasingly is performed through consumption.

## Self-identity and the blurring of retirement

How do these social changes affect the transition from work to retirement? Do the continuities of consumption mask the changes from working to post-working life? Retirement has occupied a key position within social gerontological research since its inception. Traditionally researchers examining the impact of retirement have assumed it was a major life event causing personal and emotional upheaval – to both men and their wives. A number of longitudinal and cross-sectional studies have sought to track the impact of retirement on 'well-being' in later life.[7] The results have shown few signs of such upheaval.[8] If retirement had any impact it was largely the consequence of factors pre-dating and often precipitating retirement – such as deteriorating health.

Nevertheless, considerable weight has been given to the post-retirement transition. The functionalist approach postulated that individuals went through a 'non-traumatic' adaptation to retirement, which represented the normatively successful process of mutual disengagement by individuals and by the institutions of society. For Cumming and her colleagues retirement was simply a particular instance of a more general process of social withdrawal that formed an intrinsic accompaniment of human ageing.[9] Later life was thus characterized by the gradual, but necessary, shedding of all forms of social identity.

Criticism of this functionalist dismissal of older people's needs for a social identity led to the re-formulation of retirement as a structurally imposed identity thrust upon older people by a society dominated by the interests of the capitalist economy. Retirement enforced a social idleness and loss of role and thereby contributed to the very ageing to which it was supposed to be a response. As we noted in the last chapter, structured dependency theorists saw retirement as a means of removing individuals from a significant and productive role within the community and placing them in a position of economic dependency upon the state.[10] The detailed working out of these positions for understanding the civic status of older adults will be addressed more fully in a later chapter. For now it is sufficient to note that while disengagement and structured dependency theories both made retirement a key element in the transition towards a less socially valued identity, the former assumed that the transition suited older people while the latter saw it as an imposition that distressed and disadvantaged them.

Postmodern writings question the centrality of retirement in late-life identity, raising doubts that it is such a crucial structure determining how people in late life construct their identities. While the lack of evidence of significant post-retirement dissatisfaction might be taken as supportive of this position, as we have seen this was also the outcome expected in the functionalist theory of disengagement. However, other changes, occurring particularly over the last two decades, provide evidence that retirement has become an increasingly blurred transition. This loss of definition is true as regards the age at which people actually seek retirement, the status that people ascribe to themselves during the move from working to post-working life, and the nature and degree of the economic transition associated with retirement.[11] Many of those recently retired continue or increase their pursuit of consumption-based identities that were not possible for previous generations of retirees. Retirement is longer and richer than ever before. People who are retiring at the end of the twentieth century are able to access a material culture that is more extensive – richer – than ever before. As a result,

TABLE 3.1  Secular change in mean income by age of householder:
*US Historical Income Tables*[12]

| Age group | 1968 | 1978 | 1988 | 1998 |
|---|---|---|---|---|
| 25–34-year-olds | $38 986 | $42 752 | $44 248 | $47 960 |
| 35–44-year-olds | $45 947 | $53 177 | $57 995 | $60 103 |
| 45–54-year-olds | $47 746 | $57 226 | $62 701 | $67 293 |
| 55–64-year-olds | $39 617 | $46 930 | $50 875 | $57 952 |
| 65–74-year-olds | $24 098* | $28 564 | $33 172 | $38 850 |

* Estimate based upon linear regression of income data from 65 years+ population adjusted to the changing proportions of 65–74-year-olds in the US 65 years+ population during this period.

self-expression and self-creation remain continuing possibilities sustained by the continuities of consumption and the increased access to socialized capital that present-day pensioners possess.[13]

Illustrative of this gradual blurring of the 'economic' transition into a post-working life are the figures for average income of various age groups in the United States. Table 3.1 shows the mean income of US householders in different age groups for 10 year periods from 1968 to 1998, adjusted to constant 1998 US dollar equivalents.

The 1968 income of post-retirement householders (65–74-year-olds) was just half that of middle-aged householders (35–44-year-olds) and just over half (60 per cent) of that of young-adult householders (25–34-year-olds). By 1998, their average income had increased to two-thirds of that of middle-aged householders and over three-quarters (80 per cent) of that of young adults. While the latter age cohort has experienced a 23 per cent increase in average income over the last three decades, post-retirement householders have seen an increase of over 60 per cent in their income.

## The state, retirement policy and the economic structure of later life

Compulsory retirement at age 65 was made illegal in the United States in 1978. Since then, workers in their sixties have been entitled by law to work as long as they and their employer see fit. Despite this anti-discriminatory legislation, the number of people retiring in their fifties and sixties has steadily increased in America as much as it has in other

Western societies. The ban on 'age discrimination' has done little to reverse the trend for an increasing number of older Americans to choose to leave work. In Britain compulsory retirement at age 60 for women and 65 for men was instituted as part of the 1946 National Insurance Act. The introduction of a universal old age pension combined with a statutory age for men and women to retire form one of the main planks of the 'structured dependency' critique. According to this view 'the concepts of retirement and pensionable status have been developed . . . in ways which have created and reinforced the social dependency of the elderly'.[14] Yet in Britain as in many other countries increasing numbers of people aged 55 and over are choosing to retire. The break between ages 64 and 65 for men, and 59 and 60 for women, has become a less distinct transition within what amounts to a continuum of 'ages at retirement'.[15] Structured dependency theory as explanation of the social construction of ageing is, to say the least, outdated. What evidence there is suggests that a combination of state benefits and occupational and private pensions have enabled more people to withdraw themselves from the market, rather than continuing to sell their labour and mortgage their lifetime. For many the good life now comes after rather than before retirement.

In most countries which developed old age pensions, the principal motivation driving those policies was to prevent the emiseration of old people who could neither continue in their existing job nor find alternative work as well as those who as a result of widowhood had been left bereft of economic support. In that sense the state 'took over' the identity-forming role previously exercised within the productive process. But rather than assume that state pensions were introduced to drive older adults out of the workforce into some reserve army of labour, it seems more credible to see the old age pension – wherever it was introduced – as an act of civic welfare born out of a growing sense of economic confidence and aimed at those whose marginalization posed little or no threat as a 'dangerous class'.[16] Pensions thus permitted large numbers of people to retire where before only hard necessity led people in later life to drop out of the workforce. Even in Britain, as Harper and Thane have pointed out, 'neither the Beveridge Report nor the National Insurance Act 1946 intended state pension provision unnecessarily to remove able elderly workers from the labour market'.[17]

Old age pensions were introduced at a time when the labouring poor were expected to have enough to live on but not enough to engage in surplus consumption. State old age pension policies in Australia (1899–1908), Britain (1908), Canada (1927) and New Zealand (1899) all started with the premise of providing a largely subsistence income for the aged poor, a goal which expanded only in the aftermath of the Second World War.[18] Such a perspective must itself be seen against the general expectations about work and leisure, for it is impossible to understand the meaning and impact of retirement without reference to the experience of contemporaneous working life. As numerous commentators have noted, the evolution of a mass consumer society has been a characteristic of the twentieth century. Since the Second World War, working people have been able to 'build a life for themselves' from the profits of their labour. For the first decades of this century, however, life for most people was a fairly relentless daily cycle of domestic and paid work, or desperate idleness. With each passing decade, there has come an expansion in the retail market, further developments of the mass media, growth in popular sports and entertainment, an increase in holidays, and the growth in public and increasingly private transport.[19] Following in the wake of retirement pensions, this improved standard of living has become part of the experience of successive generations of pensioners. According to Leslie Hannah, 'the generations retiring in the 1960s and 1970s enjoyed a lifetime of continually improving standards in which their retirement was truly a golden age'.[20] Establishing an economically attractive retirement from the 1960s onwards has reframed the experience of age – a change that is reflected in the widespread preference amongst older adults for the term 'retiree' or 'senior citizen' rather than pensioner, elderly or old person.[21]

In the last chapter of his book *Inventing Retirement*, Hannah writes of the ambivalence inherent in the idea of retirement. He notes the steady decline evident throughout this century in the number of men and women over 60 who remain in paid employment. This pattern of declining economic activity is evident in most Western countries[22] and was originally related to the rise in pension coverage and the decline in the agricultural sector in modern economies.[23] The interpretation of this decline has vacillated between those advocates of 'structured dependency' theory who see mandatory retirement as an enforced exclusion of older people from the world of work and those who see the development of universal pensions as the triumph of social democracy and the establishment of full social citizenship. Retirement policy itself reflects this mixture of motives – shared by labour and capital – to manage unemployment as well as to ensure social welfare.

The contrasting positions represented by retirement/pension policies are reflected in the debates in Britain in the 1940s over the introduction of a universal old age pension linked to mandatory retirement and in the debates in the United States during the 1930s that led to the Social Security Act of 1935. In the latter case an explicit goal expounded by one of the main protagonists of the Act, Frances Perkins, Chair of the Committee of Economic Security that drafted the old age provisions of the bill was to use old age security as a means of stimulating economic recovery through spreading purchasing power[24] as well as ensuring the economic security of older Americans.

In Britain in contrast, the debate leading to the 1946 Social Insurance Act arose out of explicit concerns to improve the economic and social well-being of older people. This debate took place in the immediate aftermath of the Second World War, a war fought very much as 'the people's war', serving as a powerful trigger to implement policies to cement a gender- and class-fragmented society of the pre-war era into 'one nation'.[25] The desirability of improving the economic well-being of older people was little questioned – Beveridge's main concern was the economic basis from which to fund the new state pension scheme. The labour movement, represented by the Trades Union Congress, was also keen to balance a fair pension with retirement from the workforce in order to make room for younger workers and prevent wage reductions for older employees.[26] These differing American and British perspectives had a major impact on the images of retirement they engendered.

According to Graebner, in his book on the history of retirement in the United States, from the late 1940s onwards 'the retired and those approaching retirement age were [ . . . ] exposed to a barrage of propaganda . . . The selling of retirement had begun. Life insurance companies deeply involved in the pension business were the leading purveyors of the message that retirement, far from being evidence of maladjustment was a bounty bestowed by the society and the pension. . . . Retirement . . . was the joy of being at the ball park on a weekday afternoon.'[27] He draws attention to the magazines that began appearing on American news-stands in the 1950s that exemplified this new approach to later life: *Lifetime Living, Modern Maturity, Retirement Planning News, Senior Citizen*, etc.

In Britain, in stark contrast, retirement was very much framed around the term 'OAPs' (old age pensioners), a shorthand form of describing a group of people whose defining characteristic was their semi-charitable status conferred by the Attlee government in the aftermath of the people's war. Despite their new civic status, it would be another two decades before retired people in Britain would move *en masse* from their impoverished status as OAPs. In contrast to the explicit consumerist perspective of US social security/retirement policy, Britain pursued a primarily welfarist perspective which did little to encourage consumption beyond the basic needs of subsistence.

However, by the late 1960s and early 1970s a significant surplus began to find its way into the pockets of a growing number of Britain's pensioners. The rise in occupational pension coverage in the post-war period, and the rise in the value of such benefits, contributed significantly to increased savings and an improved income in later life.[28] Subsequent pension policy has sought to stimulate still further private and occupational pension provisions, although the changing nature of work may place constraints on the future growth of personal pension plans.[29] Associated with the general trend toward greater affluence amongst the retired population over the last two decades has been a distinct change in the social identity that this period of life has had for people in Britain – with evidence of increasing fragmentation of the retired population reflecting class-, cohort- and gender-based divisions. Accompanying this change has been the rise of 'third ageism' as a distinct position accommodating the leisure and potential affluence of the newly retired. It is a position outlined most cogently in two relatively recent British books, one by Peter Laslett entitled *A Fresh Map of Life*, first published in 1989, and the other, entitled *Life after Work*, by Michael Young and Tom Schuller which appeared in 1991.[30] Both propose a new formulation for later life – a new life stage, the 'third age' – that deserves particular consideration as a key element in the search for a 'post-working-life' identity, independent of both the state and the productive processes. Both outline a position for retired people that is also quite distinctively

British. 'Third-age' positions have been outlined by US writers – Gail Sheehy particularly – which share the same celebration of agency in later life. But what sets each apart are their differing historical roots. In Laslett's and Young and Schuller's books can be found a vision of a third age that emphasizes the citizenship that pensioner status was meant to provide to British older people. In Sheehy's book *New Passages*, in contrast, is a very different emphasis upon consumerism, one that is based on the exercise of spending power and independence by retired people and one that US social security policy pursued from its outset.[31]

## Third-age identities and post-work society

This most recent transformation of old age – from pensioner to senior citizen to third-ager – demonstrates three important characteristics. In the first place it recognizes the increasing fluidity within the retired community. As noted earlier, the age at which people retire has become much less well defined[32] – despite the mandatory retirement ages of 65 and 60 for men and women in the 1946 Act. This fluidity reflects, and in some senses demands, increasing choice. Both Laslett and Young treat the acquisition of a third-age identity as the outcome of an individual decision – though Young and Schuller describe the decision in terms of choosing to become a 'positive' third-ager.[33] In the second place, the third age demands deliberation and planning – the active construction of a 'post-work' identity. In this sense it contains as its central element precisely that reflexivity which Giddens and others have noted as characterizing the late modern 'project of the self'. It involves not only the creation of a narrative of the self, but also a continuing responsibility 'in which the question "how shall I live?" has to be answered in day-to-day decisions about how to behave' measured against the 'flows of social and psychological information about possible ways of life'.[34] Finally, third-ageism assumes that pre-existing social structures – work, the state, the family – are not able to provide sufficient support and status to enable the expression of individual agency that third-ageism requires in our 'postmodern' society.

Central to all these characteristics of 'third-ageism' is a stress upon the agentic construction of a life-world. Both Laslett and Young insist that older people 'can create their own structures around lives more free than they ever had while they were solely workers'.[35] Not only is such agency required as a means of improving the social and personal well-being of retired people; it is also expected as the principal means of improving physical health in later life. Young and Schuller suggest that 'it should become possible in the future for more and more people to ward off the diseases associated with old age so that more and more can avoid decline almost until the end'.[36] While Laslett is a little less sanguine about the prospects of banishing physical debility to some smaller and smaller fraction of a life, Young and Schuller are keen to push the whole way to an agentically constructed later life in which individuals act to ensure their economic, social and physical well-being. Without such totalizing aspirations, they see themselves ending up in the invidious position of merely stabilizing a final, fourth age of 'dependence, decrepitude and death'[37] – which as both they and others note elevates the third age principally 'by treading down the fourth'.[38]

Despite the dispute over the nature and status of a fourth age and its intrinsic role in sustaining a meaningful third age, both Laslett and Young stress the agentic construction of a 'third-age' lifestyle which marks it as unique from other periods and other lifestyles. Both define it by its independence from work and the leisure opportunities that people of a certain age can enjoy. Both also stress that such leisure opportunities can benefit not just third-agers themselves but society as a whole. It is in their role as social agents that third-agers will reacquire the prestige, the social and cultural capital that they have steadily lost during the course of this century. While this emphasis upon an agentic third age invites the obvious criticism that no period of life exists as autonomous and unconnected with previous lives and previous periods of life what is significant is this declaration that the third age is historically 'new' and thus free to be defined by the choices of its constituents.

Do such positive freedoms seem probable? Are the newly retired really likely to serve as a radical force creating some new form of society where education work and leisure become inextricably fused?[39] Are they going to act as the guarantors of all that is good, beautiful and true?[40] The idea of a vanguard 'age class' pushing forward radical change in society seems a uniquely British notion.[41] In America, views concerning the emergence of a 'new' age group are expressed, but with a rather different perspective. The American emphasis is upon the new-agers themselves – how they live, what they think, what values they illustrate, what lifestyles they lead.[42] In a sense the individual lives of 'third-agers' are taken to represent new possibilities for personal identity rather than representations of a new ideology of citizenship. The American interest is not to establish a new class of citizen but rather to advertise to those who wish to listen that a new style of being an older person is possible; that it is exciting, desirable and ultimately attractive and consumable.

Behind much British third-age rhetoric is the expectation that the state should heed this project, and modify its institutions accordingly. State action is demanded and justified because third-agers are really working on behalf of all other groups and classes in society. Detractors of third-ageism question the positive freedoms claimed for third-agers and stress the continuing influences of class and gender in shaping the experience of later life.[43] They point out how many pensioners remain poor; how women and minorities make up the bulk of the downtrodden fourth-age class; how the unemployed and the part-time employed fail to benefit from occupational pensions; how men rarely face the prospects of institutionalization in late life, or indeed the experience of being a lone pensioner, isolated from the community and maintained economically and socially only through the state. Such critics point to the continuation of health inequalities in later life, the severe restrictions placed upon those living on benefits. They point to the continuities established across the lifespan through the differential distribution of economic power and privilege.

Other arguments exist that seek to place 'foundationalist' barriers in front of the progress of third-age ideology – not just class and gender, but also the irrevocability of physical ageing. At bottom it is claimed there is no escape from the fact that bodies age, deteriorate and give out. The 'Alzheimerization' of ageing is but one elaboration of this general thesis – namely that the very hardware resources to sustain, let alone fashion, an identity in later life will eventually give out, bringing all such self-projects to a suitably mocking end. All these arguments coalesce in expressing scepticism about the potential of individual agency in later life and instead seek to 'improve' the circumstances of older people by improved health care, increased pensions, economic equalization of men and women's work opportunities and a greater redistribution of resources across classes and across the lifespan.

In response it can be argued that age is a great equalizer: that class differences – in health and well-being – are less marked later in life compared with early in life; that gender becomes a less salient source of social differentiation at older ages than it does at younger ages; that historical economic development has ensured that older people have acquired sufficient income and wealth (typically in the form of housing equity) to provide most if not all with sufficient means to reshape their work-related identities; that with increasing technology, physical age differences will matter less and less; and finally that with the rise of the user/consumer movement, recipients of health and welfare will increasingly be able to position themselves as informed and questioning clients of health and welfare services to which they feel historically entitled as 'paid-up' senior citizens.[44]

The problem with this sort of argument is that it can be sustained not through any enhancing of the position of older people but by a process of equalizing down. Thus gender matters less, because sexuality is expressed weakly if at all; income ceases to matter as age debilitates and robs all of their well-being; consumer status has little meaning in structuring power relations when that status is acquired through illness, lack or disability. Structures in short become less powerful when agency declines, but such a loss of influence merely deprives all older people of the opportunity to exercise agency. In the absence of alternative structures, agency cannot be exercised simply in the spaces that age has come to occupy. The scope to create a self-identity based upon age alone is inevitably problematic – a point Young and Schiller recognize in their proposal to 'banish' age from the social landscape, along with any idea of age-related 'entitlements' or requirements.

The tyranny of the past is most evident in traditional societies – not normally associated with the devaluing of old age. Traditional societies of course are stable and repetitive – enabling older members to accrue benefits from familiarity. Agricultural work rarely fosters retirement and it sustains patterns of inheritance that ensure a degree of interdependency amongst the generations. Modern societies in contrast have pursued change and innovation, and moved away from intergenerational dependency. Until recently, however, such societies have been locked into class and gender relations that in many ways have served as rigid a framework over the course of people's lives as had land inheritance and

41

religiously framed statuses in earlier 'traditional' societies. The coming of what has been termed by some as 'postmodern' or 'postindustrial' society has altered many of the structures that frame adult life. It is these most recent changes that offer a glimpse of how later life may indeed become less a shadow of a fixed and inherently disadvantaging past.

## Class, cohort and retirement

Despite the experience of two cataclysmic world wars, those who started work at the beginning of this century and retired some 40–50 years later saw little change over the course of their working lives. Work took place largely in factories, fields and mines and the casual labour of the construction industry. In Britain and elsewhere in Europe and America, only a minority had access to an occupational pension. In 1950, the value of the British state pension (and occupational pensions too) was considerably below that of the wages of the employed workforce.[45] Two out of three people in poverty at that time were pensioners. They lived mostly in poor-quality rented accommodation. Holidays of any sort were rare – holidays abroad almost unheard of. Their expenditure was largely confined to household necessities. Hardly any pensioner households had access to a car, to central heating or to a telephone.

Contrast this with the position of those who entered the workforce in the 1950s and who are now retiring. Some form of occupational or personal pension covers almost 90 per cent of the British workforce. Less than one-fifth are employed in manufacturing industry, agriculture or mining. In the last two decades, income from occupational pensions has risen by more than 150 per cent for recently retired people; investment income by just under 150 per cent and overall income by 85 per cent.[46] Set in the context of the steady rise in pensioners' incomes from the 1950s to the late 1970s, these more recent increases confirm a continuing growth in retired people's incomes throughout each decade since the 1950s.[47] Figures for the United States were illustrated earlier in this chapter.

Improving wages over the same period have meant that those now retiring will almost invariably have a telephone, TV and VCR, central heating, automatic washing machine and a fridge-freezer. They will most

probably own their own house, have a car and eat out at least occasion-
ally. They are more likely than earlier cohorts of newly retired people to
exercise, deliberately eat healthier foods and take short-break holidays.
They are also more likely to choose to live abroad – to make a radical
break in their lifestyle after retirement.[48] Their previous work history
will have involved more job changes, greater upward occupational
mobility and increased geographical mobility than any previous cohort
had experienced. Put simply their lives are more varied, contain a greater
sense of movement and self-improvement, are less spatially confined
and as individuals they are better informed than any previous generation of retired people.[49]

As a consequence, present-day cohorts of retirees are more heterogeneous than ever before. Their lives reflect a more varied pattern of
accumulated material and cultural capital arising from differential
exposure to work-related benefits, local, national and international consumer fashions, the growth in the 'personal finance' market, particular
shifts in the housing market and the varied acquisition of household
luxury and 'special-interest' goods, arising especially from frequent house
moves. Associated with and contributing significantly to this greater
heterogeneity is a greater level of income inequality with increasing
age. US gerontologists Crystal and Shea have referred to the cumulative
advantage/cumulative disadvantage thesis as a means of explaining and
exploring the greater disparity in income evident during the 'post-work'
period of life. They argue that members of a pension/asset elite benefit
cumulatively not only from their work-related income but also from
work-related (latent) investment resources enabling them later in life to
move increasingly above the average economic trajectory of adults, while
those 'systematically excluded from or marginalised within the employment system become more dependent on the compensatory mechanisms
of the state that operate at the margins and preserve inequalities'.[50]

Crystal and Shea have conducted a careful analysis of the sources
of inequality arising out of the income and assets of older Americans.
While supplementary security income promotes equality and old age
social security produces very little inequality, they found that dividend,
investment, state and local contributory pensions and annuity incomes
contribute considerably to late life income disparities.[51] Assuming that
the very real increase in average incomes experienced by older people in

most Western societies has been contributed to by both improved state provision and greater private (including work-related) investments and pensions, the implication of Crystal and Shea's work is that the gap between the well off and the (relatively) poor older adult population will continue to widen unless there is a massive expansion of state provision – a scenario that seems extremely unlikely.[52]

How far such growing heterogeneity fosters multiple lifestyles and increases the range of options available to older people to construct new 'third age' cultures remains to be seen. If 'third-agers' are predominantly drawn from white, male, younger and well-off married retirees, in short the major beneficiaries of current social and economic practices, then the lifestyles chosen and celebrated by such third-agers seem unlikely contenders for the life cycle revolution that writers such as Laslett and Young are predicting. But whether a richer group of retirees will have an inflationary impact on lifestyle depends upon more than wealth and income alone. Although it is tempting to redefine the 'third age' as shorthand for older and richer adults, it would be a mistake to do so. Equally significant is the differential accumulation of cultural capital that successive cohorts of older people have acquired – which in turn reflects the changing times through which they have lived.

Cohort and generation obviously are interlinked. Each cohort of retired persons is the product of a particular generation and each possesses a unique as well as a common culture. These sources of cultural distinction are varied and have accelerated over the twentieth century. They include such elements as the rise of feminism and the slow growth towards parity in earning power between men and women, the expansion of the market and the commodification of lifestyle through the clothing, food and entertainment industries, the blurring of distinctions between 'elite' and 'popular' art that has been facilitated through the design, marketing and advertising industries, the growth of psychological, social and geopolitical information arising through the technological development of the mass media and the expansion of identity and issue politics that have made such inroads into traditional class politics. All these processes of cultural change that make up 'high' or 'late' modernity permeate the adult lives of the various generations of retirees at different times in their life. Further they also interact with such vertically-structured influences as gender, education, ethnicity and class – affecting the level and rate of such cultural penetration. To collapse such complex patterns of cultural and social change that contribute to fashioning individual 'third-age' narratives into the vertical constraints of class position is to ignore much of what is most distinctive about the post-war era and the 'regimes of signification' that have been established throughout post-modern society.

The third-age agenda is not one marked out by its homogeneity or its capacity to represent collective interests. Retirement has become an arena more fragmented and heterogeneous in its social, economic and physical expression than ever before. The largest point of rupture is itself a complex matter of culture, class, gender and generation. Those with the greatest material and cultural surplus who might be thought the leading protagonists for 'new-age' consumerism are precisely those most likely to distance themselves from the collective plight of the fourth age. The economic dynamo behind the third age is evident. It seems improbable that it will lead toward greater collective provision for the frail elderly. In a later chapter we shall discuss in more detail the relationship between income in retirement and its role in shaping the physical experience of age and infirmity. For now it is sufficient to note that third-age identities are likely to be elaborated through increasing material consumption, a sense of 'packing life in' to a period of adulthood of uncertain length and a wary and ambivalent position in relation to providing for 'old age'. Third-agers, while acknowledging old age, are likely to prefer to live at a considerable physical and psychological distance from it.

## Gender and retirement

In discussing the heterogeneity arising from the increasingly complex histories of consumption and production in the second half of the twentieth century we have only touched upon the role that gender may play in constraining the identities such social and economic processes make available. Under-theorizing the role of gender in our understanding of ageing has been a common complaint against social gerontologists whether they be functionalists expounding disengagement theory, structured dependency theorists critically examining the role of the state in shaping later life or activists championing a third-age lifestyle. In this next section we consider how men's and women's 'adult life trajectories' differ and what implications this may have for the various cultures of ageing that emerge in retirement.

Consideration of the gendered basis of the adult lifecourse has until relatively recently focused upon the emergence of women within the public arena of work – their entry into and maintenance of work-based adult identities – rather than their 'exit' from an adult identity in retirement. The menopause has been the only central topic that researchers – feminist and non-feminist alike – have pursued for its 'exit-like' properties. Feminism 'discovered' old age relatively late in its own evolution and – possibly in consequence – has approached the issue of ageing with many of the essentialist assumptions that traditional gerontologists have long held. Harrington and Kunkel state 'Mainstream feminism of the 1960s, 1970s and early 1980s assumed that "woman" was a unifying category separable from other dimensions of oppression'.[53] As such there was little interest in examining how the category 'woman' served different functions and was subject to different influences at differing points in the lifecourse. Although this last decade has seen a new interest in how age and gender influence each other as identities,[54] much of the 'age and gender' writing has tended to concentrate upon the menopause as a marker of age (even if to 'deconstruct' it). Considerably less attention has been paid to the constraints that working life may impose on women's post-work incomes and their opportunities to develop consumption-mediated identities in later life. We shall focus upon three factors potentially constraining women's third-age identities – women's differential access to pensions and consequently their differing economic position in later life; women's relationship to the domestic economy and the influence of caregiving obligations upon women's freedom to create themselves in later life; and finally the significance of ageing and sexuality and their relationship to 'feminine' identity.

## Gender and retirement income

Several writers have noted that older women are less likely to have an occupational pension and if they have one it is unlikely to yield the same benefits as men's.[55] This is a reflection of less stable employment histories, greater occupational segmentation, higher rates of part-time work and more limited opportunities for career progression. While single and divorced women are much more likely to have occupational pensions than either married women or widows, whether or not marriage is a benefit or disbenefit to women in later life is a complex question. In general new widows experience a growth in their individual income while suffering a loss in household income. Whether this results in an overall deterioration in economic well-being depends in part upon the level of income enjoyed as a joint household. Since widowhood early in retirement affects poorer households more than rich ones, the lower incomes of households headed by widows are not straightforward to interpret. Although studies in Europe and America confirm that households headed by older women have lower income and lower net worth than those headed by men, these differences tend to be more marked at later ages than immediately on retirement – i.e. amongst earlier cohorts of retirees.

There are signs of gradual progress toward parity in the household income of retired single men and women, primarily as a result of rises in the lifetime earnings, labour market attachment and occupational attainment of working age women. As Phillip Levine and his colleagues have noted:

> closing the sex gap in years of work, average pay and occupational attainment . . . [will] . . . almost eliminate the retirement income gap for nonmarried people.[56]

The changing economic potential for women to exercise a third-age identity can be examined in other ways. Table 3.2 illustrates the proportions of over-65-year-old households characterized as falling within the 'middle income range' for US households from the late 1960s to the 1990s.

The slow erosion of differential rates of 'poverty' amongst older men and women evident in the above table is not confined to single people.

TABLE 3.2 Percentage of US 'late-life' households enjoying 'middle level' incomes[57]

| Household type | 1969 | 1978 | 1987 | 1996 |
|---|---|---|---|---|
| Married couple 65 years+ | 58% | 65% | 70% | 69% |
| Single male 65 years+ | 42% | 46% | 52% | 57% |
| Single female 65 years+ | 29% | 40% | 43% | 46% |

Amongst the over-65-year-old population, all the newly retired – those best placed to take on third-age identities – will be progressively less affected by gender-based income and asset inequalities. Irrespective of marital status, men and women, in the US at least, are starting off their retirement with more equal access to the opportunities afforded by the growing consumer orientation in later life. To quote the findings of another recently published US study of gender differences in pension wealth:

> the dramatic reduction over the past thirty years in gender differences in employment characteristics, which account for most of the pension gender gap among workers currently approaching retirement, suggests that the gap in pension wealth between men and women will narrow . . . [and] the likely result of these trends will be greater pension wealth for women, leading to more equitable labor outcomes for working women and improved economic security for elderly women in the next century.[58]

As this trend continues, inevitably it will add to the horizontal inequalities of cohort and generation at the same time as it erodes those vertical inequalities associated with gender.

### Gender, caregiving and retirement

Despite signs of growing parity in women's life cycle pattern of earnings, other factors may constrain their opportunities to construct a consumer-oriented third-age identity – in particular the ties of sustaining the domestic economy. Non-working women in their late fifties and sixties, for example, are much more likely than men to describe their status as 'looking after the home', in contrast to describing themselves as 'retired', 'unemployed' or 'long-term sick'.[59] The duty older women feel toward maintaining the domestic economy is reflected in one recent German survey of 'daily life in very old age'. The authors found the one significant gender difference in the frequency and duration of various categories of activity was the time spent on instrumental activities of daily living – shopping, cooking, cleaning and other forms of housework.[60] How far do these demands of household maintenance and personal caregiving constrain women's opportunities for an agentic third age?

Numerous studies have reported that women more than men feel an obligation toward housework, to keeping in touch with their family –

both children and grandchildren as well as their own parents, if still alive – and to maintaining the health and well-being of their partner. This combination of nurturing duties seems likely to inhibit the opportunities to engage in that 'culture of narcissism' that some might consider to be represented in 'third-age' lifestyles.[61] Studies of caregiving, grandparenting and time budgeting indicate quite marked gender differences in the extent and range of activities that men and women perform in later life. The accumulated evidence of such studies reinforces the point that women much more than men are tied to their lifelong roles as unpaid domestic workers and that these roles continue even in later life.[62] While it is difficult to judge how far such role differentiation can or will change – and indeed whether such change is inevitably beneficial to women's capacity to experience later life positively – it is important to acknowledge the potential constraints of domestic life in exercising the social citizenship of the third age.[63]

## Gender, sexuality and retirement

Finally, the positive choice of an age-related status – particularly the relatively privileged status of the third age – may prove more difficult for women than for men, because women have rarely benefited socially or personally from the ascription of 'maturity' or 'seniority'. As many writers have been at pains to point out, older men can still command sexual goods; can still be presented as 'attractive' partners; and can still play the role of lover, both in the hyperreality of film as well as in 'real-life' encounters in a way that is still culturally acceptable to most, if not all, sections of the community.[64] Masculinity in short is less compromised by social ageing. As a result, more women than men choose to disguise their age; internalize ageism and feel uncomfortable with the desexualized albeit democratic status of 'third-ager'. Those unable or unwilling to choose age-irrelevant domestic roles – playing the part of wife, daughter or grandmother at home – may find themselves either facing a desexualized existence as a third-ager, with the attendant risk of being publicly misinterpreted as a failed fourth-ager, or chancing all on the transgressive denial of ageing, through elaborate and effortful routines of self-care.[65]

We shall consider the broader issues arising from the alignment between women's identity and their sexual role in more detail in the next chapter. Here we consider the potentially inhibiting effect of gender and sexuality on the way in which third-age identities can be exercised. Feminist writers such as Margaret Gullette see mid-life women oppressed by current discussions over the menopause and the need for women to 'restore' their compromised sexuality through HRT. She argues that this 'personal health' discourse serves only to divert women from exercising a more civic role which their improving economic and political position now allows.[66] Germaine Greer has drawn attention to 'the utter invisibility of middle-aged women in English literary culture' and the general failure of modern culture to offer a positive image for older women. She too has argued – though from a slightly different premise – that the medicalization of the menopause has served women ill: 'One thing . . . seems certain: the women who imagine that the solution to the complex of problems they must surmount during the climacteric can be supplied by the medical establishment have historically turned out to be the unluckiest of all.' For Greer, as for other mid-life feminists, loosening the links between sexuality and womanhood offers the opportunity and hope for older women to experience a new sense of personal serenity and to derive a new sense of freedom and power from this liberation from the sexual.[67]

The Australian gerontologist Diane Gibson has also written of the silence over older women's lives. She draws particular attention to the silence over the positive aspects of later life for women. She feels that social gerontologists – including those writing from a feminist perspective – have too easily problematized older women as the typical fourth-ager – very old, living alone and seriously disabled. This she argues ignores: 'the fact that the experience of being old and female is [also] one characterised by . . . better social support, higher social participation, [and] greater continuities'.[68] What Gibson and other writers seem to be alluding to is the greater social capital from which women can express a 'self-identity' in later life that is determined neither by past activity within the realm of production nor by current reproductive vigour.

This raises the question of whether older women are more able to live their later lives protected from the effort of having deliberately to engineer a new identity for themselves as 'third-agers', 'senior citizens' or 'retired persons'; in short whether women are less oppressed by the postmodern demands of self-reflexivity. Part of the social capital that older women possess may be the continuity that women's lives express in their unending involvement and care in the reproduction of home and family life. Intergenerational links may prove a more powerful means of rendering women's age irrelevant by enabling their roles as wife, mother, sister and daughter to continue to evolve in later life – despite the menopause and despite retirement.

## Ageing in private: the role of family in suppressing/repressing later life identities

Discussion of gender leads to consideration of the general significance of the family in structuring identity in later life. While the social processes of production and consumption dominate the public sphere, any discussion about the exercise of identities that embraces or excludes age cannot be concluded without reference to the role played by family life. Numerous studies have indicated the importance of family life in maintaining people's sense of feeling good about themselves and their lives.[69] Roles within the family are of course less centrally affected by changes in economic status (e.g. retirement) or in biological age markers (e.g. menopause) and relations between spouses, between siblings and between parents and children are less subject to such age-related discontinuities.

While statuses such as grandparenthood might seem to confer a kind of age-related social identity upon individuals, people are now becoming grandparents across an ever-widening portion of their adult lifespan – some people in their late thirties, some in their late eighties. While there is little doubt that grandparenting offers older men and women opportunities to experience new roles and act as transgenerational resources within the family, personal identities within a family are more age-irrelevant than identities outside. To that extent, families offer little in the way of socially recognized identities for older people. Instead they provide the setting for constructing more idiosyncratic and essentially more personal identities. The very lack of social ascriptions may thus enable people to escape the whole issue of establishing and enacting some form of social identity as a third-ager/retired person/senior citizen etc.

Finch and Mason provide an interesting perspective on the nature of identity in their study of family obligations. They draw attention to the way that family members appear to construct what they term 'moral identities' within the family system. By this they mean the ways in which individuals within a family seek to establish a reputation for themselves – seeking to present themselves in a particular light *vis-à-vis* others in the family. Drawing upon Goffman's symbolic interaction model, they outline how individuals 'manage' their conduct of family relationships in order to establish a moral reputation/identity from which they may draw in both present and future family exchanges.[70] The seemingly 'private' sphere of family life, however, is not immune to the destabilizing effect of late modernity. Thus their research led them to conclude that such negotiations over a moral identity within the family take place within a broader context of uncertainty regarding the rules by which family members are supposed to conduct themselves:

> we can say with some confidence that . . . there is nothing approaching a clear consensus about family responsibilities. In the late 1980s in Britain people were not acknowledging clear identifiable principles about what . . . family members should offer each other.[71]

Whether or not this apparent lack of a cultural compass is the direct result of our 'postmodern times', their work demonstrates the lack of any horizontal (class and gender) influence on the process of moral negotiations over identity in contemporary families. This reinforces the notion that domestic identities as much as 'post-work' identities increasingly are enacted with little reference to those familiar structures that 'modernist' social theory saw as conferring meaning and shape on household roles. Only when the older person becomes 'a dependent', and family members are transformed into 'carers', do the boundaries of the family become redrawn. It is at this precise point that responsibility for the older person's identity is transferred to those institutions of the state that manage care and deal in the identities of lack, need and infirmity of which the fourth age is such a part.[72]

## Notes

1 Miller, D. (1991) *Material Culture and Mass Consumption*, Blackwell, Oxford, p. 47.
2 Giddens, A. (1991) *Modernity and Self-Identity*, Polity Press, Cambridge, p. 244.
3 'The "struggle for recognition" is fast becoming the paradigmatic form of political conflict in the late twentieth century' (Fraser, N. (1995) 'From redistribution to

recognition? Dilemmas of justice in a "post-socialist" age', *New Left Review*, 212, p. 68). See also Wolfe, A. and Klausen, J. (1997) 'Identity politics and the welfare state', *Social Philosophy and Policy*, 14: 2, pp. 231–55.

4 For a more extended discussion on the transformation of work in modern society, see Crook, S., Pakulski, J. and Waters, M. (1992) *Postmodernization: Change in Advanced Society,* Sage, London, esp. Chapters 4 and 6.

5 In place of the relatively homogenizing uniform of factory overalls and strict workplace codes about suitable attire, today's office-based employees are relatively free to wear what they choose, display what jewellery and make-up they like, what hairstyles they prefer etc. Increasingly this applies to and affects both sexes. See Bauman, Z. (1998) *Work, Consumerism and the New Poor*, Open University Press, Buckingham, and his discussion of the transfer from an ethic to an aesthetic of work, pp. 32–6.

6 See Veblen, T. (1899) *The Theory of the Leisure Class*, Macmillan, New York.

7 See, for example, Thompson, W.E., Streib, G.F. and Kosa, J. (1960) 'The effect of retirement on personal adjustment: a panel analysis', *Journal of Gerontology*, 15: 165–9; Kierckhoff, A.C. (1964) 'Husband–wife expectations and reactions to retirement', *Journal of Gerontology*, 19: 510–16; Stokes, R. and Maddox, G. (1967) 'Some social factors in retirement adaptation', *Journal of Gerontology*, 29: 329–33.

8 See, for example, Streib, G.F. and Schneider, C.J. (1971) *Retirement in American Society: Impact and Process*, Cornell University Press, New York and Atchley, R.C. (1976) *The Sociology of Retirement*, John Wiley, Chichester.

9 See Cumming, E. and Henry, W.E. (1961) *Growing Old: the Process of Disengagement*, Basic Books, New York.

10 See Townsend, P. (1981) 'The structured dependency of the elderly: a creation of social policy in the twentieth century', *Ageing and Society*, 1: 5–28; Phillipson, C. (1982) *Capitalism and the Construction of Old Age*, Macmillan, London; Walker, A. (1980) 'The social creation of poverty and dependency in old age', *Journal of Social Policy*, 9: 45–75; Estes, C. (1979) *The Aging Enterprise*, Jossey Bass, San Francisco, CA, for examples of structured dependency theorists outlined earlier.

11 Reviewing several international studies of early retirement conducted in the 1980s, Guillemard and van Gunsteren concluded: 'The end of the life course is becoming more variable, imprecise, and contingent since chronological milestones are being torn up. Nowadays no one working in the private sector knows at what age and under what conditions he or she will stop working. Retirement as a social situation . . . no longer constitutes the horizon where everyone foresees the pathway to be taken one day out of the labor force toward old age . . . The social construction that closely associated definitive withdrawal, old age, and retirement is breaking up . . . The meaning of the last stage of life is blurred'. (Guillemard, A-M. and van Gunsteren, H. (1991) 'Pathways and their prospects: a comparative interpretation of the meaning of early exit', in M. Kohli, M. Rein, A-M., Guillemard and H. van Gunsteren (eds), *Time for Retirement: Comparative Studies of Early Exit from the Labor Force*, Cambridge University Press, Cambridge, p. 383).

12 Source: http://www.census.gov/hhes/income/histinc, Table H-10.

13 Using data from the British Family Resources Survey 1993/94, Barrientos has shown that some form of occupational or personal pension scheme covered over 90% of the employed population of Britain. As each cohort of workers reaches retirement age over the course of the next few decades the cumulative value of the various

contributory pension schemes will entail a greater return as the period of working life covered by occupational and private pension schemes extends. (Barrientos, A. (1996) 'Supplementary pension coverage in Britain', *Economics Paper 18*, Working Paper Series, University of Hertfordshire.)

14 Townsend, P. (1981) *op. cit.*, p. 23.

15 Tanner notes that the proportion of men aged 55–64 in Britain who are retired 'has been increasing steadily' over the last two decades. Similar trends are evident in the USA. While 'spikes' exist – at ages 60 and 65 – these exist against a background of rising rates of retirement at other ages, typically before age 60 (see Tanner, S. (1998) 'The dynamics of male retirement behaviour', *Fiscal Studies*, 19, 175–96).

16 It is illustrative that the only social security measure that was extended to the black African population during colonial rule in South Africa was the provision of an old age pension (see Lund, F. (1993) 'State social benefits in South Africa', *International Social Security Review*, 46: 5–25).

17 Harper, S. and Thane, P. (1990) 'The consolidation of "old age" as a phase of life, 1945–1965', in M. Jefferys (ed.), *Growing Old in the Twentieth Century*, Routledge, London, p. 47.

18 To some extent this was still true when US president Franklin Roosevelt introduced old age social security legislation in the early 1930s. Quadagno and Hardy note: 'Initially OAI (Old Age Insurance) benefits were so low and coverage so limited that few workers could afford to retire . . . [such that] . . . as late as 1967, poverty rates for people over 65 were about 30%' (Quadagno, J. and Hardy, M. (1995) 'Work and retirement', in R. Binstock and L.K. George (eds), *Handbook of Aging and the Social Sciences*, 4th edn, Academic Press, New York, p. 330).

19 See for example Benson, J. (1994) *The Rise of Consumer Society in Britain 1880–1980*, Longman, London, esp. Chapter 2, pp. 35–55.

20 Hannah, L. (1986) *Inventing Retirement: the Development of Occupational Pensions in Britain*, Cambridge University Press, Cambridge, p. 126.

21 In one recent survey of older adults – people over 60 – 75 per cent liked the term senior citizen, 73 per cent the adjective 'retired', 70 per cent 'retiree' and a similar proportion 'senior'. In contrast less than 10 per cent liked 'old', 'oldster' 'old man/ woman' and 'old person' and less than half 'older adult' (Chafetz, P.K., Holmes, H., Lande, K., Childress, E. and Glazer, H.R. (1998) 'Older adults and the news media: utilisation, opinions and preferred reference terms', *The Gerontologist*, 38: 481–9).

22 See Katz, S. (1996) *Disciplining Old Age: the Formation of Gerontological Knowledge*, University of Virginia Press, Charlottesville, VA, p. 66.

23 See Pampel, F.C. and Weiss, J.A. (1983) 'Economic development, pension policies and the labor force participation of aged males', *American Journal of Sociology*, 89: 95–102; Gurkan, A.A. and Gilleard, C.J. (1987) 'Socioeconomic development and the status of elderly men in Turkey: a test of modernization theory', *Journal of Gerontology*, 42: 353–7.

24 Graebner (1980), pp. 191–2 describes the countercyclical role envisioned by Roosevelt and his advisors for the bill seen as 'inextricably linked' to its welfare functions (Graebner, W.A. (1980) *History of Retirement: the Meaning and Function of an American Institution 1885–1978*, Yale University Press, New Haven, CT).

25 May, T. (1996) *Restating Political and Social Change*, Open University Press, Buckingham.

26 See Macnicol, J. and Blaikie, A. (1989) 'The politics of retirement, 1908–1948'. In M. Jefferys (ed.), *Growing Old in the Twentieth Century*, Routledge, London, pp. 34–7.

27 Graebner, W. (1980) *op. cit.*, p. 231.

28 See Hannah, L. (1986) *op. cit.*, pp. 126–7.

29 See Barrientos, A. (1996) *op. cit.*

30 Laslett, P. (1989) *A Fresh Map of Life: the Emergence of the Third Age*, Weidenfeld and Nicolson, London. Young, M. and Schuller, T. (1991) *Life after Work: the Arrival of the Ageless Society*, HarperCollins, London.

31 Sheehy, G. (1996) *New Passages*, HarperCollins, London.

32 Guillemard, A-M. and van Gunsteren, H. (1991) *op. cit.*

33 Young, M. and Schuller, T. (1991) *op. cit.*, pp. 105–25.

34 Giddens, A. (1991) *Modernity and Self Identity*, Polity Press, Cambridge, p. 14.

35 Young, M. and Schuller, T. (1991) *op. cit.*, p. 179.

36 Young, M. and Schuller, T. (1991) *op. cit.*, pp. 19–20.

37 Laslett, P. (1989) *op. cit.*, p. 4.

38 Young, M. and Schuller, T. (1991) *op. cit.*, p. 181.

39 See Young, M. and Schuller, T. (1991) *op. cit.*, pp. 178–9.

40 Laslett, P. (1989) *op. cit.*, pp. 196–203.

41 See also Midwinter, E. (1985) 'Old Age: Vanguard of the revolution', in A. Butler (ed.), *Ageing: Recent Advances and Creative Responses*, Croom Helm, Beckenham.

42 See, for example, Downes, P., Tuittle, I., Faul, P. and Mudd, V. (1996) *The New Older Woman*, Celestial Arts, Los Angeles, CA, or Sheehy, G. (1996), *op. cit.* In the latter, Sheehy expounds on the 'birth of second adulthood' from 45 to 85+, a period filled with such exciting events as 'passage to the age of integrity', life in the 'flaming fifties', 'serene sixties', 'sage seventies', 'uninhibited eighties' right up to the 'nobility of the nineties'. She describes 'a revolution in the life cycle . . . the whole shape of the lifecycle has been fundamentally altered'. Sheehy exhorts her readers thus:

> Stop and recalculate. Imagine the day you turn 40 as the infancy of another life. That is what this book is all about, an entirely new concept of the life cycle – a Second Adulthood in middle life. (Sheehy, (1996) *op. cit.*, p. 7)

In *The New Older Woman*, the talk flips easily from 'taking control of one's life' to the problems of 'fighting the fashion wars' and the lack of smart fashionable clothes in sizes 14 and over. As one participant says:

> We want the vitality, energy, enthusiasm and excitement that's associated with youth but we have to select the kind of youthfulness we want: extract the good part, throw out the idea that we exist for someone else. . . . (Downs *et al.* (1998) *op. cit.*, p. 58)

43 Bury, M. (1998) 'Ageing, gender and sociological theory', in J. Ginn and S. Arbor (eds), *Ageing, Gender and the Lifecourse*, Sage, London, pp. 15–34.

44 Recent Eurobarometer studies indicate that, among the older populations of European Union countries, there is a marked preference for the term 'senior citizen' as a means of socially identifying older people (Walker, A. (1993) *Age and Attitudes*, European Union Commission, Brussels, p. 3).

45 See, for example, Fiegehen, G.C. (1986) 'Income after retirement', *Social Trends*, 16: pp. 13–18; Hannah, L. (1986) *op. cit.*, pp. 30–45.

46 Data from Department of Social Security (1998) *The Pensioners' Income Series 1996/7*, The Stationery Office, London, Tables 1, 2, 3 and 4.

47 'Older pensioners are poorer than the more recently retired. This fact has been confirmed in numerous studies in the UK . . . as well as in the US . . . and elsewhere'

(Johnson, P., Stears, G. and Webb, S. (1998) 'The dynamics of incomes and occupational pensions after retirement', *Fiscal Studies*, 19, pp. 197–8). That this is a cohort effect rather than a progressive impoverishment over the course of retirement is suggested by the same authors' longitudinal study of pensioner incomes which they found 'tend on average to be quite stable' (p. 213).

48 The steady increase in the number of British couples retiring to France, has been the subject of a study by Hoggart and Buller, who have shown clearly the importance of 'middle-class' background and 'couple' status in influencing these retirement decisions (See Hoggart, K. and Buller, H. (1995) 'Retired British home owners in rural France', *Ageing and Society*, 15: 325–54).

49 See, for example, *Social Trends*, vol. 29, Tables 10.4 and 13.13, and the various General Household Surveys, 1974–1995, HMSO, London, for this and much other related information concerning the income, resources, activities and expenditure patterns of pensioner households. Similar comments on the improvements in the material aggregate well-being of older Americans have been made by Robert Hudson (Hudson, R.B. (1996) 'The changing face of aging politics', *The Gerontologist*, 36: 33–5).

50 O'Rand, A.M. (1996) 'The precious and the precocious: understanding cumulative disadvantage and cumulative advantage over the life course', *The Gerontologist*, 36, p. 233. See also Crystal, S. and Shea, D. (1990) *op. cit. infra*.

51 See Table 2 in Crystal, S. and Shea, D. (1990) 'Cumulative advantage, cumulative disadvantage and income inequality among elderly people', *The Gerontologist*, 30: 437–43.

52 Sheila Shaver has provided evidence of the impact of various combinations of selective and universal provision of state support in alleviating poverty amongst older people. Her findings imply that where universal social insurance is provided there is less inequality in later life and by implication less cumulative advantage/disadvantage than in those economies where voluntary supplementary pensions and personal investments account for a greater proportion of the total income of the older population (Shaver, S. (1996) 'Universality and selectivity in aged income support', in V. Minichiello, N. Chappell, H. Kendig and A. Walker (eds), (1996) *Sociology of Aging: International Perspectives*, International Sociological Association, pp. 278–303).

53 Harrington, C.L. and Kunkel, S. (1996) 'Feminist politics, critical gerontology and the sociology of aging', *ibid.*, p. 9.

54 Arber, S. and Ginn, J. (1991) *Gender and Later Life*, Sage, London.

55 See Laczko, F. and Phillipson, C. (1991) 'Great Britain: the contradictions of early exit', in M. Kohli, M. Rein, A-M. Guillemard and H. van Gunsteren (eds), *Time for Retirement: Comparative Studies of Early Exit from the Labor Force*, Cambridge University Press, Cambridge, pp. 222–51, p. 242 and Moen, P. (1995) 'Gender, age and the life course', in R. Binstock and L.K. George (eds), *Handbook of Aging and the Social Sciences*, 4th edn, Academic Press, New York, p. 174.

56 Levine, P.B., Mitchell, O.S. and Phillips, J.W. (1999) 'Worklife determinants of retirement differentials between men and women', *NBER Working Paper No. 7243*, National Bureau of Economic Research, Cambridge, MA, pp. 20–1.

57 Source: http://www.census.gov/hhes/income/mednhhld, Tables 11–15.

58 Johnson, R.W., Sambamoorthi, U. and Crystal, S. (1999) 'Gender differences in pension wealth: estimates using provider data', *The Gerontologist*, 39, pp. 332–3.

59 Laczko, F. and Phillipson, C. (1991) *op. cit.*, Tables 7.10 and 7.11.

60 For a European perspective see Horgas, A.L., Wilms, H-U. and Baltes, M.M. (1998) 'Daily life in very old age: everyday activities as expression of successful living', *The Gerontologist*, 38: 556–68, Table 8. In the USA, evidence of gender imbalance is illustrated in a study by Keith (1994) who found older women spent 35 hours per week on housework, contrasted with 7.5 hours by men (Keith, P.M. (1994) 'A typology of orientations towards household and marital roles of older men and women', in E.H. Thompson (ed.), *Older Men's Lives*, Sage Publications, London, pp. 141–58).

61 See Lasch, C. (1980) *The Culture of Narcissism*, Abacus, London, esp. pp. 207–17.

62 Gibson, D. (1998) *Aged Care*, Cambridge University Press, Cambridge, p. 77.

63 Pavlako and Artis have noted that 'Over the course of the twentieth century more recent cohorts of women have been more likely than earlier cohorts to be involved in both caregiving and employment'. They found that employment status was largely unrelated to whether or not women took on caregiving responsibilities but that caregiving invariably led to a reduction of hours worked with a cost to both short-term and long-term income. The implication was that the reduction in hours worked had a long term impact on earnings and subsequent income in retirement – further compromising women's economic potential to fulfil consumer driven retirement lifestyles (Pavlako, E.K. and Artis, J.E. (1997) 'Women's caregiving and paid work: causal relationships in late midlife', *Journal of Gerontology*, 52B: S170–9). However, the same issue of the journal contains another study which suggests caution in overemphasizing the restrictions that caregiving imposes upon older women's participation in leisure and other social activities. Older women who had caregiving responsibilities were found to have similar levels of participation in social and leisure activities to women without such responsibilities (Farkas, J.I. and Himes, C.L. (1997) 'The influence of caregiving and employment on the voluntary activities of midlife and older women', *Journal of Gerontology*, 52B: S180–9).

64 See the article on 'Star Power' in the March–April 1998 issue of *Modern Maturity* for a brief overview of the continuing attraction of male stars aged 60 and over.

65 One example of this potentially risky strategy is illustrated by the way Jane Fonda's status has been compromised through her decision to have aesthetic surgery for breast enhancement – see for example Gloria Steinem's ambiguous comments in the recent issue of *Modern Maturity* (May–June 1999, p. 53).

66 'We're all more vulnerable because of . . . menopause discourse . . . Middle-ageism in general constructs self-centredness in the bad sense, distracting women from our dense, multilayered, interesting lives, draining energy and confidence and subverting midlife power that could go into politics – ending war, hunger, poverty, sexism and ageism itself' (Gullette, M.M. (1997) 'Menopause as magic marker: discursive consolidation in the United States and strategies for cultural combat', in P. Komesaroff, P. Rothfield and J. Daly (eds), *Reinterpreting the Menopause: Cultural and Philosophical Issues*, Routledge: London, p. 191).

67 See for example the interview with Gloria Steinem in *Modern Maturity*, May–June 1999, when she speaks of the release from 'the expectation of looking and behaving a certain way, of always having a man in your life' (p. 53).

68 Gibson, D. (1998) *op. cit.*, p. 144.

69 See, for example, Coleman, P.G. (1984) 'Assessing self-esteem and its sources in elderly people', *Ageing and Society*, 4: 117–35 for the salience of the family as an enduring source of well-being in later life.

70 See Finch, J. and Mason, J. (1993) *Negotiating Family Responsibilities*, Routledge, London, esp. pp. 129–61.

71 Finch, J. and Mason, J. (1993) *op. cit.*, p. 21.

72 The concept of family boundaries and their significance in relation to mental infirmity in later life has been developed by Pauline Boss (see Boss, P. and Greenberg, J. (1984) 'Family boundary ambiguity: a new variable in family stress theory', *Family Process*, 23: 535–46; Boss, P., Caron, W., Hornal, J. and Mortimer, J. (1990) 'Predictors of depression in caregivers of dementia patients: boundary ambiguity and mastery', *Family Process*, 29: 245–54).

# CHAPTER 4

# Identity, self-care and staying young

If 'third-ageism' represents the positive reframing of later life as a chosen identity, characterized by active choices and later-lifestyle commodification, other cultural strategies can be discerned that more emphatically resist any notion of a status change in retirement. Taken together these cultural practices emphasize the theme of 'staying young'. Unlike those practices that constitute 'third-ageism', those that constitute 'staying young' are not confined to adults of any particular age group. Rather they are shared and expressed by growing segments of the whole adult population. In this chapter we examine the broader cultural forces that seem to be operative within these 'anti-ageing' identities in later life. In so doing we address issues that go beyond the specific concerns, behaviours and attitudes of the retired population. This widened perspective is needed because within the cultural practices that make up adult 'lifestyle' and the socialized desire for self-definition 'ageing' has come to play an important role, not so much as a key element of adult identity, but because of its capacity to constitute an ever-present risk to the success of the identity project itself. Resisting not just old age but ageing itself is becoming an integral component of many adult lifestyles. While the former strategy marks the central issue for 'third-ageism', it is the latter that forms the central theme to the cultural practices and 'lifestylism' that makes up 'staying young'.

## Self-definition and the technologies of the self[1]

In considering 'age-resisting' practices, we are examining one of the most acute manifestations of postmodern malaise, namely the desire for individual lives to be conducted according to an unspecified but pervasive lifestyle aesthetic.[2] The place of this new and decidedly 'physical' culture is explored in relation to the widespread concern with physical exercise, self-control and the disciplining of the body. Lacking clear external reference points by which to judge the success of these cultural practices, the demand for self-expression and self-definition encourages the apparent transgression of externally constrained social identities. Awareness of ageing serves as the ever-present premonition that such aspirations are in the end beyond our reach. As such, ageing remains unaccommodated, and increasingly an identity framed through resistance – an identity of staying young, choosing not to grow old.

Foucault coined the term 'technologies of the self' to describe those practices:

> which permit individuals to effect by their own means or with help from others a certain number of operations on their own bodies and souls thoughts conduct and way of being so as to transform themselves in order to attain a certain state of happiness, purity, wisdom, perfection or immortality.[3]

Using various historical sources dating back to the Hellenic era, he sought to illustrate how themes of self-control and self-care have been well-established 'technologies' possessing a history comparable with other more widely discussed technologies – of production, signification and power. At the same time it is evident that our contemporary technologies of the self are of a very different order from those described in Greco-Roman philosophy and the early Christian manuals on confession and self-examination. The reflexive play that characterizes contemporary self-preoccupations derives from practices that are far more varied and unstable than in the past. Not only do present-day technologies of the self exhibit a greater fluidity in the forms they take, but as Foucault himself points out they possess a further and more important characteristic – namely their intent 'to constitute, positively, a new self' – a feature of modernity that represents the most decisive break with the self technologies of the past.

More recently Giddens, in his book *Modernity and Self-Identity*, has discussed many of the key features that such contemporary technologies of the self display. He writes:

> In the post-traditional order of modernity . . . self identity becomes a reflexively organised endeavour. The reflexive project of the self, which consists in the sustaining of coherent yet continuously revised biographical narratives, takes place in the context of multiple choice. . . . because of the 'openness' of

social life today the pluralisation of contexts of action and the diversity of 'authorities', lifestyle choice is increasingly important in the constitution of self-identity and daily activity.[4]

Thus characterized, self-invention seems to be a central organizing principle in the conduct of life. But what Foucault also observed was that such practices of 'self'-care and 'self'-control are themselves contained within other technologies of control. The manner in which such 'control of control' is exercised is what Foucault termed the processes of 'governmentality'. While Giddens acknowledges that there exist 'standardizing influences' affecting these technologies, he is at pains to point out the deliberate life planning that defines the modern self project. Thus, for example, rather than seeing 'psychotherapy' as a cultural practice reflecting the inherent commodification of contemporary self technologies, Giddens prefers to frame it as 'an expert system deeply implicated in the reflexive project of the self', one that 'should be understood and evaluated essentially as a methodology of life planning', a technology for taking control,[5] a natural extension of the rise of expert systems in contemporary society.

Illustrative of the 'agency', which Giddens attributes to the project of the reflexive self, is the resurgent interest in what he refers to as 'life politics'. Life politics are defined as sharing the following features: 'political decisions flowing from freedom of choice and generative power; the creation of morally justifiable forms of life that will promote self-actualisation [and the development of] ethics concerning the issue "how should we live?" in a post-traditional order'.[6] Thus the freedom to define one's identity is intimately linked to the general concern with defining the conduct of lives and the role of the state in enabling individuals to participate in a pluralist 'lifestyle' strategy.

The declared freedom to define one's identity is also central to much of third-age discourse. Laslett's seminal book on the third age repeatedly stresses the importance of individual choice in establishing a 'third age' as part of one's life planning. Young and Schuller echo the same point in their book *Life after Work*. They redefine retirement as the opening of the third age, ushering in a future of 'positive liberty', to be shared by all ages, which 'will be much more fully attained than it has at any time since the industrial revolution'.[7] What Foucault recognizes, however, is that the cultural privileging of 'self-care' and 'self-control' systems exists within technologies of influence and power which direct and fashion these self-creating technologies toward other goals and other priorities than might be articulated by the social actors who feel they 'choose' to choose their lives.

The 'transgressive' nature of the self project itself has to be explored with care. Are there limits to such transgressions, and if so how are those limits defined? Do they derive from 'natural' systems that lie outside social control or from systems of control established by the 'economic interests' of particular groups or collectivities? This is a central issue for the sustainability not just of 'anti-ageing' cultural strategies but of all forms of 'life politics'. Foucault made clear in his later writings that technologies of power constitute but one side of the practical systems through which individuals are governed. As Burchell has pointed out:

> if techniques of the self are more than the insubstantial complement or effect of technologies of domination, if they are not just another way of securing ends sought through technologies of domination, then the study of their interaction with these technologies would seem to be highly relevant to the ethical problems of how freedom can be practised.[8]

Viewing the emergence of anti-ageing, 'staying young' culture as illustrative of these 'technologies of the self', we need to consider two important contextualizing processes. The first is the political shift that has been evident in most Western countries from the late 1970s and early 1980s and which shows every sign of continuing into the next century, namely the expectation that individuals themselves should take prime responsibility for achieving and maintaining health, wealth and well-being throughout their adult life. Such a perspective represents later life as the culmination, or final reckoning, of how well such responsibilities have been exercised. Too much government is seen as constraining the space where individual liberty can be expressed. Following the collapse of world communism, we have seen the much vaunted 'end of history' thesis pronouncing not just the positive viability but the indestructibility of 'liberal democracy' as the 'no-contest' winner in the competition to determine how best to govern and how best to be governed. While interpretations of this political shift may vary, the outcome is everywhere evident in the growing emphasis upon reducing public expenditure, privileging the role of 'market forces', criticizing state paternalism, resisting the collectivization of social identity and expressing scepticism toward all 'grand narratives', and their attempts to claim the ideological high ground.

The second contextualizing influence is the changed relationship that exists between age and cultural capital. Prior to the 1960s, what carried both economic and cultural weight in most societies was the value system expressed through the lives of the middle-aged men of the 'upper-middle' classes of that society. The arrival of 'pop culture' destabilized all of that. That which was middle aged and middle class was devalued in a more comprehensive and more complete manner than any earlier attempts *pour épater la bourgeoisie*. The cultural – if not the economic – currency of the elite underwent a devaluation that has never been restored. Pop stars, fashion photographers, hair stylists, disk jockeys and sports stars emerged as the proponents of a new 'informal' lifestyle and the icons of consumer society. The improved technologies developed from the machinery of two world wars were redirected in peacetime toward the pursuits of leisure and profit. From transistor radios to compact disks, from walkie-talkies to mobile phones, popular culture and popular technology proceeded hand in hand in a continuing celebration of the new. The desire for the new stimulated economic growth, expanded markets at home and abroad and consolidated a mass consumer society where young adults could establish a position for themselves in direct (and profitable) conflict with the 'establishment'. New technologies of mass communication provided the platform for a wholesale assault on 'old values' and a championing of the new by a generation of pop artists, popular musicians, film directors, playwrights, journalists and writers who spoke with, for and to the newly empowered youth of post-war society.[9] By the end of the twentieth century, youth culture has become the site of immense cultural capital – a cultural capital made substantial by its integral links with the economic and commercial capital that makes up the 'leisure industry'. Popular musicians of the 1960s and 1970s count amongst the richest members of society. Pop artists not only have been incorporated into the academy but have achieved a dominating position and influence within it. Pop art can realize millions of dollars. Novelists shoot into positions of wealth particularly by the conversion of their books into

63

film. Sports stars command salaries that vie with those of movie stars. Youth has become institutionalized and is now central to most of contemporary culture. Under these conditions of cultural dominance, traditional middle age has difficulty in establishing arenas in which it can flourish or exercise a mass influence. The ageing protagonists of youth culture – the wrinkled artists, the grey-haired rock musicians, the 'lean and leathery' film stars, the footballers turned managers and TV commentators – seem to command a 'natural' place for themselves within contemporary culture. But that place is precarious because of the very contradictions embodied in the personal and social identities of those concerned. As third-agers, these individuals occupy significant positions within 'grey capital'; but they are required at the very same time to continue to invest that capital within markets dominated by youth-oriented modes of consumption.

It is in the context of these processes, the individualization of life-styles, the shrinking role of the state and the decline of traditional middle-aged middle-class cultural capital, that 'age-resisting' technologies of the self must be examined. Anti-ageing/staying young involves not only exercising consumer choice and possessing the material means to resist the marginal 'state-determined' identity of the 'old age pensioner', but also the cultural capital to avoid getting locked into a generational ghetto increasingly distanced from the global 'youth' culture of the late twentieth century. It is a tension that pervades an ever-widening span of adult life as the horizontal structuring of society by generation and cohort competes with the more traditional structures of class, race and gender.

## Anti-ageing: resisting change by embracing the new

After half a century spent democratizing fashion, Levi jeans are beginning to fall out of fashion. For much of the second half of the twentieth century, jeans extended their appeal across barriers of gender, class and generation, endlessly adaptable and never unfashionable. Jeans have been worn as readily by those too young to have learned to walk as those too old to be able to. They have turned men's as well as women's bottoms into objects of the sexual gaze. They have been able to signify both youthful defiance as well as earthy wisdom. But the rise of designer jeans in the 1980s introduced a new degree of segmentation into the market that threatened this intergenerational cross-gender communality. Just as jean manufacturers had begun to expand their waistlines and their markets, so the desirability of an increasingly undifferentiated item of clothing began to pall amongst those whose consumption patterns marked them out as signifiers of style. But despite this 1980s re-orientation toward youth, older people with the means to keep their waistlines narrow and their spending power directed toward signification could and did keep pace. Although as consumers, they do not drive the process of market diversification, they retain the capacity to keep up with the style vanguard. Musicians, movie stars and artists in their fifties and sixties occupy particularly iconic positions, enabling them to continue their engagement with the 'hyperreality' of designer culture. Those who have aged with them – contemporaries who attend their concerts, buy their music, watch their films, who still connect with their originally 'youthful' role as lifestyle models – can still share some critical elements of this common cultural dynamic.[10]

Along with Levi's, some commentators consider the cinema too will soon become an 'outmoded' form of modernist culture. Whether or not this is as prescient as those Macluhanites who back in the mid-1960s foretold the end of the book, remains to be seen. Whatever may be the eventual fate of film, the videotape currently occupies a position similar to jeans in its versatility to appeal to the desires of young and old, men and women. Over the last 25 years, video rental shops have flourished – in marked contrast to most other small retail outlets that have declined. Supporting this trend has been a remarkable growth in the ownership of video cassette recorders (VCRs). In 1983, the General Household Survey first began to obtain data on the ownership of VCRs. Three years earlier, the survey began collecting data on the ownership of automatic dishwashers. At that time (1980) few VCRs were available to the general public and it seems probable that fewer than 1 per cent of the general population had one. Subsequent ownership of these two technologically sophisticated household goods by 'pensioner households' provides a fascinating illustration of the impact these two very different types of domestic goods have made in the modern 'pensioner' household (Table 4.1).

TABLE 4.1 Ownership of VCRs and automatic dishwashers in UK pensioner households, 1980–95

| Household goods | 1980 Household type | | 1986 Household type | | 1990 Household type | | 1996 Household type | |
|---|---|---|---|---|---|---|---|---|
| | Couple | Single | Couple | Single | Couple | Single | Couple | Single |
| Dishwasher | 3% | 1% | 4% | 1% | 9% | 2% | 16% | 5% |
| VCR | 1% | <1% | 17% | 4% | 49% | 14% | 80% | 42% |

While an automatic dishwasher might seem desirable as a means of escaping the drudgery of washing up, at least in shared households, growth in ownership of dishwashers is relatively minor compared with the growth in ownership of VCRs. Over a 15-year period more than three-quarters of pensioner households in Britain acquired a non-essential piece of leisure technology. Watching a hired video film at home has become a cultural pursuit where age is largely irrelevant. Access to a common canon of film, music, news, TV and radio soap operas and documentaries provides adults of all ages with the ready means to participate in the contemporary cultural mix.[11]

Similarly the growth in home computers and access to the Internet illustrates how readily adults of all ages and backgrounds have become integrated into and participants in the cultural mix that the technologies of the late twentieth century shaped and served.[12] In Britain around 10 per cent of pensioner households have access to a home personal computer (PC); figures from the US are around 20 per cent. The consequence is increasing choice over what music to listen to, which films to watch, which internet services to access and which versions of the news one chooses to listen to. Although possession of these goods varies by socioeconomic group, age, ethnicity and gender, these structuring features are increasingly unstable sources of differentiation in postmodern society. The fundamental openness of the media itself provides an important means of revising and reversing dominant cultures and fostering more individualized alternatives. While the costs and benefits of these processes of structural dissolution are impossible to judge, they clearly represent those points where technologies of the self and technologies of power intersect. The outcome of such interaction is less predictable now than it was in those earlier modern times encountered at the beginning of the last century.

## Technologies of the self and personal care

If ownership of 'leisure goods' is one index of an individual's capacity to participate in popular 'neophiliac' culture, consumption of 'leisure services' is an even more salient one. The cinema has provided one of the most powerful vehicles for establishing consumer desires. Present generations of retired people are the second- and third-generation inheritors of these effects. Movies have been important in introducing audiences to new technologies such as psychoanalysis and space travel, providing social commentaries on urban life, politics and the role of the media in public affairs, and offering vicarious opportunities to enter worlds far removed from their daily lives. The movies have also displayed the idealized faces and bodies of our dreams. The iconic significance of the film star has been pivotal in influencing how we dress, how we look and how we act. Film and subsequently television have provided one of the most important cultural institutions fashioning twentieth-century life.

The role played by the cosmetic industry in creating a culture of anti-ageing can be traced back to the cinema. Prior to the emergence of the cinema, the purchase of make-up was confined to society's elites. While 'society' women seem to have been concerned with their looks, their shape and their smell for much of recorded history, prior to the twentieth century the opportunities for most women to 'make themselves up' were scant indeed. The cinema called for new methods of make-up suited to the realism of film rather than the artefact of theatrical stagelights. Movie actresses became famous as much because of their looks as their roles. And those who made up their looks – the make-up artists – were particularly well placed to expand their activities beyond the dressing rooms and into the growing number of chain stores that were springing up in the 1920s and 1930s. Max Factor rose to prominence by transforming theatrical make-up into a more photogenic commodity. His success encouraged him to produce and sell cosmetics on the basis that they had been designed 'for the stars'. The film industry created a mass consumer market for cosmetics.[13]

Lipstick became the easiest and cheapest way for working-class girls to become 'fashionable'. After the end of the First World War, American chainstores such as Woolworths and Wallmark opened cosmetic counters selling the newly produced lipsticks and eyebrow pencils. These modern 'aids to beauty' took an important slice of the earnings of young working women who had started to join the post-war work-force in increasing numbers throughout Europe and the United States.[14] Their introduction in the 1920s marked a significant and apparently irreversible shift toward 'a world where youth and beauty are thought to be synonymous', encouraging cosmetic manufacturers 'to produce a range of preparations and treatments designed to erase wrinkles, discourage double chins and generally preserve a youthful complexion'.[15] Despite many of the privations suffered by people in Europe during the Second World War, by the time the war was over, make-up had become an intrinsic part of a woman's face. As cosmetic technology developed and marketing and advertising became increasingly sophisticated, working women in the 1950s, 1960s and 1970s became a huge market for firms such as Elizabeth Arden, Clairol, Estee Lauder, L'Oreal, Revlon and Yardleys who increasingly sold their products as the necessary elements of a woman's identity.[16] Unlike those who became pensioners in the immediate post-war era, women who grew up in the 1950s and 1960s had become accustomed to cosmetics as an intrinsic part of their public persona. They were used to 'putting on their face'.

They were also used to 'having their hair done'. The rise of the hair salon follows a history comparable to that of cosmetics. Although women began to visit hair salons toward the end of the nineteenth century, the techniques and styles were confined pretty much to the elite and a small but rising number of middle-class professional women. After the First World War, hairdressing salons began to emerge as the sites of a new popular culture – and the rise of the hairdresser as the creator of individualized 'hair styles'[17] expressing/shaping the identity of the consumer. The manufacture of electric hairdryers, synthetic shampoos and semipermanent dyes (tints) established hair-styling, colouring and cutting as central features of pop culture. As the number and range of activities that were subsumed under the general practice of hair culture rose and hair stylists became recognized as artists and popular celebrity figures, so the marketing of hair products also grew. Synthetic hair dyes were introduced onto the counters of drug stores, department stores and supermarkets during the 1950s and 1960s.[18] Grey hair became as much a sign of personal neglect or transient weariness as an intrinsic feature of ageing. Once hair dying became a widespread cultural practice, the colour of one's hair was dislodged as a predetermined individual characteristic – an intrinsic marker of temperament and national origin.[19] In its place came an acceptance that women would experiment with style, cut and colour much in the same way that fashion demanded experimentation with clothing combinations and colours. By the 1980s there was no longer a fixed fashion or style code required as a 'generational' marker for 'new' entrants to adulthood. Just as clothing and hair styles lost their significance in delineating between generations, hair dyeing too became age irrelevant. Hair dyes were ceasing to be bound by 'natural' colours and cosmetics transformed as much as concealed identities. Women's appearance moved toward the realm of the 'hyperreal'. Grey, white, green and gold became permissible shades that women might choose for their hair.[20] Hair established itself as social text.

Just as working women in the 1920s and 1930s were able to buy a new lipstick when they could not afford a new dress or a new pair of shoes in order to express a 'fashionable' identity, from the 1950s onwards, going to the hairdresser and having one's hair cut, styled and coloured became a similarly affordable way of engaging in the general culture of self-transformation – 'negotiating the endless succession of changes that make up even the most tranquil of contemporary lives'.[21] These commodified technologies of the self have enabled more and more people – women more than men, although as in many areas of personal care the gender gap is narrowing– to actively resist being defined by their appearance as 'old and grey'. The transformation of self achieved through visiting the hairdresser becomes a common way of resisting identity closure – of participating in the contemporary 'transformational culture' where grey hair may be seen as 'the accident of our present biological condition and no necessary marker of the authentic self'.[22] Despite being embedded within the general cultural shift toward indeterminacy and flux such age-resisting practices do not eliminate the spectral presence of age. But 'age' as a social category no longer occupies the simple foundationalist position it once did. Age exists but it is harder and harder to define what exactly it is and to whom it applies/should be applied.

## Age identity and the politics of the self

Conditions of personal uncertainty seem to foster non-traditional political responses. They also foster widespread political apathy, a point Baudrillard made in his essay *In the Shadow of the Silent Majority.*[23] The social expression of private experience has played a large part in the rise of identity politics in late twentieth-century life. The subjective experience of being ignored, devalued and disadvantaged has served as a trigger for many individuals who possess 'minority' group status to seek collectively to obtain due hearing in the political process. This has not happened to any substantial degree with older people. Significant political mobilization around 'retirement/pensioner' issues has occurred periodically throughout this century, but it has been limited and reached perhaps its greatest prominence during the 1930s with the Townsendite movement in America.[24] 'Pensioner' movements remain active but subdued. Despite the growing political power of 'the grey vote' there is little evidence that policies directed at the specific circumstances of older people are higher up the agenda now than they were 50 years ago. One must ask why age has not taken off as a political identity.

If pensioner-based movements can be thought of as the 'redistributional politics of age', 'grey power' movements might seem their equivalent in the area of 'representational' or identity politics.[25] However, an identity politics based around 'age' has been even less well articulated than that around pension policies. When the comparison is drawn with the way that significant social movements have emerged around the experiences of disabled people, of women, of people from cultural, racial and sexual minorities, age has proved a politically inert form of identity.

We shall discuss in a later chapter social policies toward old age and the positioning of the citizen in retirement. Our intention at this point is to consider the broader 'political' dimension of 'age-resisting' versus 'age-identifying' practices. While a number of attempts have been made to extend the kind of cultural politics that have been practised by gay and disability movements to the arena of ageing, their impact has been at best small and quite transient. Various international years for celebrating older people or marking 'age' have come and gone with little impact on the lives and experiences of older people. In Britain, the current 'debate of the age' sponsored by Age Concern, the major charity addressing ageing issues in Britain, has had a limited impact on public consciousness and has hardly made the headlines of newspapers or reached the main news bulletins on national radio and TV.[26]

Within the context of the pervasive commodification of lifestyle issues, age itself cannot be developed as an obvious point of resistance. Age does not sell either such obvious consumables as cars and clothes or those more subtle commodities that constitute 'issue' and 'identity' politics. Marginalized as a civic status, public 'agedness' conveys little beyond vulnerability and risk. Those older people with sufficient material and cultural capital to attract the interest of retailers are not seduced by appeals to their aged status. Their social value lies in being 'still young'. Indeed, whether it is meaningful to engage in a politics of the personal based upon any age group is open to doubt. Age or rather some of the experiences that come with personal ageing connect to issues that have a well-established agenda, but ones that are not limited to any particular age group – for example, issues that concern feminists, ecologists, movements representing disabled people, advocates of assisted suicide or simply Neighbourhood Watch groups. Such issues may well engage significant numbers of older people, but through personal identification rather than through their social identity as an ageing person.[27] Embracing age as a politicized identity is, and we would argue will remain, too transgressive a step for even the most radical groupings. Perhaps resistance can only be expressed by inertia – not bothering to participate as an age-graded consumer. The 'silent majority' appears to be doing just that. Rather than imagine this to be a position that will be expressed ever more determinedly by the ageing masses (as Baudrillard seemed to suggest was happening/would happen) what seems likely is that 'resistance' will be expressed increasingly through the very economic systems that sustain the expansion of capital. As such, changes in the worldwide sales of anti-ageing cosmetics might provide a better index of social resistance to ageism than evidence of political mobilization around social policies toward 'the aged'. Such consumer indifference towards the incursions of ageism seems improbable, at least in the immediate future. For now, at least, resisting age rather than ageism greases more palms, oils more deals and turns more dollars.

## Age, sex and power

Many age-resisting cultural practices are predominantly the province of women. This is true of cosmetic surgery; of anti-ageing make-up creams and preparations; of hair dyes; of age-denying fashion. Books offering 'anti-ageing strategies' are directed at and bought principally by women.[28] Does this mean that rather than 'resisting' the oppressive bio-social processes of ageing, women are party to even more oppressive practices that dominate and subjugate their true nature – their natural ageing? Seduced into consuming such products, are women demonstrating once more their lack of material and cultural capital and their general inability to resist socially 'ageist' practices by devaluing the 'natural' processes of ageing?

There has been much popular debate about the (un)desirability of resisting the natural – reflecting the postmodern antipathy toward ideas of technological progress. One of the most recent aspects of this concern is the potential costs and benefits of genetically modified foodstuffs. Over the last two decades innumerable concerns have been expressed over such issues as the dangers of human cloning; the threat posed by 'designer babies'; the dangers of artificial hormones and lowered sperm counts; hydrocarbon emissions and global warming; radiation leaks and cancer; the mutagenic potential of herbicides and pesticides, etc. Numerous writers have drawn attention to the growth of 'risk society' and the ambiguous position that 'scientific expertise' has come to occupy, both creating and controlling risk.[29] One distinct theme within this discourse is that women are somehow closer to nature than men; that because they are more dependent upon their performance of 'natural' roles – typically defined by the activities of sex, reproduction and nurturance – they are more vulnerable to the technological fall-out arising from 'man's' attempts to control nature. Men perform or induce women to perform unnatural practices upon themselves – at men's behest and mostly for men's benefit[30] – ostensibly to support or enhance women's capacity to perform their natural roles. Technology is thus viewed as another version of pornography that oppresses as a direct function of its appropriation and distortion of that which is natural and thus 'truly' female.[31]

This dichotomy of 'maternal nature' versus 'patriarchal technology' provides a central tension in those technologies of the self that adopt an

explicit anti-ageing strategy. There is a sense that age does not comprom-
ise men in the way it does women; that men can afford 'third-ageist'
strategies that merge age, power and autonomy while women cannot.
The increased risk of death that men face in later life might suggest that
age is in fact a more threatening (and oppressive) process for men than
for women. However, it can be argued that it is precisely because men
face an increased risk of dying from chronological age that anti-ageing
strategies hold less appeal. As long as such strategies fail to alter the
association between chronological age and dying, they can be seen as
vain and ineffective – pandering to the views of others rather than
achieving the truly transgressive impact of overpowering nature by throw-
ing ageing into reverse. In short technologies of the self that seek to
resist the 'death of beauty' may be seen to occupy a weaker position
than those that seek to resist not the appearance of age but the decline
of 'power and influence' by which the adult world is run. Succumbing
to those technologies of the self that are controlled by the cosmetic,
food and pharmacological industries, women remain abject[32] before both
science technology and global capital.[33]

In a later chapter we shall discuss what influence social processes may
have in influencing bodily ageing. Here we wish to acknowledge that
beneath those technologies of the self that seem to illustrate choice and
agency may lie technologies of power determined by gender imbalances
in the control of culturally defined 'expert' discourse. Acknowledging
this possibility does not mean that anti-ageing/age-resisting practices
are inevitably pseudo-agentic acts, acts of false consciousness into which
women as an oppressed group are duped for the overall benefit of the
existing, male-dominated economic order. The question is rather how
to distinguish truly 'transgressive acts' of self-definition from the self-
deluding practices that consumer culture solicits.

Current debates within popular feminist/post-feminist writing provide a particularly acute illustration of this problem. Naomi Wolf's
book *The Beauty Myth* is a powerful critique of the role that retail
capital plays (particularly the diet and cosmetic industries) in the creation and expansion of such features of the 'beauty myth' as the fear
of ageing which still oppress women, irrespective of their economic
status. Despite growing financial independence, Wolf argues, women
remain subordinated to men in part through the endless dissatisfaction

engendered by relentless advertising that fuels and elaborates a fear of ageing and the expected loss of identity that accompanies the end of beauty.[34] The critique of the beauty myth and its power to oppress women has been elaborated by older feminists who seek to celebrate the 'asexualism' of ageing embodied by the menopause. Veteran feminists such as Gloria Steinem and Germaine Greer have both written and spoken enthusiastically of the menopause as the ultimate source for women's liberation.[35]

On the other hand writers such as Jane Fonda, Nancy Friday and to a lesser degree Betty Friedan exhort mid-life women to use their new-found power to continue the potentially 'ageless' pursuit of a sexualized lifestyle that incorporates both intimacy and attractiveness.[36] The divergent ways in which Wolf and Friday regard the cosmetic industry provide a fascinating reflection of the multipositionality that typifies much of postmodern culture – with the industry cast either as a grasping manipulator of women's thoughts and values (Wolf) or as a daring interpreter of what women secretly desire but otherwise find difficult to acknowledge (Friday). Whereas Wolf seeks to locate women's heightened fear of physical age in the restless destabilization of identity that retail capital seeks to achieve, for Friday the fear is located intrapsychically – from the fear generated by the relationship between mothers and daughters. The task for women in mid-life, according to Friday, is to slough off the fear of sexual autonomy that mothers induce in their daughters and which inhibits the self-assertion that men in mid-life display. A sexualized identity in later life – for both Betty Friedan and Nancy Friday – becomes a continuing necessity achieved through the personal struggle that women must undertake in order to become a whole person. Framed as a personal voyage, a quest for true liberation, the task of becoming a more fully sensuous woman is seen not so much as resisting ageing as resisting the stereotype that mothers impose upon their female children. The site of resistance lies within the personal sphere and the personal sphere is itself 'the political'.

Friday writes:

> ... there is no test for autonomy that carries as much fear of losing mother/ other women's love as that of conquering fear of sex ... despite everything we have won, women refuse to see ourselves as owning mother's witchy

power, preferring instead the very effective image of little mistreated people at the mercy of the big bad wolf . . . there is absolutely nothing we women could not accomplish – including the abolition of this double standard of aging – if we could get the deadwood out of our houses and encourage one another to take in power of our sexual beauty which lives beyond the menopause and which is not restricted to and defined by youth.[37]

Managing the menopause becomes a key task; maintaining an economically powerful post-menopausal status at the same time as retaining an identity that still embodies sexuality and sexual beauty.[38] For Friday and for other 'post-feminists', the growing economic power that women are beginning to exercise means that women can express their autonomy both through physical culture and through acts of 'serene' consumption. Taking care of oneself expresses a real rather than an illusory power. In Foucault's terms, the technologies of the self provided by fashion and physical culture reinforce rather than undermine the growth in economic and social power that women have begun to realize.[39] If age resistance defines this culture, it is so because it expresses the power that arises from redefining nature rather than capitulating to an oppressive version of it. In another sense, it is also part of Donna Haraway's 'Cyborg Manifesto' that seeks to blur the boundaries between nature and culture.[40]

## Men and women and the postmodern menopause

Menopause provides a key arena where such technologies jostle for power. Is there a change taking place in women's 'post-menopausal' identity? Does the increase in women's consumer power offer new opportunities for women to go through the menopause with no loss of status, no decline in cultural capital? Is the growing equalization of men's and women's income and power in middle age leading to a growing convergence toward an ungendered but uncertain menopause? In this next section we shall examine the emergence of the menopause as a socially recognized 'life event' serving as a mid-life marker for the transition into an irreversible agedness – for both men and women.[41]

Although the phrase 'male menopause' was introduced into medical discourse in the nineteenth century,[42] it excited very little interest until more recently when it seems to have undergone a re-birth assisted along the way by a newly coined term, the 'andropause'. This term was coined by the Belgian endocrinologist Alex Vermeulen to describe a male version of the climacteric, characterized by loss of sexual desire, poor memory, fatigue, mood disturbance and an increased risk of osteoporosis (brittle bones).[43] While reviews of this topic frequently conclude that the male menopause is a poorly developed and probably misconceived idea, much the same can be said for the female climacteric. Whether there is a clear and coherent set of symptoms that women or men experience around age 50 is probably irrelevant. What is significant is the idea that the term 'menopause' can be used to serve as a marker for 'ageing' potentially shared by men and women. It reflects the diffusion and fragmentation of the gendered lifecourse that characterizes postmodern society and is made most evident in the new discourse of personal health that has emerged within the last two decades of the twentieth century.[44]

Until the mid-1970s, the menopause had been a socially invisible event.[45] The social silence that surrounded the menopause and its lack of socioeconomic significance enabled the 'menopause' to become a site easily subject to unstable, personalized interpretation. In Kristeva's terms it represents one of the 'abject' features of life, embodying a complex of wishes and fears which offers considerably more scope for consumerist 'self-technologies' than, say, the publicly constructed status of retirement. Creating a post-menopausal identity is a task that is both more fluid and more open to the contradictory elements that define consumer society.

In common with other cultural practices of age resistance, two very different transgressive approaches can be observed in constructing this potentially new identity. The first is the 'elimination of the menopause' strategy, typified by anti-ageing consumer-oriented medicine, with its emphasis upon the use of synthetic hormones (hormone replacement therapy) or the newer eco-friendly phytoestrogens both of which aim to reverse or minimize the signs and symptoms of the change. The second strategy, equally but differently transgressive, redefines the menopause as a re-birth – 'the chrysalis . . . [out of which] . . . the female woman [is] finally to emerge'.[46] The former strategies are considered by protagonists of the latter to be no more than by-products of an internalized 'age phobia' highlighted and then amplified by the marketing strategists of the patriarchal 'global' pharmaceutical industry. The latter in turn may be seen as buttressing a political position that privileges the personal by shifting responsibility upon the individual to 'define' not only this particular stage of life, but more generally their own mode of entering 'old age'.[47] By reinforcing a 'do-it-yourself' approach to ageing – exhorting women to resist the defining of their identities by both the pharmaceutical industry and the patriarchal state – the onus is placed firmly upon the individual woman. It is up to her to determine when and how she is to 'emerge' from the chrysalis of engendered adulthood to become a truly liberated woman. It requires a personal act of resistance – a self-determined gesture to overthrow the snares of retail capital. Such a position might fit the beliefs and experiences of some middle-class, already 'powerful' women, but it may not have the same resonance for those for whom accepting 'irreversible ageing' is to incorporate yet one more devalued status along with a host of others (class, race, gender etc.).

Characteristically for our postmodern times, the rhetoric of liberation is used by both sides. Wendy Cooper, author of an early anti-ageing book called *No Change*, speaks of the 'biological liberation' that hormone replacement therapy (HRT) offers women. She describes HRT as 'a second biological revolution . . . for the older woman'.[48] While HRT for men has proved less popular, various compounds including DHEA and testosterone are beginning to occupy a rather similar position. Most evident on the west coast of the United States, there has been a steady increase in the number of 'anti-ageing' clinics offering various treatment plans to sufferers from the andropause. In Britain, a key event has been the government's quandary over family doctors prescribing the synthetic compound sildenafil citrate (Viagra) for male impotence. Despite initial government recommendations that treatment target those whose impotence arises from non-age-related pathology such as that induced by diabetes, Viagra has rapidly bypassed its role as a treatment for specific pathologies to become the means for older men to 'reverse' their ageing and restore a synthetic youthful sexual performance that is widely seen as crucial to their self-esteem.[49]

What both positions share is a common concern with the body and its central role in framing postmodern identities. As many commentators have pointed out, consumer society privileges the body both as the overt focus of consumption and as the defining element of individuality.[50] Until quite recently, the menopause has been seen as one of the silent modes of entry to 'old age' that was the sole preserve of women: intimate, domestic and largely unaffected by the economic sphere of production. As consumption has come to have a more powerful influence on post-modern society, it is unsurprising that there should be a growing public interest in the signification of the menopause. The previously defining biological feature of the menopause – i.e. the cessation of menses – has been overshadowed by the broader significance of the menopause as a threat to identity. That identity is not presaged upon fecundity; it is about continuing engagement with the dominant culture of 'youth', 'sexuality' and 'fitness'. HRT is offered not as a treatment for amenorrhea. Instead it is advocated as a means to restore the vagina to youthful fitness; ensuring adequate genital lubrication; stimulating a positive mental attitude and warding off those cardiovascular, musculoskeletal and neurological diseases that have come to signify old age/fourth age.

This focus upon 'mid-life' well-being has distanced menopause even further from the physiology of menstruation. On the one hand it transcends gender. Both men and women can share the common goal of managing their mid-life crises.[51] On the other hand it can create a revived, feminist identity – enabling a new woman, serene and powerful, to emerge. Developing a post-menopausal lifestyle shares an increasingly common cultural space with Laslett and Young's advocacy of a post-retirement third age. Like third-ageism, it has acquired a range of complex and often contradictory signifiers. Like third-ageism, it advocates a new periodization of the lifecourse – establishing a period of life and associated lifestyle that is neither youth nor age, though participating in elements of both. Like third-ageism, it is defined as much by its rejection of old age as it is by the positive assertion that it offers a new form of being an adult. And, as a characteristic element of postmodern culture, it is imbued with risk and uncertainty.

## Fit to face down ageing: exercise and the work-out

If strategies to combat the menopause seem to emphasize passive acts of consumption – swallowing pills, applying creams, fixing patches or having implants – other models of 'menopausal resistance' adopt a more masculine emphasis upon activity and self-control. A growing number of people of all ages have adopted exercise and work-outs as a means of staying fit, maintaining health and preventing the diseases and general deterioration that are seen to constitute ageing and old age. Viewing oneself and being viewed by others as fit involves engaging with a post-modern physical and symbolic culture – with its privileged sites such as public parks, leisure centres and health clubs – and its defining attire of trainers, tracksuits, sweatshirts, cycling shorts and other visible markers of pace and movement. The development of an age-resisting culture of active leisure began to acquire significant cultural capital in the 1970s. The steady disappearance of manual labour as a significant element in the economy and the rising expectation that health could be achieved through personal effort rather than professional ministrations served to make fitness – and the public appearance of fitness – one of the most valued currencies in contemporary culture. Increasingly working-out has overtaken making-up as a source of personal expenditure.[52]

Exercise has become an increasingly important topic in academic gerontology as well as public health. 'Ageing and activity' is one of the central themes of current gerontology.[53] Exercise occupies an important position too in certain forms of popular feminism. Perhaps the 'classic' example is the Jane Fonda work-out programme.[54] The Fonda work-out is sold to women as part of a general cultural package helping women reclaim their bodies and 'take control' of their lives. It is part of a 'sell' which has evolved and generalized across the lifecourse – naturally enough – represented by a growing number of self-help books on the 'change' and women's identity in mid-life. A similar rhetoric to that used in the work-out books and videos is used, exhorting women to take control of their mid-life change – invoking the myth of the 'pioneers' staking out 'new territory' for mid-life women. Other US women writers – Gale Sheehy in her book *New Passages* is one example[55] – have emulated this style of pep talk. It has been used more politically in some of Gloria Steinem's writings, such as her essay 'The politics of muscle'.[56] It is the kind of writing that can be found in most of the pages of *Modern Maturity* where older people's physical achievements are celebrated by standards that are established by reference to con-temporary 'youth culture'.[57]

Survey evidence indicates that the rate of 'self-directed' exercise amongst 50- and 60-year-old men and women has been increasing steadily since the late 1970s, when jogging to keep fit first hit the streets and parks of most American and European cities.[58] In Britain, leisure clubs have almost entirely replaced the old-style public swimming pool; interestingly leisure is defined primarily as the activities provided by gymnasiums, sports halls and swimming pools.[59] While the leisure centre and 'health club' provide the most advanced opportunities for those who are able or desire to exercise their selves in public (typically the young and/or well-off), do-it-yourself mini-gymnasiums, exercise bikes, fitness videos and TV work-out programmes offer private access to the new physical culture for a much wider population, including of course self-conscious older adults.

Public health researchers have accumulated considerable evidence that leisure-oriented exercise benefits older people, reducing both their morbidity and their mortality. Exactly how this happens is not quite so clear. Empirical support for the belief that exercise in later life has a direct impact upon cardiorespiratory fitness is quite weak.[60] It may well be that activity influences well-being more through its symbolic than its physiological impact, which might explain why social participation possesses apparently equal effectiveness in reducing later-life morbidity and mortality.[61] The exact position that activity occupies as an identity-shaping practice is complex. Factor analytic studies of activity and ageing suggest different patterns of association between men and women – with men's exercise much more 'a thing apart'. In general women engage less in self-consciously directed exercise; rather, women's everyday life and activity seem to be more closely integrated.[62] It may be that levels of overall activity – rather than that undertaken self-consciously as leisure – better strengthens the heart and lungs – though contributing little to strengthening a sense of identity as a 'fit' person. Jane Fonda and writers like her may have helped women develop a more distinctive role 'resisting age' by regaining control over their bodies. While such work-out strategies seem to occupy the masculinist pursuit of physical culture and self-control, they can also be viewed as 'artifice' – strategies designed as much to deny ageing as to build a stronger sense of an agentic self. The benefits of self-determined physical culture may be different from and maybe less effective than the benefits of activities arising out of a busy and 'engaged' life within and outside the home.[63] Exercising solely as a means of resisting age may establish an identity defined principally by the dangers it seeks to ward off. To that extent it may be no more effective a strategy in resisting old age than the habit of wearing expensive trainers and a pair of tracksuit bottoms when shopping or driving to the off-licence/liquor store.

As with many of the activities that constitute 'technologies of the self' in postmodern society, the emphasis upon consuming on the basis of signification and pursuing lifestyles derived from expert discourse of the personal health industry creates inherent uncertainties and instabilities. Specifically age-resisting technologies require the spectral presence of old age. Following an agenda that privileges choice and agency, age-resisting fitness regimes promote a positive self image of non-agedness that further reinforces the undesirability and fear of old age. Rather than transgressing the current social construction of old age, such practices subtly reinforce it. This is of course one more instance of that paradox that Beck has noted of contemporary 'risk society' – that the more people seek to identify and eliminate risks, the more risky life becomes.

## Age, identity and the 'experience society'

Alongside the alertness to risk in postmodern society is the cultural devaluing of status 'in favour of' the authenticity of 'inner experience'. Gerhard Schulze argues that the social values of late modernity have created a shift in the reference point by which the good life is signified. He argues that increasingly it is defined by self-referential experience rather than social position.[64] Postmodern consumption is directed principally toward achieving particular inner states – of well-being, self-esteem, self-actualization and so forth. These internal states are nevertheless pursued through the selection and acquisition of external goods, whose signification as markers of a valued lifestyle relies less and less not only on their use value but also their worth as indicators of social differentiation. Instead commodities are sold according to their capacity to signify, suggest and stimulate particular 'inner states'. Schulze draws attention to how people use consumer experiences as the means to achieve particular inner states of well-being, self-esteem or self-respect. He sees a reciprocal relationship developing between the

increasing commodification of everyday life and the increasing centrality of consumers' choices in determining 'the good life'. Given this
emphasis upon consuming in order to 'be' – to achieve a subjective self-
referential position – Schulze argues that consumers are expected to act
as if they know what they want and what they want to be. As a result,
importance is attached to acquiring self-knowledge. The individual consumer is expected through the development of self-knowledge and self-
expertise to be able to achieve a particular internal state – through his
or her choices. The desire for such effective self-knowledge creates one
of the core dilemmas of postmodernity – namely the indeterminacy of
the self identity that is being sought out.

Schulze writes:

> The naïve thought that one can search for and find oneself as if this 'self'
> were a given camouflages the fact of reflective self-construction at the moment
> of discovery. Nothing is a given and everything remains open. One is faced
> with incalculable possibilities of self-discovery.[65]

Each act of 'identity-determining' consumption establishes new possibilities of being. Lifestylism creates a restless condition of infinite desire,
a pervasive and permanently destabilizing phenomenon of postmodern
life. Achieving a stable inner state of self-regard and self-confidence
implies not only the successful avoidance of failure – failure implied
through feeling bad, feeling unfit, feeling excluded, feeling old – but also
of finding oneself in a position where no more can be wished for: an end
of desire.

Because of the implied relationship between external circumstances
and internal states – and because of the assumption that individual
agency is the *sine qua non* to achieve control of these inner states – an
enormous value is attached to identities that have been achieved through
self-referential actions. This is as true for feminist-inspired calls to choose
to be freed from patriarchal institutions as it is for advertisements that call
upon men and women to choose not to let 'nature' deprive them of their
right to eternal youth. Even calls for renunciation – not to consume –
end up conveying an identical message. By dieting one can become a
fitter, better person; by not dyeing one's hair one can become more truly
'oneself'; by resisting alcohol and other drugs one can grow in strength
and worth; by not making up one's face one can be 'more natural', etc.

The identity conveyed by old age is everywhere resisted – whether the resistance is focused upon the social category of 'old age', the internal state of feeling oneself 'old' or the physical features that characterize 'agedness'. Whether the message is made explicit in Jane Fonda's workout programme or whether it remains hidden within the paradox of Germaine Greer's search for power through serenity, the practice remains one of resistance and a resistance prefaced upon the assumption that control and care of the self are sufficient to prevent the impoverishment that is old age. And both Greer and Fonda sell books. Transgressive strategies are themselves commodifications of lifestyle.

In so far as old age symbolizes individual failure – 'losing it' by a failure to ward off disease, a failure to act positively, a failure to be selective, a failure to actively engage with modern lifestyles – it is impossible to imagine old age becoming a reference point for any culture that most adults would aspire to. Most if not all lifestyle cultural practices are institutionalized 'anti-ageing' strategies. Old age cannot escape its association with personal failure and the risks of failure are omnipresent. All lifestyle practices are performed against a background of risk and potential/eventual failure; the failure ultimately to deliver the infinite jouissance to which the postmodern life endlessly beckons. But there are no other choices open except resistance. Choices now exist and do offer more – more opportunities to practise third-ageism; to practise strategies of staying young; to practise challenging and contradictory images about age and its signification. They also share a common resistance to old age and a belief that such resistance is possible and practical.

The absence of resistance to old age has traditionally been the product of lack; its 'acceptance' presaged upon the absence of choice and agency in later life. In the early part of the twentieth century, even as late as the 1940s, for all but a small minority, retirement and old age were looked upon as unwanted, unwelcome and inevitable impositions.[66] Exhortations to accept old age and mortality, though still widely preached, represent a type of discourse that is no longer supported by practice. The refusal to choose to go on choosing is in the end simply another choice.[67] Death is increasingly somebody's responsibility. We are no longer – and perhaps we never were – in a position to choose whether or not to develop 'cultures of ageing'. Those cultures are emerging because of the widening choices and the increasing numbers of people in a position to act out those choices.

The increasing number of social agents acting within the complex structures that currently shape the experience of 'ageing' will continue to create an ever more complex cultural space where more and more individualized versions of ageing and age resistance will be expressed. This reflects the growth in the number of people living long enough to face the prospect of old age as well as the increasing opportunities available to all social agents in late modernity to talk about their lives, to reflect upon them and also to act within them. It also reflects changes in the relationship people have with their own bodies and the changes in their relationship with the state. Changes in both these arenas are central influences upon postmodern culture. The contemporary operation of these two 'limiting conditions' of citizenship and the body on the cultural processes and practices that constitute resisting/ageing provides the focus for the subsequent two sections of the book.

## Notes

1 See Foucault, M. (1988a) *The History of Sexuality*, vol. 3, *The Care of the Self*, Penguin, London, and Foucault, M. (1988b) 'Technologies of the self', in L.H. Martin, H. Gutman and P.H. Hutton (eds) *Technologies of the Self: a Seminar with Michel Foucault*, Tavistock Publications, London, pp. 16–49.

2 See, for example, Bauman's account of the growing significance accorded aesthetic criteria in regard to both work and consumption. Bauman, Z. (1998) *Work, Consumerism and the New Poor*, Open University Press, Buckingham, esp. pp. 30–2.

3 Foucault, M. (1988b) *op. cit.*, p. 18.

4 Giddens, A. (1991) *Modernity and Self-Identity*, Polity Press, Cambridge, p. 5.

5 See Giddens, A. (1991) *op. cit.*, pp. 179–80.

6 See Giddens, A. (1991) *op. cit.*, p. 215.

7 'We are not by any means resting our argument on the claim that all people at this stage of like being free, merely that they can be' (p. 21). See also pp. 18–20 and pp. 176–7, in Young, M. and Schuller, T. (1991) *Life after Work: the Arrival of the Ageless Society*, HarperCollins, London.

8 Burchell, G. (1996) 'Liberal government and techniques of the self', in A. Barry, T. Osbourne and N. Rose (eds) *Foucault and Political Reason*, UCL Press, London, p. 21.

9 A related account of the post-war overthrow of the middle-aged middle-class culture of the nineteenth and twentieth centuries can be found in Elias' description of the transformation of intergenerational relationships during the course of the twentieth century, which he refers to as the 'informalisation process' – see Elias, N. (1996) *The Germans*, Basil Blackwell, Oxford, pp. 35–43.

10 Paul Wallace comments: 'By failing to come out with new styles in the early 1990s Levis came to be identified by teenagers as the jeans their parents wore . . . In this way the continuing success of Levis with the now ageing baby-boom generation had backfired' (Wallace, P. (1999) *Agequake*, Nicolas Brearley Publishers, London, p. 100).

11 Roughly similar proportions of young, middle-aged and older adults read *TV Times*, *Radio Times* and *What's on TV* – weekly British magazines concentrating on 'terrestrial' television programmes put out by the BBC and ITA (*Social Trends*, vol. 29, Table 13.10). Age differences do emerge, however, for magazines focusing upon the 'newer' satellite TV channels.

12 The rise in 'seniors in cyberspace' is described in the March 1995 issue of *Ageing International* in an article devoted to SeniorNet Online. The same article illustrates the potential for 'anti-ageing' strategies emerging from the internet. Thus one senior net citizen stated: 'I'm an old lady except when I'm online. Then I'm 37, blonde and ready to roll' (quotation from Furlong, M. (1995) 'Communities for seniors in cyberspace', *Ageing International*, p. 33).

13 'The factor which determined the growing acceptance of cosmetics was initially the cinema' (Angeloglou, M. (1970) *A History of Make Up*, Studio Vista Ltd, London, p. 119).

14 'The office girl of 1932 spent what was in the values of the time a large part of her weekly salary on cosmetics' (Gunn, F. (1973) *The Artificial Face: a History of Cosmetics*, David & Charles, Newton Abbot, p. 153).

15 Gunn, F. (1973) *op. cit.*, p. 151.

16 According to Key Note – a leading UK market research company – UK sales of toiletries and cosmetics in the 1990s exceed £10 billion.

17 See, for example, 'The hairdresser as guru' in Cox, C. (1999) *Good Hair Days: a History of British Hairstyling*, Quartet Books, London, esp. pp. 80–92.

18 Eugene Schueller, founder of the French cosmetic company L'Oreal, has been credited with inventing the first synthetic hair dye a couple of years before the First World War. Successful production of safe and lasting synthetic hair dyes for the mass market, however, only took place after the Second World War (Cox, C. (1999) *op. cit.*).

19 Passports and identity documents throughout the world had '[hair] colour' as a category in the list of features defining the owner. Hair colour was seen as indicative of innate character – at least prior to the widespread use of hair dyes in the 1950s – which in turn prompted much of the earlier fashions regarding 'desirable' hair colours to dye for (see Cox, C. (1999) *op. cit.* and also McCracken, G. (1997) *Big Hair: a Journey to the Transformation of Self*, Indigo, London).

20 McCracken quotes a London department store announcing 'that young women were using grey "as a fashion statement"' (McCracken, G. (1997) *op. cit.*, p. 144).

21 McCracken, G. (1997) *op. cit.*, p. 14.

22 McCracken, G. (1997) *op. cit.*, p. 146.

23 Baudrillard, J.F. (1983) *In the Shadow of the Silent Majority*, Semiotext(e), New York.

24 Elman provides a useful account of the Townsend movement which successfully mobilized one tenth of the US elderly population, triggered by the events of the Depression – see Elman, C. (1995) 'An age-based mobilisation: the emergence of old age in American politics', *Ageing and Society*, 15: 299–324.

25 The distinction between redistribution and recognition politics refers to that described in Nancy Fraser's essay 'From redistribution to recognition' (Fraser, N. (1995) 'From redistribution to recognition? Dilemmas of justice in a "post socialist" age', *New Left Review*, 212: 68–93). She refers to the politics of the former as being concerned with correcting socioeconomic injustices in the distribution of primary goods while the latter politics is concerned principally with correcting cultural injustice in the form of disrespect, non-recognition and cultural marginalization. As she and others acknowledge, the two processes are necessarily intertwined.

26 The debate of the age has been set up in 1999 to act as a series of public forums that are meant to raise awareness and promote reflection upon the 'ageing' of the twenty-first-century's population structure. In Britain it has been supported and sponsored by Age Concern, a UK-based lobbying charity for older people and various financial institutions such as Norwich Union and General Accident.

27 Surveys in Britain indicate similar concerns about traffic pollution, radioactive and toxic waste, acid rain and urban decay amongst both young and old – though age differences do exist around global warning and depletion of the ozone layer. See Table 11.2, 'Future environmental concerns by age', in *Social Trends* (1999) vol. 29, The Stationery Office, London, p. 184.

28 Recent examples on British bookshelves include Blackman, H. (1997) *How to Look and Feel Half Your Age: for the rest of your life*, Virgin Books, London; Kenton, L. (1996) *Rejuvenate Now*, Vermilion Books, London, and Lalvani, V. (1998) *Stop the Age Clock*, Hamlyn, London. There are many others.

29 See Beck, U. (1992) *Risk Society: Toward a New Modernity*, Sage, London.

30 See, for example, Germaine Greer's book on the menopause: 'the campaign to eliminate menopause has been initiated and is run by men' (Greer, G. (1991) *The Change: Women, Ageing and the Menopause*, Penguin Books, Harmondsworth, p. 18); also Coney, S. (1993) *The Menopause Industry*, Spinifex, Melbourne, and Fausto-Sterling, A. (1985) *Myths of Gender: Biological Theories about Men and Women*, Basic Books, New York, particularly Chapter 4.

31 For the historical origins of this 'enlightenment' perspective on masculinity and femininity see Jordanova, L. (1989) *Sexual Visions: Images of Gender in Science and Medicine between the Eighteenth and Twentieth Centuries*, Harvester Wheatsheaf, London, and Battersby, C. (1989) *Gender and Genius*, The Women's Press, London.

32 The term 'abject' is used in Kristeva's sense reflecting the impure defiling elements of the body – that which needs to be concealed/repressed (see Kristeva, J. (1982) *Powers of Horror: an Essay on Abjection*, Columbia University Press, New York).

33 Of course, this polarization of gendered positions itself is diffused by postmodern society's blurring of sex roles, the increasing sexualization of the male body and the elision of 'health, youth and beauty' as a measure of social worth.

34 See Wolf's chapter 'Religion' in her book *The Beauty Myth*, where she writes: 'Women die twice. Women die as beauties before their bodies die. Women today in the full bloom of beauty keep a space always in mind for its diminution and loss . . . for women to be urged to think continually of beauty's fragility and transience is a way to try to keep us subservient' (Wolf, N. (1991) *The Beauty Myth*, Vintage, London, p. 103).

35 For Gloria Steinem's comments see her essay 'Doing sixty' in Steinem, G. (1994) *Moving Beyond Words*, Bloomsbury, London, pp. 249–83, as well as her recent interview published in the May–June 1999 issue of *Modern Maturity*. Germaine

Greer, in her book *The Change*, writes: 'The climacteric marks the end of apologising. The chrysalis of conditioning has once for all to break and the female woman finally to emerge' (Greer, G. (1991) *op. cit.*, p. 440).

36 Nancy Friday makes her own position clear in her latest book, *The Power of Beauty*, where she writes: 'as we extend youthful beauty with exercise, surgery, better health and self chosen work, my own vote goes to the risk taker who flaunts the rules of morality and dares to wear paint, show leg, cleavage and flesh, who goes for surgery so long as she carries it off with confidence' (Friday, N. (1998) *The Power of Beauty*, Arrow Books, London, p. 703). Friedan's position is much more nuanced than that, but it is clear that she is as much an advocate of 'both the necessity and the possibility of intimacy and passionate sexual being beyond the dreams of our youth' as Friday (Friedan, B. (1994) *The Fountain of Age*, Vintage, London, p. 218).

37 Friday, N. (1998) *op. cit.*, p. 657.

38 A similar point has been made by Natasha Walter in her book on the 'new' feminism. She argues that 'Fashion . . . can no longer be seen as a monolith of oppression . . . or: the contrary fashion movements . . . [help] create the freedom we now take for granted . . . Today . . . women can link fashion with power rather than powerlessness' (Walter, N. (1998) *The New Feminism*, Little, Brown and Company, London, pp. 93–9).

39 Walter, N. (1998) *op. cit.*, p. 90.

40 Haraway, D. (1991) *Simians, Cyborgs and Women*, Routledge, London.

41 This is not the transition into 'old age' but rather the transition into an age-determined status that is not seen as 'reversible' in the way that feeling old at earlier ages can always be thought of – by more rest, better diet, a change of routine, etc.

42 Featherstone, M. and Hepworth, M. (1985) 'The history of the male menopause 1848–1936', *Maturitas*, 7: 252–3.

43 Dr M. Carruthers, personal communication.

44 Benson cites a 1994 article in the *Guardian*, which captures this theme: 'The ageing process is genderless; as unspeakably vile for men as for women. Men do not have menses to pause or cycles to interrupt when they reach the stage of life when intimations of mortality are not just misfortunes that strike other people. But they do sweat. They do lose their beauty. They do suffer the damnably humiliating side effects of menopause: the depression, the fatigue, despair, irritability, shame, panic and loss of libido' quoted in Benson, J. (1997) *Prime Time: a History of the Middle Aged in Twentieth Century Britain*, Longman, London, p. 14.

45 Greer expounds at length on '[t]he social invisibility of the menopause' and its consequences in her chapter 'No rite of passage' in Greer, G. (1991) *op. cit.*, pp. 36–62, esp. p. 39.

46 Greer, G. (1991) *op. cit.*, p. 440.

47 Again, using Greer as an advocate for this transgressive approach, it is apparent in many parts of her book that she sees the ignominy that ageing women face as a function of a centuries-long campaign by 'the patriarchal bureaucratic state' 'to destroy the power of the mother' (Greer, G. (1991) *op. cit.*, p. 73).

48 Cooper, W. (1987) *No Change: a Biological Revolution for Women*, Arrow Books, London, p. 16.

49 In May 1999 the UK Department of Health circulated new instructions to general practitioners enabling them to prescribe the drug to men whose impotence 'caused great personal distress' – irrespective of their medical diagnosis (DoH 1999).

50 Cf. Sulkunen, P. (1997) 'Introduction', in P. Sulkunen, J. Holmwood, H. Radner and G. Schulze (eds), *Constructing the New Consumer Society*, Macmillan, London, pp. 6–7.

51 Two examples might suffice to illustrate this point. The first concerns dehydro-epiandrosterone (DHEA). DHEA is a neurosteroid that has been promoted to combat the effects of fatigue and depression in post-menopausal men and women – see Regelson, W. and Kalimi, M.Y. (1997) 'Dehydroepiandrosterone (DHEA) – a pleiotropic steroid. How can one steroid do so much?'. In R.M. Klatz (ed.), *Advances in Anti-Aging Medicine*, vol. 1, Mary Ann Liebert Inc, New York, pp. 287–317. The second concerns phytoestrogens – plant-derived compounds that mimic the functions of estrogen. There is increasing popular and scientific interest in the use of these compounds to help both mid-life men and women stave off the dangers of cancer, heart disease and osteoporosis (see, for example, the 1998 special supplement on phytoestrogens in the *American Journal of Clinical Nutrition*, vol. 68).

52 Over the last two decades (1980–2000), growth in sports centres, leisure and health clubs and the related expenditure on sportswear and sport-related cosmetics has overshadowed the growth in cosmetics – which are now showing signs of a downturn in sales. See the two *Key Note Reports: Health Clubs and Leisure Centres and Cosmetics and Fragrances*, Key Note Ltd, London, 1996–98.

53 See Shephard, R.J. (1988) *Activity and Ageing*, Croom Helm, Beckenham. Also Buchner, D.M. (1992) 'Effects of physical activity on health status in older adults', II. Intervention studies, *Annual Review of Public Health*, 13: 469–88.

54 Hilary Radner provides an extensive discussion of the role the *Jane Fonda's Workout Book* has played in directing a generation of women toward 'self mastery' through aerobic exercise – and its explicit contrast with women's more passive involvement with fashion and make-up. Thus Radnor quotes from an interview with Fonda when she says: 'I may dress for a man but I exercise for myself'. As Radner points out such positions tend to be riven by their own internal contradictions – witness Fonda's later choice to undergo cosmetic surgery for her breasts and eyes. But like capitalism itself such internal contradictions may provide the dynamo for further development rather than undermine the whole endeavour. See Radner, H. (1997) 'Producing the body: Jane Fonda and the new public feminine', in P. Sulkunen, J. Holmwood, H. Radner and G. Schulze (eds), *Constructing the New Consumer Society*, Macmillan, London, pp. 108–33.

55 See, for example, Sheehy's 'New map of adult life' – Sheehy, G. (1996) *New Passages*, Harper Collins, London, pp. 16–17.

56 Steinem, G. (1994) 'The politics of muscle'. In *Moving Beyond Words*, Bloomsbury, London, pp. 93–8.

57 Consider as example this *Modern Maturity* profile of 77-year-old Marjorie Newlin: 'She works out four times a week at Rivers Gymnasium in Mount Airy [but] what really knock's everyone's socks off is when [she] strips down to a bikini for body building contests.' (*Modern Maturity*, vol. 41R, March–April, 1998).

58 See Benson, J. (1997) *op. cit.*, pp. 128–9.

59 The number of 'dry' indoor leisure centres in Britain rose from 20 in 1970 to over 1200 in 1996. Even 'wet' leisure has changed. 'Swim aerobics' have acquired a weekend popularity that exceeds that of swimming lessons. (*Key Note Report on Health Clubs and Leisure Centres*, 2nd edn, Key Note Ltd, London, 1997.

60 'Based on these data self reported leisure time physical activity cannot be considered a useful surrogate for physical fitness in older subjects' (Tager, I.B., Hollenberg, M. and Satariano, W.A. (1998) 'Association of self reported leisure time physical activity and measures of cardiorespiratory fitness in an elderly population', *American Journal of Epidemiology*, 147, p. 929).

61 See Glass, T.A., De Leon, C.M., Marottoli, R.A. and Berkman, L.F. (1999) 'Population based study of social and productive activities as predictors of survival among elderly Americans', *British Medical Journal*, 319: 478–83. 'Social and productive activities that involve little or no enhancement of fitness lower the risk of all causes of mortality as much as fitness activities do' (p. 478).

62 See Morgan, K. *et al.* (1991) 'Customary physical activity, psychological well-being and successful ageing', *Ageing and Society*, 11: 399–415, and Benson, J. (1997) *op. cit.*, pp. 142–3.

63 See Lantz, P.M., House, J.S., Lepkowski, J.M., Williams, D.R., Mero, R.P. and Chen, J. (1998) 'Socioeconomic factors, health behaviors and mortality: results from a nationally representative prospective study of US adults', *Journal of the American Medical Association*, 279: 1703–8; Haan, M., Kaplan, G. and Camacho, T. (1987) 'Poverty and health: prospective evidence from the Alameda County Study', *American Journal of Epidemiology*, 1225: 989–98.

64 Describing what he calls 'the rationality of experience' in contemporary society, Schulze argues that contemporary lifestyles are directed toward arranging the external circumstances of one's life towards the end of achieving the best possible internal effect. 'We choose taste exchange travel throw away affiliate leave each other eat this drink that – always trying to improve the relation between situational input and subjective output' (Schulze, G. (1997) 'From situations to subjects: moral discourse in transition'. In P. Sulkunen, J. Holmwood, H. Radner and G. Schulze (eds), *Constructing the New Consumer Society*, Macmillan, London).

65 Schulze, G. (1997) *op. cit.*

66 Wentworth reported in a 1943/4 survey that only 5 per cent of US retirees did so in good health and as a positive choice. Wentworth, E.C. (1945) 'Why beneficiaries retire', *Social Security Bulletin*, 8: 16–20.

67 To choose, in the present context, is primarily to choose how not to enter 'old age'. The contemporary consumerist approach to suicide is exemplified well by Derek Humphry in his book *Final Exit* and marks merely the most extreme version of choosing not to choose (Humphry, D. (1991) *Final Exit, The Hemlock Society*, Eugene, OR).

# CHAPTER 5

# The old person as citizen

The development of individualized 'cultures' of ageing is constrained by two factors – the framing effects of social policy and irreversible changes in physical health. Both have traditionally been conflated in the concept of 'citizenship'. The category of 'senior citizen' demarcates both old age and the lifecourse. While the idea of the citizen may be relatively easy to accept in a world of nation-states and passports its genesis and significance is less well understood. As we have seen, structured dependency theorists have argued that old age is a product of social policy. The establishment of state old age pensions is based on some form of personal entitlement. This entitlement also extends to other welfare provision that may include various domiciliary and residential services. Citizenship is usually the rubric under which government takes responsibility for the well-being of its non-working population. Whatever the inadequacies of the political economy approach, the concept of citizenship remains crucial to our understanding of ageing in the modern world. The idea of universal entitlements is bound up with the creation of citizenship. The entitlements created by citizenship have established the pensioner as a generic category of person who shares the same experiences and needs, and who has the same interests.

From its very beginning the modern state and its social policies have always played an important part in fashioning the expression and experience of old age. Old age pensioners existed in Britain at least as far back as Tudor and Stuart times.[1] The claim of structured dependency theorists, however, is that the emergence of the modern welfare state at a particular stage of capitalist development imposed universalist social security provisions and mandatory retirement which, while protecting older people, kept them in poverty.[2] The appearance of an all-encompassing relationship between the individual and the state embodied in the idea of citizenship establishes the potential for the modern state – through its laws and policies – to structure to varying degrees the pattern and expectations that individuals have of each stage in the human lifecourse. This is the essential message of the political economy approach. That it has become increasingly limited as a means of understanding ageing is in large part due to the changing nature of citizenship that has been evident during the second half of the twentieth century. In order to chart these changes we have to go back to the immediate post-war era where the idea of welfare citizenship was first articulated.

## T.H. Marshall and all that

T.H. Marshall's model of citizenship provides a point of departure for most discussions on the nature of citizenship in the twentieth century. Written in 1950 during the period of reconstruction following the Second World War, Marshall's work was seen as providing a theoretical justification for the 'post-war consensus' that underpinned the existence of the welfare state. This approach sought to create a society where individuals and classes would be integrated into a wider community through social policy. Historically founded on an optimistic interpretation of the evolution of freedom in the United Kingdom, Marshall saw a progressive movement towards twentieth-century social rights beginning with the establishment of civil and economic rights in the eighteenth and nineteenth centuries. Post-war Britain and its welfare state represented for many the triumph of social development in dealing with the problems of market capitalism.[3] The inequalities created through the market were to be contained by the state in order to establish social harmony. Citizens would therefore have a stake in society; one which removed the desire to radically change the institutional order or challenge the centrality of the market. It is important to note that Marshall's account of citizenship was not just a theory, but also a justification of the social-democratic and collectivist strategies pursued by post-war governments.

The full title of Marshall's *Citizenship and Social Class* highlights his view that citizenship needed to be seen in the context of profound class differences. This focus on social class points to the collective nature of the rights he was advocating. While citizenship rights may be seen as belonging to individuals, in reality they resided in whole classes of the population. Consequently, it was not individual inequality that was important but social inequality. Whole classes had to be freed from the negative effects of market capitalism. In order to achieve this, Marshall pointed to the significance of a secondary system of industrial citizenship created by the trade unions. The mass membership of the trade unions allowed collective bargaining to become an instrument for raising workers' social and economic status and thus promote social unity. Central to the way citizenship was conceived from this perspective was its collective nature. Social rights were about collective security and integration; they were there for every one who would otherwise be disadvantaged by the inequalities thrown up by the operation of the market. This was equally true of the intentions behind many welfare policies such as health, social security and education.[4]

Marshall's account of citizenship has not survived the last few decades without serious criticism. Rees challenged its historical accuracy and its conflation of nationality with citizenship, Michael Mann questioned its narrow geographical focus on Britain while Anthony Giddens pointed out its failure to acknowledge the importance of conflict in creating the possibilities for various forms of freedom.[5] Equally important is his failure to see the gendering of citizenship that was implicit in the original design to the extent that women often failed to qualify for pensions as of right and only achieved them through marriage.[6]

Citizenship understood in terms of Marshall's paradigm has been remarkably successful in generating debate but rather less so in limiting class conflict or promoting social justice. The heyday of citizenship theory and practice is generally thought of as occurring between 1948 and 1964, a time when mass benefits and mass entitlements came into being in health and social security.[7] As with nationalization the social effectiveness of the Keynesian welfare state did not always live up to its potential. Class inequalities remained and often widened. On top of this, it was often the middle class who received maximum benefit from the welfare state either directly through employment or indirectly through increased opportunity.[8]

That the vision of citizenship outlined by Marshall was not succeeding can be gleaned from what became known as the 'crisis of the welfare state' which occurred after 1976. While Pierson has pointed to the multiple meanings this phrase has come to represent,[9] what is important is that the negative connotations of the concept became crucial for political debate and marked the end of a consensus about the role of the state in securing social justice through social policy. Henceforth, and to differing degrees, governments would be cautious if not openly hostile to the role of the state in overcoming inequalities generated by the market. Public spending was often identified as a principal cause of economic difficulties that were in turn seen as necessitating reductions in public expenditure.[10]

In these altered circumstances the idea of what citizenship was became more confused. The nominal benefits to the working class that citizenship was supposed to provide became more problematic at the same time as expectations were increasing that they should be delivered. The social wage and the protection offered by social insurance as collective rights depended upon a prosperous economy and a low take-up. The combination of high inflation and rising unemployment in the mid- to late 1970s threw this into confusion and in so doing exposed some of the instabilities within Marshall's account of the relationship between capitalism and social class.[11]

The emergence of the 'new right' in the 1970s and 1980s on both sides of the Atlantic is well documented as is the corresponding resurgence of economic neo-liberalism.[12] Again this acted to undermine the notion of citizenship that had emerged from the post-war consensus. To the 'new right' the social rights embodied in citizenship represented the victory of socialism by stealth. The rights of citizenship, because of their collective nature, led inevitably to bureaucracy, inefficiency and the coercive power of the state over all individuals. Furthermore, these rights led to economic stagnation and decline as the leviathan of the expanding public purse crushed all individual initiative through taxation and regulation. The policies followed by the Thatcher government in the UK and the Reagan administration in the USA were deliberate attempts to limit social citizenship, as was John Major's resistance to the implementation of the 'social chapter' of the Maastricht Treaty in the 1990s.

Some commentators have argued that, the politics aside, the changes represent an inevitable response to a changing society. Peter Saunders has argued that such moves do not undermine citizenship but instead promote it so that it accords with the interests of the majority of the population who no longer perceive themselves needing the social protection that the entitlement to social security and unemployment benefits was intended to provide.[13] Neither is there a significant section of the population whose wages are so low they need the state's help in ensuring their social reproduction. There might be relative inequality in remuneration but not absolute poverty. As real incomes have risen the need for the 'socialized consumption' of state welfare by the mass of the working class has declined. This new affluence, as well as the increased cost of welfare, has resulted in a shift to 'privatized consumption'. The popularity of the sale of council houses by the Conservative government during the 1980s is a powerful example of this process. Focusing on issues of choice and consumer sovereignty as key issues in modern society also has its effects on the remainder who have to rely on public services. This marginalized sector of the population are likely to become dissatisfied as they compare their relative fate with those able to privatize their consumption.

From a different position, Zygmunt Bauman makes the same point about the impact of being a recipient of state welfare. In an era characterized by consumption and choice people use commodities to establish their self-identities. Those who do not have the resources to participate in the market become 'repressed' welfare clients subject to the controlling disciplinary mechanisms of the state.[14] In *Work, Consumerism and the New Poor* Bauman has gone considerably further, stating that the processes of consumer society 'pathologize' and 'criminalize' the poor as both individual failures and social dangers.

As Bauman writes:

As in all other kinds of society, the poor of a consumer society are people with no access to a normal life, let alone a happy one. In a consumer society however, having no access to a happy or merely a normal life means to be consumer manqués, or flawed consumers. And so the poor of a consumer society are socially defined, and self-defined, first and foremost as blemished, defective, faulty and deficient – in other words, inadequate consumers.[15]

While not everyone would accord with this view of the 'sovereign consumer', what does seem to be true is the general acceptance of the inferiority of state welfare, so much so that supporters of the Marshallian idea of citizenship have accepted that there was much wrong with the welfare state especially in its lack of respect for individuals and its concentration on 'statist' solutions or in its reliance on corporatism.[16] More recently the ideas described as the 'Third Way' have discarded the idea of the welfare state altogether.[17] Consequently, both at a theoretical and at a practical level there has been an abandonment of the conventional idea of citizenship.

## The state, status and citizenship

An alternative to the social-democratic view of citizenship and old age has been developed by Bryan Turner who, through the importance of the idea of status, sees ageing as intrinsically bound up in the nature of modern society.[18] Following on from earlier points about the decline of mass society Turner argues that the importance of status has increased as the highly stratified societies of Western industrialized capitalism give way to the more fragmented forms of consumer society. Status, like citizenship, has the power to include or exclude individuals from a community or society. Citizenship is increasingly a form of status that confirms that a person is a full member of a modern nation-state. The civil rights struggles of Black people in the USA provide an example of how the exclusion of groups from the 'public sphere' leads to a lack of status and of power. To be a citizen and to be accepted as one is therefore important in the social construction of status groups.

Following many contemporary sociologists Turner also argues that, as traditional occupational structures play less and less of a role in most people's day-to-day activities, a multitude of lifestyle choices come to replace them. Status politics based around group identities become crucial to the practicalities of policy formation and implementation in the public sphere. To extend Turner's argument, the collapse of class in society is reflected in the popular rejection of mass provision of welfare. Instead, what emerges is a form of pressure group politics. Citizenship in this formulation is about different status groups competing to get their particular needs met and being relatively unconcerned as to how this is achieved. In terms of the desirability for older people of the continuation of universalist welfare policies, it could be countered that a more flexible welfare environment with multiple providers may be more responsive to their needs than those organized by powerful welfare bureaucracies.

According to Turner, older people are in competition with other social groups because the negative experience of ageing results in them being denied their universalistic rights of citizenship. This leads Turner to describe them as a 'state administered status group' because they become the clients of the state in order to enforce their social entitlements. When Turner wrote this – in 1988 – he clearly saw the possibility of the development of a politics of old age in the mould of the US 'Gray Panthers' which would be positive. This is because, he argues, 'competitive struggle between social groups over resources [is] the essential feature of a sociology of status'[19] and has the effect of creating social solidarity and identity within the group. Conflict also provides a way in which enhanced social mobility will be possible, at least in principle. However, Turner has since become more pessimistic and sees significant generational conflicts over scarce resources leaving older people socially disadvantaged.[20] Using the concept of generations borrowed from the work of Bourdieu, he argues that each generation comprises a cohort of persons passing through time who share a common habitus and lifestyle. Membership of a generation is both inclusive in terms of shared experience and exclusive in terms of attempts to secure advantages against subsequent generations. Turner writes:

> For example, the generation of 1945 was born into a social environment in Britain that was characterised by economic growth, an emerging welfare state, access to free higher education and an international context that was comparatively peaceful. Individual access to these resources requires a generational identity and solidarity organised around exclusionary practices which continue to secure these advantages against subsequent generations. The labels which are attached to these post-war generations are indicative of generational conflicts, cohort fortunes and social resentments in for example 'The Lucky Generation', 'The Baby Boomers' or 'The Me Generation'. These generations stay on top by organising a concerted approach to successful marriage patterns, reproduction, employment and inheritance strategies.[21]

He argues that in a society that is impersonal and highly differentiated, as well as having an emphasis on young and new occupations, it is not surprising that older people find themselves discriminated against or losing out in terms of social policy. The effect of belonging to the present older generation is one that cannot be successfully articulated as a status because of its prior incorporation in a welfarist notion of citizenship.

Does the more culturally fragmented environment of globalization and postmodernization shift this pessimistic conclusion? If the nation-state has lost a considerable amount of its power to organize society does this change the perception of the older person as incorporated into welfarism? After all, the position of the old might be aided by a wider acknowledgement that being an elderly person is just another cultural identity. Does the growth of the powers of the European Union shift responsibility for social rights to supranational bodies such as the European Court of Justice and the European Parliament, and if so does this give more opportunity to older people to successfully articulate their interests? If such post-national citizenship is to have any meaning, it will have to be based on a common European identity in which no specific culture is predominant nor any group less important than others. Optimistically, Turner sees the potential multiplicity of cultural identities existing alongside one another leading to respect for one another's difference and rights. What Turner posits as 'cultural citizenship' is based on the democratization of culture that emerges from a fragmentary postmodern culture and which treats all as equal. This returns Turner to an explicit theme in Marshall's idea of citizenship; that of citizens sharing in a common culture. Turner argues that the collapse of the distinction between high and low culture that accompanies postmodernization allows all citizens to share in such a common culture where no particular set of ideas can dominate and accordingly difference must be accepted.

Tellingly, as Roche has pointed out, there is a deep acknowledged ambivalence in Turner's work about just how the nation-state-based concept of citizenship integrates with postmodern cultural fragmentation and whether the nation-state will become redundant as a result.[22] Roche makes an important point in arguing that such transnational citizenship is unlikely to be achieved because such bodies as the EU do not have the capacity to grant citizenship themselves but must establish it through the member states first. Furthermore, the issue of 'subsidiarity' allows national governments the right to set social policies in accordance with their own priorities. The strategy of gaining Euro-rights for older people is thus also limited in its effectiveness.

Anthony Giddens in his book *Beyond Left and Right* offers a slightly different reworking of the compact between citizen and state by relating old age to what he terms 'positive welfare'.[23] Accepting that the welfare state has failed to deal successfully with the individualism of modern social life, he links this with Ulrich Beck's notion of 'risk society' to argue that in a period of 'reflexive modernization' there is no need for the social security provided by mass welfare states. For Giddens the distinction between actuarial risk and manufactured uncertainty represents the difference between welfare policy and an engaged individual agency. The welfare state assumed that the risk facing individuals could be calculated and plans made to minimize it. Under the new circumstances of reflexive modernization we are exposed to levels of 'manufactured risks' which are not easy to fix or calculate. This new reality is a product of the unintended consequences of industrialization and a growing incapacity for knowledge to anticipate or adequately explain them. The issues surrounding ageing, argues Giddens, must be seen from this perspective. Reiterating many of the points made by social gerontologists, he points out the negative social impact of being separated out as an old age pensioner. However, instead of focusing on this as an issue of social policy, he locates it as one of individual agency: '[a]geing is treated as "external", as something that happens to one, not as a phenomenon actively constructed and negotiated'.[24] Giddens therefore sees as positive any action to remove this external label and make the older person more involved in their own self-creation. In practical terms this means older people taking more responsibility for their individual well-being. More controversially it means removing the state retirement pension as an unnecessary form of 'precautionary aftercare'.[25] Instead governments should concern themselves with the creation and promotion of the 'autotelic self' who not only has self-respect and ontological security but also challenges risk as a way of achieving self-actualization. The abolition of the state retirement pension may be a fundamentally radical idea as far as contemporary politics is concerned; however, it is not so far from the practice of recent British governments who have ensured that state pensions have become less and less valuable in real terms. While in a more recent (1998) popular work designed to provide theoretical gloss to the new Labour government Giddens accepts the need for some form of state pension, he also writes:

Old age is a new-style risk masquerading as an old style one. Ageing used to be more passive than it is now: the ageing body was simply something that had to be accepted. In the more active, reflexive society, ageing has become much more of an open process, on a physical as well as a psychic level. Becoming older presents at least as many opportunities as problems, both for individuals and the wider social community.[26]

In order to achieve this, pensionable age should be abolished as should the category of pensioner; instead, compulsory saving schemes should be introduced that could be accessed at any point in the lifecourse. In this way not only is the connection between old age and citizenship broken, but also the very idea of old age itself.

The work of Turner and Giddens suggests that the compact between old age and citizenship is rapidly being discarded, dislocating the usefulness of both terms as far as sociology and social gerontology are concerned. Giddens makes what is a relatively novel proposal, inverting the customary relationship between the state and its 'dependants', suggesting that older people should 'be regarded as part of the wealth creating sectors of society, and as able to contribute to taxation revenue'.[27] While this may be a rhetorical flourish it does at the same time suggest that we start to look at the economics of later life in a different way.

## Grey capitalism and the role of pension funds

The relationship between capitalism and the construction of old age through citizenship was one predicated upon a particular view of the nature of capitalism. The nature of capitalism has undergone significant change. Giddens could not be advocating the abolition of the old age pension were it not for the growing affluence of people of working age and the changes in the sources of income for retired people. The rise of what Robin Blackburn has called 'grey capitalism' provides a radically different perspective on the status and position of the retired population to that outlined within the Marshallian construction of 'senior citizenship'.

Drawing attention to the impact that pension funds have on global financial markets, Blackburn points out that a significant proportion of the world's investment finance belongs to funds tied to occupational pension schemes or to private pension funds.[28] He charts the meteoric rise of this form of financial institution in the deregulated financial markets of the 1980s and 1990s and its potentially negative impact on long-term economic growth. The validity of his criticism does not concern us here. Rather, what is significant is not the actual number of people participating in private pension schemes, but the transformation of the compact between state and citizen that underpinned the state retirement pension. Moving toward individual responsibility for the funding of retirement not only creates inequality but also justifies it. While it is true that the shift to private pensions does not necessarily alleviate any of the burden of funding retirement, what is also true is that the key role of pension funds in the economy changes the construction of the identity of the potential recipient of pensions. Their economic status is no longer determined by the state and by the taxes raised by that state, but increasingly arises from participation, actively or passively, in the investment strategies of global finance. The role of the citizen has been replaced by that of the consumer of financial services. Britain's New Labour government advocates a system of second pensions derived from investment income as their chosen a model of financing retirement. Those left without such options are expected to forgo a reasonable level of security in old age and accept, instead, benefits set at the lowest level. This is a long way from the idea of an egalitarian society in old age supported by a universal pension guaranteeing a 'national minimum' income after retirement from the workplace.

What is important, in the context of this book, is not the debate about whether or not the state should provide adequate pensions and security in retirement, but the issue of how people construct their lives. Having to make plans throughout adulthood for a post-working life creates a very different set of experiences from those of being part of a mass system of entitlements administered by the state. As we have pointed out earlier, in a consumer society the construction of identity is made up of large numbers of such choices, each contributing to the whole. To use again Anthony Giddens' phrase, we are no longer in a period where such 'precautionary aftercare' is the structure within which ageing occurs. In the past, retirement was connected to the decline in productivity of the older worker and the need to remove such age cohorts from the workforce. The circumstances in which retirement now occurs are connected more to choice and lifestyle on the one hand and to redundancy on the other. The growth of retirement as a third age – a potential crown of life – has been accompanied by a desire to see retirement as a period of leisure and self-fulfilment, an ideal closer to the market than to the workhouse. While this attitude may be fully realizable within a minority section of the population of older people, culturally this group represents the aspirations of many unable to undertake such a lifestyle.[29]

This model of organizing the funding of the post-retirement population is not confined to Britain. Indeed, it is much more familiar in the USA where the idea of universal social entitlement has never really caught on as a political objective. The history of retirement in America is one of particularistic entitlement rather than federal responsibility. However, as Blackburn points out, while the model of funding pensions through investment was initially a very Anglo-Saxon affair, being initially confined to Britain and the USA, it is now spreading to other European nations. Indeed, the Anglo-Saxon approach to financing old age is being promoted by the World Bank itself as the most desirable approach to the questions raised by ageing populations. More radical versions based upon the Chilean model of state-regulated personal investment funds are spreading equally widely especially in Latin America and the post-communist world as part of a new wave of neo-liberalism. These developments suggest that what is taking place is a global response to the nature of the link between citizen and state and the diminishing belief in the ability of state welfare systems to meet the new demands placed upon them.[30]

## Citizenship and governmentality

If the role of the older person is increasingly framed as that of consumer rather than citizen, does this mean that there is no longer a category of old age or that social policy has little to do with ageing *qua* ageing?. The answer is no. The shift towards what has been described as 'Advanced Liberalism'[31] designates a different role for social policy – one that is concerned with the Foucauldian term 'governmentality'. The idea of governmentality is a development of Foucault's idea of the disciplinary society – a society in which individuals are organized through various expert knowledges and in which the internalization of these discourses occurs through the idea of the panopticon. As we noted in the previous chapter, governmentality refers to the state's role in the 'conduct of conduct'. By this, Foucault referred to the process of mutual interaction between state and self-governance. Thus while individuals internalize the state's systems of control and surveillance, the state in its turn appropriates the various 'technologies of the self' as its means of government. Ostensibly, these self-technologies appear as free choices but increasingly they are choices sponsored by governments. Importantly governmentality equates with both rationality and free choice. Not only is the adoption of an appropriate 'technology of the self' an individual responsibility; it is also a rational response. Not to engage with governmentality is to put oneself outside society and so to be 'at risk'.

Turner has pointed out how governmentality and risk are the two concepts that locate the real tensions of modern society.[32] The tension is between the deregulation of the macro–global level, and all the agentic dilemmas that this throws up, and the micro–local requirement for a continuing politics of surveillance and control. He writes:

> As the global economy develops into a culture of risk, the nation-state is forced to invest more and more in internal systems of governmentality.[33]

Consequently the notion of governmentality locates itself within the idea of citizenship as a way of coping with the insecurities of the modern world. The technologies of the self are informed by norms, values and statistics that can be used to measure and assess the performance of individuals. Those who deviate from this frame of reference are then the appropriate targets of social policy. David Armstrong has written of the emergence of what he terms 'surveillance medicine' where the whole of the individual's life is subject to scrutiny for risky behaviours that might give rise to future health problems. Governmentality as citizenship extends to areas as diverse as education, social services and disability. In each of these areas concepts of normality or appropriateness, derived from 'expert' discourse, are utilized and those individuals causing concern by not meeting them are targeted to receive special attention. Poster argues that such forms of surveillance constitute 'a Superpanopticon, a system of surveillance without walls, windows or towers or guards. The qualitative advances in the technologies of surveillance result in a qualitative change in the microphysics of power'.[34] All parts of social life are encoded into data, not only to be used for the purposes of establishing normality and risk but also to 'create' the individual who is constituted therein.

The implications of governmentality for the state are immense. If the organization of welfare can be understood as a technical problem of risk avoidance then the nature of state welfare can be radically re-arranged. Assessment and administration become the main, if not the sole, functions of the welfare state. As Castel points out, in an era of state welfare contraction 'the interventionist technologies which make it possible to "guide" and "assign" individuals without having to assume their custody could well prove to be a decisive resource'.[35]

Governmentality, then, can provide some of the solutions to the prob-lems of modern welfare states by reordering the relationship between the citizen and the state. There are those who rise to the challenge of modern life and those who fail. Rewriting the compact with old age is an example of the transformation of collective welfare benefits into individual ones. The acknowledged connection between the state pen-sion and poverty in the UK which has been maintained in part by the decoupling of the link with average earnings is not to be dealt with by increasing the rate at which the pension is paid. Instead, compulsory secondary personal pensions are proposed which would be dependent on the amounts paid into the fund, leaving the ultimate pension to vary considerably. This policy builds upon processes that have already occurred in the restructuring of the welfare state where many different tiers of pensioner have come into existence. It involves a moral as well as a fiscal position whereby the state expects of its citizens choices that serve both the state and their own interests as private citizens.

One result is a fragmenting of the ageing population into those who can successfully exercise the appropriate technologies of the self by pro-viding for their old age and those who cannot. The relative affluence of occupational and private pension holders separates them out from those older people as primarily welfare benefit recipients. It is the latter group who now constitute the 'problem' of 'old age'. The same dichotomy is played out in relation to health care. Here people are presented with two images; one the physically frail and dependent 'fourth-ager' lacking the necessary 'self-care' skills to sustain a third-age identity, the other the active and healthy individual producing and consuming his or her 'third age'. The former is a drain on resources, especially if he or she needs high levels of care, while the latter is the acme of agency and is the target of lifestyle advertising. It is therefore not at all surprising that services for older frailer people (such as long-stay hospital beds) are being reduced or made the individual's liability (payments for nursing homes) at the same time as retired people are presented with a discourse of choice and opportunity.

These conundrums illustrate the contradictory nature of this new mode of citizenship. Ageing seems to present particular problems in a society ordered around governmentality and risk. Citizens are encouraged to take greater personal responsibility for their health and for extending the period of a fit and healthy third age; at the same time, old age is considered ultimately a non-agentic, primarily physiological process that cannot be overcome by any technologies of the self. It moves people from a post-working lifestyle into a welfare category of risk. In Britain and in other countries this has meant that surveillance (health screening) has become almost as mandatory at the age of 75 as retirement is at age 65, potentially transforming the older person's body into little more than an object of health-care discourse.[36]

In this chapter we have charted the transformation of the idea of citizenship from its Marshallian origins in the post-war social democracies to its fragmentation in the postmodern contradictions of governmentality. We have seen how correspondingly 'old age' has ceased to be a universal category created by social policy to become a residual category applied to those deemed incapable of exercising the reflexive agency demanded by contemporary consumerism. This does not mean that social policy is irrelevant or that it cannot act as a limiting factor shaping the experience of later life. However, it has lost its universal capacity to do so and can no longer play the central role previously accorded to it by populations and governments. As governments increasingly hand over responsibility for later life to the individual they do so at the same time as promoting the internalization of the spectre of enfeeblement and impoverishment of old age once externalized and embodied in the institutions of the workhouse.

While citizenship remains a key concept in understanding the nature of, and the fragmentation and contradictions of, later life, it is no longer internally consistent. Instead the notion of welfare dependency which has been created by social policy acts as a backdrop and warning to those aspiring cultures of ageing which are the concerns of our book.

## Notes

1 See Beir, A.L. (1985) *Masterless Men: the Vagrancy Problem in England, 1560–1640*, Methuen, London; Wear, A. (1991) 'Caring for the sick poor in St. Bartholomew's exchange, 1580–1676', *Medical History*, Supplement 11: 41–60.
2 See Macnicol, J. and Blaikie, A. (1989) 'The politics of retirement, 1908–1948'. In M. Jefferys (ed.), *Growing Old in the Twentieth Century*, Routledge, London, p. 22.
3 Titmuss, R. (1974) *Commitment to Welfare*, Allen & Unwin, London.
4 Timmins, N. (1996) *The Five Giants: a Biography of the Welfare State*, Fontana, London.
5 Giddens, A. (1982) *Central Problems in Social Theory*, Macmillan, London; Mann, M. (1987) 'Ruling class strategies and citizenship', *Sociology*, 21: 339–54; Rees, A. (1996) 'T.H. Marshall and the Progress of Citizenship', in Bulmer, M. and Rees, A. (eds) *Citizenship Today: the Contemporary Relevance of T.H. Marshall*, UCL Press, London.
6 *Cf.* Sainsbury, D. (1993) 'Dual welfare and sex segregation of access to social benefits: income maintenance policies in the UK, the US, the Netherlands and Sweden', *Journal of Social Policy*, 22: 69–98.
7 Hay, C. (1996) *Restating Social and Political Change*, Open University Press, Buckingham.
8 Le Grand, J. (1982) *The Strategy of Equality*, Allen & Unwin, London.
9 Pierson, C. (1998) *Beyond the Welfare State*, Polity Press, Cambridge.
10 Higgs, P. (1993) *The NHS and Ideological Conflict*, Avebury, Aldershot.
11 Hindess points out that Marshall's later work seems to recognize this instability by using the term 'hyphenated society' to describe a 'democratic-welfare-capitalism' where the elements seem to have to achieve balance (Hindess, B. (1993) 'Citizenship in the Modern West', in B.S. Turner (ed.), *Citizenship and Social Theory*, Sage, London, pp. 19–35).
12 Taylor-Gooby, P. (1991) *Social Change, Social Welfare and Social Science*, Harvester Wheatsheaf, Hemel Hempstead.
13 Saunders, P. (1993) 'Citizenship in a Liberal Society', in B. Turner (ed.), *Citizenship and Social Theory*, Sage, London, pp. 57–90.
14 Bauman, Z. (1988) *Freedom*, Open University Press, Milton Keynes.
15 Bauman, Z. (1998) *Work, Consumerism and the New Poor*, Open University Press, Buckingham, p. 38.
16 Taylor-Gooby, P. (1991) *op. cit.*
17 Giddens, A. (1998) *The Third Way: The Renewal of Social Democracy*, Polity Press, Cambridge.
18 Turner, B. (1988) *Status*, Open University, Milton Keynes; see also Turner, B. (1993) 'Postmodern culture/modern citizens', in B. van Steenbergen (ed.), *The Condition of Citizenship*, Sage, London.
19 Turner, B.S. (1989) 'Ageing, status politics and sociological theory', *British Journal of Sociology*, 40, p. 589.

20 See Turner, B. (1997) 'From governmentality to risk: some reflections on Foucault's contribution to medical sociology', in A. Petersen and R. Bunton (eds), *Foucault, Health and Medicine*, Routledge, London.

21 Turner, B. (1998) *op. cit.*, p. 302.

22 Roche, M. (1995) 'Citizenship and modernity', *British Journal of Sociology*, 46: 715–33.

23 Giddens, A. (1994) *Beyond Left and Right*, Polity Press, Cambridge.

24 *Ibid.*, p. 170.

25 *Ibid.*, p. 182.

26 Giddens, A. (1998) *op. cit.*, p. 119.

27 *Ibid.*, p. 184.

28 Blackburn, R. (1999) 'The new collectivism: pension reform, grey capitalism and complex socialism', *New Left Review*, 233: 3–65.

29 This argument closely parallels the debate over the changing nature of 'class relationships' in Western society and the growing distinction between 'poverty' and the 'working class'. The aspirations of the adult working population have shifted considerably over the last 50 years – aspirations that increasingly are associated with a 'middle-class' status (see, for example, the recent British survey of class and social attitudes, reported in *The Guardian*, 24 December 1999).

30 These new demands arise both from changing demographics (alteration in the numerical balance between those in work and those enjoying a post-work life) and from changing expectations (alteration in the expected standard of living of working and non-working people beyond the simple reproduction of their daily life).

31 See Rose, N. (1996) 'Governing advanced liberal democracies', in A. Barry, T. Osborne and N. Rose (eds), *Foucault and Political Reason: Liberalism, Neo-Liberalism and the Rationalities of Government*, UCL Press, London, pp. 37–64.

32 Turner, B.S. (1997) 'Foreword: from governmentality to risk, some reflections on Foucault's contribution to medical sociology', in A. Peterson and R. Bunton (eds), *Foucault, Health and Medicine*, Routledge, London, pp. ix–xxi.

33 *Ibid.*, pp. xviii–xix.

34 Poster, M. (1990) 'Foucault and data bases: participatory surveillance'. In B. Smart (ed.), (1995) *Michel Foucault 2: Critical Assessments*, vol. 7, Routledge, London, p. 87.

35 Castel, R. (1991) 'From Dangerousness to Risk', in R. Burchell (ed.), *The Foucault Effect*, Harvester Wheatsheaf, Hemel Hempstead, pp. 281–98, p. 295.

36 Gilleard, C. and Higgs, P. (1996) 'Cultures of ageing: self, citizen and the body', in V. Minichiello, N. Chappell, H. Kendrig and A. Walker (eds), *Sociology of Aging*, International Sociological Association, Melbourne, pp. 82–92.

# CHAPTER 6

# Senior citizenship and contemporary social policy

Peter Townsend's contribution to one of the most influential collections of work on structured dependency theory, *Ageing and Social Policy: a Critical Assessment*, drew attention to the key role played by the state's policies on pensions, old age residential provision and 'community care' in the social construction of dependency in later life. Drawing on earlier work, he wrote:

> Twentieth century processes of retirement, establishment of minimum pensions, residential care and delivery of community services have created forms of social dependency among the elderly that are artificial.[1]

Current British pension policy enforced retirement and paid retired people a universal 'subsistence pension' which had the combined effect of sustaining their dependency and marginalization: 'after decades of struggle the percentage of elderly dependent on means tested social assistance is almost identical to what it was . . . in the 1890s'.[2] In a similar fashion, writing about residential care policy he argued:

> residential homes for the elderly serve functions for the wider society and not only for their inmates. While accommodating only a tiny percentage of the elderly population they symbolise the dependence of the elderly and legitimate their lack of access to equality of status.[3]

Nor were pension policy and the use of residential care the only means of imposing dependency and depriving older people of their status as equal citizens: 'Artificial dependency is fostered . . . not just in . . . the existing structures of residential care but in the community services'.[4] Community health and social care services failed to address the reality of older people's lives and resources and Townsend concluded:

> Elderly people are conceived as isolated recipients of service and the stultifying restricted and restrictive character of that service is not . . . acknowledged. As a consequence the conception and development of community services helps to foster and deepen public images of elderly people as dependent wards of the state.[5]

Whatever the flaws in his formulation, Townsend's approach highlighted some of the key aspects of social citizenship that shaped people's post-work lives in the second half of the twentieth century. In this chapter we examine how the changes in the nature of citizenship over this last half century have been expressed with respect to pension policies, the provision of long-term institutional care and the delivery of domiciliary health and social services.

## Citizens, stakeholders and pension policies

The origins of the old age pension in England can be traced as far back as the sixteenth century. At those times, however, the pension was a very local affair, largely offered as alms to those in evident need and determined by parish councils. State-administered 'universal' old age pensions originated in Germany in the late nineteenth century. In Britain they were introduced by Lloyd George in the Old Age Pensions Act of 1908, which entitled all those aged 70 and over to claim up to five shillings a week, depending upon need. This means-tested scheme was eventually abandoned by the Beveridge reforms culminating in the 1946 National Insurance Act. This Act provided a flat rate universal state pension to men who retired at 65 and women who retired aged 60.

Pensions became a central plank in the welfare state of most Western democracies, making up a key element of post-war citizenship. They were represented as a pact between the generations. In Britain, those in work and their employers contributed their national insurance payments which provided the funds out of which pensions and social security were paid – to those out of work and those retired from work. As the labour force's economic condition improved, so it was assumed would the state pension rise in value enabling those who had left work to benefit from the improved living standards of those in work. Similar contributory schemes have been implemented in most Western countries with some variation in the balance between funds derived from contributions and funds derived out of general taxation.[6]

By the late 1970s a growing note of scepticism began to emerge about the long-term viability of this model of 'pay as you go' contributory social insurance schemes and the indexing of pensions to average wages, especially in the light of high rates of inflation. This was first evident in Britain but such doubts about 'social insurance' systems have also been expressed in most Western countries, if not at that time, certainly subsequently. After the return of a Conservative government in Britain in 1979, an immediate re-think of the state pension took place. In 1980 the state pension was indexed to prices rather than wages, a move that signalled the gradual transformation in the nature of income in later life. As the value of the state pension declined – as a proportion of average wages – an increasing amount of retirement income derived from non-statutory sources, particularly occupational and personal pensions. As a result, despite the decline in the real value of the flat rate state pension there has been no concomitant rise in poverty amongst pensioner households. In 1948, at the start of the British welfare state, more than half of 'old age pensioners' received supplementary benefits. In 1980 less than one in five did so. By 1997 that figure had fallen so that less than one in seven pensioners received income support.

The change in government in Britain in 1997 has not led to any change in direction with regards to pension policy. Increasingly older people are expected to derive their income from their own savings and investments rather than from their citizenship as 'old age pensioners'.[7] One direct consequence of this transformation of the state as the provider of later life income is the growing disparity between the economic position of those with supplementary pensions and those without. According to one recent report, those with occupational pensions receive a weekly income over 80 per cent higher than those without.[8]

In the United States, pension policy has followed a rather different route, although some of the consequences for income inequalities in later life are very similar. As mentioned in Chapter 4, a contribution-based federal social security fund was established in the 1930s and has been extremely successful in providing increasing prosperity to America's retired population. This exists alongside a well-established tradition amongst large sections of the population of obtaining income in retirement from personal pension plans and other retirement-focused investments. Currently these funds make up over a quarter of total equity holdings in the US.[9] Since the Carter administration in the mid-1970s, concerns have been raised about the overextension of the social security programme. Various proposals have been made to alter the age of entitlement, merge private and federal income security systems, introduce means testing of benefits and, most recently, to 'privatize' a part of the massive social security fund by creating a retirement fund that could be invested in stocks and bonds. Proposals to establish individualized retirement funds – termed personal security or universal savings accounts – allowing individuals to opt out from the social security contributory scheme are also being put forward.[10]

The recent interest in individualizing social security accounts has been seen by some as a flirtation with the Chilean model of compulsory privatized pension arrangements. Since 1981 when it was first introduced the Chilean model of pension funds has received widespread praise from the institutions of global capitalism. Jose Pinera, the Chilean finance minister, established the principle of individualized savings accounts based upon compulsive contributions that were set at one-tenth of the individual's gross wage. These are paid into a choice of government-approved private pension funds. The Chilean model of state-ensured 'individualized' pension funds has been widely influential in many newly capitalized economies – in Latin America and more recently in Eastern and Central Europe. More than the British and US systems it pushes the idea that individual choice throughout adult life should be the determining influence upon the income one will receive after retiring from paid employment. The implication is that those who end up needing the state's support to ensure an income in later life are more easily viewed as the feckless poor – poor by their failure to make the right choices as consumers of financial services. The return to a reliance upon individual decisions has led some to comment upon a new turn in social policy, back to the 'voluntarism' of the nineteenth century, pre-dating the welfare state. While the principles may be articulated in terms of increased choice the general thrust is to seek to wean successive generations of older people from being 'dependent' upon the state.[11] If social policy in the first half of the twentieth century was to culminate in the universal state pension, policy in the second half can be seen as leading to the return of individual responsibility – but this time from a base of relative affluence spread across a much wider range of the population.

## Community care: the clientization of citizenship

Having transformed the pension system, it took the Conservative government a further 10 years before introducing similar transformations to the British systems of health and social care. The NHS and Community Care Act, passed by the British parliament in 1990, gave a powerful impetus to the creation of a bounded market for health.[12] One of the most significant effects of achieving this was the creation of a consumerist or 'user' perspective in health care intended to operate as a proxy for a health care market. This was achieved by first separating the responsibility for providing health and social care services from the responsibility for purchasing or commissioning such care. For health care, responsibility for commissioning was retained by slimmed-down local health authorities reframed as the collective representation of the 'purchasing power' of the local population. The accountability of the health authorities to the state was, however, unaltered. Providers remained by and large the hospitals and clinics whose professional structures had dominated much of nineteenth- and twentieth-century health care. Now they found themselves increasingly 'under contract' to the purchasers of public health. For social care, the responsibility for provision was meant to shift away from the local authority – with the explicit goal of stimulating a local economy in privatized social care. Although the social care component of the Act was deferred for over two years, when it took force early in 1993 one of its key features was the explicit rationing and targeting of resources – dependent in part upon need and, as emerged from various court judgements made in the 1990s, upon a chosen level of resources. Consumerism as a discourse was given free rein – always provided that its demands remained within the 'cash envelope' offered by local and central government.

Under the terms of the Act, local authorities were charged with the responsibility to publish annual community care plans setting out their priorities for the provision of social care. These plans typically were based around several 'vulnerable' groups which included 'the elderly' or 'older people', 'the disabled' and 'the mentally ill'. Following on from various government-sponsored inquiries into the future of 'community care', the new planning system was designed to target resources to those considered in greatest need. Since the reforms were first enacted – for health in 1990, for social care in 1993 – limited attempts have been made to assess their impact upon health and well-being amongst older people. One of the more consistent features in determining their impact has been on the 'control' over expensive long-term care in hospitals and increasingly in nursing homes – a topic that we shall address in more detail later.

Within UK community care policies, 'the elderly' remains a prominent category amongst the various impoverished groups of consumers of health and social care. Treated for much of the post-war period as a silent but deserving minority, attempts have been made to 'give them a voice' or to 'empower them' so that they can be represented as more effective consumers. Such attempts at citizen advocacy continue to figure prominently on the social policy agenda and seem to be favoured by the liberal research community.[13] While such discourse may seem to offer opportunities for a shift in power from those who provide to those who receive services, the very constructed nature of this voice belies its intent. The current developments in consumerist discourse in the health and welfare field must be placed in the more general context of the evolution of welfare systems within the United Kingdom, and the shift away from universal levels of provision to provision determined by level of need – or level of risk.[14] Most retired people do not characterize themselves or accept their characterization as 'the elderly' – nor do they wish to identify themselves as 'old' for consumerist purposes. Hence the 'voice of the elderly' that is sought is in effect one constructed out of the neediness of those poor, disabled and dependent individuals within the retired population who are the targets of home and institutional care. The size of this constituency varies from country to country – but is at most around one-sixth the over-65-year-old population, and in most countries no more than 5 per cent.[15] While Townsend concentrated upon the depersonalizing nature of community care, what he ignored is the automatic elision of 'the elderly' as a category of need – evident since the onset of welfare legislation in the 1940s and perpetuated in the governmentality of contemporary discourse around 'user empowerment' and 'the assessment of individual needs'. Despite the withdrawal of universal provision and the targeting of need, the discourse of community care continues to construct categories out of an age grouping – reframed as 'elderly users' or 'elderly clients'. The majority who have nothing to do with this system remain uncomfortably a reserve army of consumption.

Similar trends can be detected in many developed countries – namely the transforming of universal state provision of care, the establishment of a social market in health and social care and the enhancement of 'local voices' representing consumer, not human, rights. As in Britain, many continental European countries have moved toward a separation of purchasing and providing roles in both health and social care. Increasingly the emphasis is upon the control of the providers of health care to demonstrate that they offer 'value for money'. Following 1992 legislation in Italy, local health authorities have been cast in the role of commissioners of health care while public hospitals compete with the private sector for health-care contracts. One explicit aim has been to establish 'a more active role for patients and other service users'.[16] In Holland the Decker commission has recommended fostering competition amongst providers and an increase in 'consumer choice', although according to Maarssen and Janssen the successful implementation of these reforms still remains some way off.[17] Purchaser–provider splits have been proposed in Sweden too – with its government seeking to establish greater consumer choice.

By effecting this division between purchasing and providing health care, these new European models are becoming more like the model of health care that was first adopted during the Nixon era in the United States. The Republican government at the time sought to stimulate the development of Health Maintenance Organizations (HMOs), operating as the 'preferred providers' for private health insurance schemes. Subscribing to an HMO was meant to ensure that consumer choice would drive down costs and cause providers to reduce their operating costs basically by ensuring a good level of health for their subscribers. Unfortunately little successful cost cutting occurred. Arising out of such failure to effectively regulate health care, the new Clinton administration announced plans in 1994 to radically reform health care by imposing a compulsory comprehensive health insurance system paid by employers and employees – by the government for the poor – that would be administered through regional commissioning bodies that would enable patients to get 'the best deal' for their money. Fearing the emergence of socialized medicine the reforms met widespread professional and institutional opposition and have been abandoned, with US health care remaining very much in the hands of private and not-for-profit insurers and suppliers. Nevertheless the steady growth in HMOs in recent years has meant that greater controls are being introduced over the providers of health care. That control, however, is in the hands of the health insurance companies whose primary interest is to reduce the risks they run as health insurers and minimize their costs as health purchasers. Given the 'for-profit' nature of the private insurance companies and the inevitable overheads introduced as part of the competitive market, such 'privatized' representation of consumer interests inevitably offers a costlier deal than state-sponsored schemes (much in the same way that private pension schemes do).

US health care for older people has been managed differently. Since 1966 Medicare has operated as a federal health insurance scheme funded largely by general taxation and covering most acute home- and hospital-based health-care costs. Together with Medicaid – a similar scheme that covers those too poor to make any contribution to Medicare – these two systems have significantly increased older people's health purchasing power. While Medicaid is responsible for funding the majority of long-term nursing-home care, the majority of community health-care services for older people are funded through Medicare. Because Medicare is an open-ended system there continues to be considerable anxiety about the federal government's capacity to bankroll these schemes. Various plans to cut, transform or privatize Medicare and Medicaid have been made, although very little thought seems to have been given to controlling the costs of providing the health care itself – by greater use of the existing regulatory controls over fee schedules and other payments. As Jonathan Oberlander has recently pointed out, the cost controls achieved by HMOs mean that 'in many markets Medicare is now the high-payer'. There is thus good reason for lowering Medicare payment rates to health-care providers.[18]

The social care component of community care in the US comes from a variety of largely non-federal sources but has never formed part of the US government's universal health and social insurance schemes – i.e.

social security and the related health insurance schemes of Medicare and Medicaid. Each state has developed its own versions of homecare services and its own methods of funding those services. Most are means tested. The providers of domiciliary services have been private for-profit or voluntary organizations and so there has not been any tradition of government planning of social care provision. Models of extreme consumer sovereignty coexist with state provision. More significantly the 'categorization' of the elderly as state-sponsored recipients for social care has been much less pronounced, and, it could be argued, as a result there has been less association of the retired community with categories of 'neediness' and lack. Indeed, the universality of Medicare and the absence of federal policies around social care can be seen as enabling retired people in America – on the whole – to be less burdened by the state structuring of dependency in old age than retired people in those Western countries whose governments impose a greater level of government-controlled welfare provision.

## Long-term institutional care: choice and social exclusion

Townsend saw the threat of institutionalization – evident in the nineteenth-century workhouse and largely re-created in a more benign form by the 1948 National Assistance Act – as a means of 'disabling' older people from seeking appropriate help in managing their daily living. He viewed the tripartite divisions of long-stay hospital, nursing home and residential care home as a means of exercising social control over the inmates, disciplining the older person to accept whatever care was offered by the threat of transfer to an even more dependency-inducing setting.

If maintaining a significant control over its older citizens by the selective application of long-stay institutional care was ever the government's intention, such 'governmentality' has undergone a radical change in the 1990s. Before considering the situation in Britain – which appears to present an anomaly in relation to nursing-home care – it is worth considering the broader international picture. Since the 1960s, the number of nursing-home beds relative to the size of the over-75 population has risen significantly in many developed countries. More recently it has begun to fall – in some cases very dramatically. This 'transition' took place during the mid- to late 1980s.[19] Britain presents an apparent anomaly because, unlike in other OECD countries, there has been a steady rise in the number of nursing-home beds relative to the over-75 population. The biggest transformation in Britain is in the decline of long-stay hospital beds rather than in the number of nursing-home beds. The reason for this is that most severely disabled older people in Britain were looked after in so-called geriatric and psychogeriatric hospitals, right up to the mid-1980s. In 1983 the then Conservative government introduced changes to the social security supplementary benefits system that allowed retired people on income support to gain 'board and lodgings' payment in both nursing and residential homes. This led to a large rise in the provision of long-term care out of the National Health Service and local authority social services into the private and voluntary nursing-home sector. Various attempts were made to regulate this sudden growth in demand (and the increasing demands on the public purse for additional supplementary benefit payments) but the die was cast and the government was faced with the dual task of both sustaining the revitalized private sector long-term care industry and controlling social security costs.[20] Although these changes effectively halted the expansion of state-provided long-term care institutions – both in the National Health Service and in local authorities – it was another decade before the government undertook to shift not just the provision but the funding of long-term care from the health service into the local social services.

It is important to recognize that, despite the variations in system of institutional provision, the greatest amount of government control over the last two decades has been to halt and where possible put into reverse the expenditure on long-term nursing care beds. Most writers would agree with Gibson that despite some cross-national diversity 'it is possible to observe an increasing co-incidence of policy directions toward home-based care and away from systems heavily reliant on institutional provision'.[21] Consequently the number of people in nursing homes and long-stay hospitals in many Western countries has begun to fall relative to the rise in the over-75-year-old population. This transition is evident not only in countries where there is considerable regulation of levels of provision (e.g. Australia, Sweden) but also in countries where a (state-supported) market for long-term care operates (e.g. United States – see Figure 6.1). This raises questions about the relative significance of

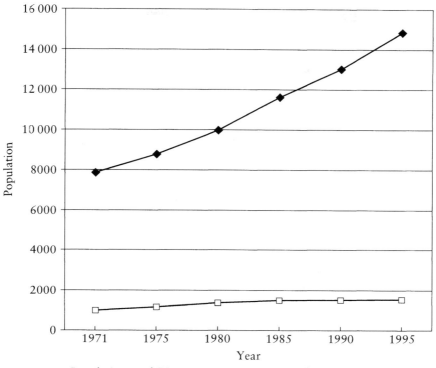

**FIGURE 6.1**  Changes in the nursing-home population and the size of the over-75-year-old population in the USA 1971–95

government policies, changing demographics and changing social expectations in accounting for the change.

Purely economic accounts of the decline in the ratio of nursing-home beds to the size of the over-75 population have concentrated upon two main factors – the change in health status and the change in the gender balance of the older population. In their detailed analysis of determinants of population-based rates of nursing-home entry in America, Lakdawalla and Philipson suggest that improvements in health in later life together with a gradual equalization of the rise in the numbers of elderly men and women accounted for much of the relative decline in nursing-home entry.

These authors suggest that, in the absence of severe mental disabilities, family or marital support makes entry into nursing-home care a highly unlikely event for both retired men and women.[22] On the other hand, widowhood, and the loss of income associated with widowhood, adds considerably to the risk for both men and women. Also of relevance is their observation that 'market-based homecare' does not function as a substitute for family care – at least not as far as protecting older people from entering a nursing home. Whether from private or public means, they suggest that purchasing homecare services by the single and/or the widowed older person has very little impact on the total numbers of older people entering nursing homes.

Of course what Lakdawalla and Philipson's study does not address is the role of the state in influencing the chances of older people ending their lives in long-term-care institutions and hence the state's role in contributing to the 'structured dependency' of retired people by the disciplinary power of 'institutionalization'. Given their focus upon the American nursing-home industry where federal government regulation is limited, this is understandable. What these authors illustrate is the impact of non-policy factors on the 'risks' of nursing-home entry – providing a more balanced perspective against those views which treat institutional care as simply a product of social policy.

Granted that non-policy factors can play a significant part in slowing or reversing trends in long-term nursing-care provision for older people, it is important to recognize also the key role played by recent government policy in most Western countries in shifting provision of long-term care towards an emphasis upon care at home and away from care in long-term institutions. Such policies have been articulated most clearly over the last two decades. They have involved not only the encouragement of community case management practices to manage long-term-care costs but also the introduction of a market element into the long-term sector together with increasing regulatory and systems control. In Britain this has meant a widening of means testing in the provision of long-term care, a cutback in health spending on long-term care, tighter budgetary controls within local authorities and more stringent systems for determining 'need'. The private sector now dominates the 'market' for long-term nursing-care beds while health and local authorities play largely a rationing, monitoring and service-auditing role.

Similar processes have been evident in Australia – with the exception of the shift from hospital to nursing-home provision since Australia had no large and established network of long-term hospital beds of the kind that Britain had inherited from its system of workhouse infirmaries and mental asylums. In 1987 case management systems were introduced under the Community Options programme as a means of preventing 'premature' entry into nursing homes. Geriatric Assessment Teams (now termed Aged Care Assessment Teams) were set up as a means of screening all potential entrants into nursing homes with a view to reducing 'unnecessary' admissions of people whose medical or social conditions could be altered to alter their apparent 'neediness' for care. Subsequently, the ratio of nursing home beds per 1000 people over age 70 years in Australia declined by 15 per cent.[23] At the same time legislation was passed mandating clear standards of care within the nursing-home industry.

In the USA the principal form of regulation has been through the 'certificate of need' (CON) programme introduced in the late 1970s as a means of regulating the expansion in the supply of nursing-home beds. The responsibility for instituting CON programmes rested with the states rather than the federal government but originally federal funding was made contingent upon the application of CON programmes. Subsequent legislation cut back the role of central government in regulating health planning. Despite this apparent withdrawal from government 'interference', research suggests that states have continued to use CON programmes as a means of controlling the growth of nursing homes.[24] By 1995 the National Center for Health Statistics (NCHS) observed the first drop in the number of nursing homes offering long-term care, confirming the impact of these supply control mechanisms in the USA. Interestingly there were also clear signs that nursing homes, like supermarkets, were getting larger and were increasingly operated as part of a chain. This response to consumer demand reflects most clearly the reality behind the actual purchasing mechanisms of long-term care, whatever the rhetoric of client choice.

Nevertheless, these processes of control are the very obverse of what were Townsend's concerns. Rather than induce unnecessary dependency, government policies now focus upon minimizing – even ignoring – the neediness of disabled older people and encouraging them to manage at home. Rather than increasing the threat of dependency as a way of disciplining older people not to seek help, current policies pursued in most Western countries seek to reduce to a minimum older people's dependency upon the state. Indeed, several governments are exploring or instituting ways of establishing some form of personal insurance against the 'risk' of long-term care, shifting the 'public' responsibility for long-term care provision further onto individuals and away from the state. Although it is perfectly plausible to see this as the direct result of the crisis in public spending that arose in the mid-1970s, the outcome is that the role of the state in making old age a period of dependency is very much more marginal now than it was in the 1950s and 1960s when many provisions existed that offered a wider range of accessible institutional care for vulnerable members of the retired population.

Of course social policy continues to frame old age in policy terms as a category of need – or of risk. The 'elderly' remain conceptually linked to dependency and want – a potential 'charge on the parish'. At the same time the absolute numbers of retired people to whom such epithets apply are a small and, in relative terms, shrinking minority. The dilemma is that by retaining the links between old age, 'elderly' status and social provision, most retired people are personally and socially still further distanced from having anything to do with old age. While people increasingly may seek to make provision for their own ageing, perceiving their lives as much as consumers as wage earners, there is now much less likelihood that collective citizenship can be forged either from a common status as 'old age pensioners' or as a consumer constituency of aggrieved and ill-served 'elderly' clients. Targeting need ever more tightly frees more retired people from the restrictive attributions of a social-policy-determined old age. The costs to those users who cannot escape their status as targets of the newly regulated and standardized long-term care services remain to be seen. It seems doubtful that their lot has worsened in consequence and relatively speaking their numbers have diminished; nevertheless they remain as an iconic warning against 'improvidence' – both during and after working life.[25]

## Senior citizenship – avoiding closure

Underlying much policy debate in many Western countries is the 'problem' of a rising elderly population – framed around concerns over the public costs arising from demands for income support and long-term care in managing daily life. Rather than the state seeking to capture 'old people' and contain them in positions of structured dependency, it seems clear that the state is seeking to do precisely the opposite, namely to rid itself as much as possible from the responsibility of having to pay for these 'dependency-inducing' structures. This is as true whether the target is 'stakeholder pensions', as in Britain, or in mandatory long-term care contributory insurance schemes, as in Germany. In the United States the debate centres on privatizing social security, Medicare and Medicaid as well as proposals for public long-term-care insurance. As we have already pointed out, the common theme behind all these debates and policy proposals is a significant reconceptualization of the relationship between the state and the individual, from a framework of common citizenship to one based around sectorized consumers. As the lot of the average working person has improved over the last half-century, there has been a growing experience of surplus income – surplus in the sense of having more than enough to secure the means to reproduce one's own daily life – and a concomitant interest in the choices that individuals make in how they spend this surplus income. The expansion of retail capital to profit from this surplus income has helped to lead individuals towards an increasingly consumer-oriented, signifier-dominated lifestyle. Much of the establishment of lifestyle consumerism began with the rise of 'youth culture' and the surplus income of those newly entering the workforce. Increasingly it has spread to encompass more and more of the lifecourse, both downwards as parental spending on goods and services for their children and upwards in the form of investment to support continued spending after leaving work. Increasingly the nature of that consumption has become dominated by the symbolic value of goods and services – fostered by retail capital but predicated upon the 'surplus to use' value of such consumption. Under these changing economic circumstances, the necessity for public safeguarding of an adequate national minimum income (one that incorporates the opportunities for surplus consumption) becomes a matter for a relatively small section of society: those who could be but are not in work, those who are retired after a history of not having worked and those who are unable to work. Universal provision seems a less pressing requirement to maintain the stability of social and economic structures and the focus shifts to a concern over those minorities whose lack of economic and social capital threatens social order, rather than the economic system itself.[26]

As the state seeks to disinvest in universal social insurance programmes, concern has moved toward ensuring that the new 'citizen consumers' fulfil their requirements as 'rational economic agents'. Various attempts are being proposed from state encouragement of second-pension schemes to the developments of incentives for individuals to take up long-term-care insurance. While the former does resonate with individuals' desires to enjoy a well-earned retirement, attempts to push people toward private long-term-care insurance seem to have achieved very limited success, no doubt because an emphasis upon lifestyle consumerism fits badly with the images conjured up by life in a long-term-care institution.[27]

Relatedly attempts have been made to reframe the language by which long-term care is described. Some economists speak of individual's demand for long-term care, treating them very much as potential consumers; governments introduce systems of monitoring consumer satisfaction; introduce mechanisms to assess compliance with standards; seek to consult with users and develop proxy systems of advocacy. This new language of welfare seeks to construct a universalism based on consumer not social rights. It seeks in effect to foster the myth of consumer sovereignty – whether what is consumed is a 'wished-for' or 'needed' good. Of course, long-term care is mostly neither wished for nor a good, in the sense that it contributes little to the richness, diversity or even length of life. Increasingly as policies target those in greatest need – and by greatest need is usually meant those who demonstrate the highest risk for some other costlier outcome – the characteristics of those entering nursing homes become less and less desirable. Agency in particular becomes more problematic and the qualities of Marshallian citizenship – reflected in social participation, social contribution and social responsibility – become less and less evident. Attempts to construct a citizen's voice, attempts to put in place standards for 'residents' rights' and attempts to suggest consumer choice become an increasingly strained practice sustaining the illusion of a form of 'citizenship' with which most citizens wish to have nothing to do.

Defining older people as citizens who consume long-term and community care services adds to the distance between the lived experience of retirement and the state discourse of ageing. If retired people are to exercise citizenship, it will not be through their client status but through the extension of a lifestyle built during their working lives. Increasingly the gap between pre- and post-retirement is less stigmatizing, less economically jarring and less culturally distinct. Citizenship – in the sense of having common cause to preserve a national health service, in the sense of wanting to preserve an economically rewarding working life that will in turn guarantee an economically satisfactory retirement and in the sense of being concerned to preserve and build an environment that is pleasant to live in, clean and healthy and rich in the opportunities it affords to participate in its common public space – is not likely to be rejected or framed as constructing a dependency in retirement. Such senior citizenship will not be expressed by being categorized as 'the elderly' or by receipt of an 'old age pension'. If government policies continue to treat 'the elderly' simply as another category of need, alongside the disabled, the mentally ill and other 'marginalized communities', then few retired people are likely to find such a 'politics of age' either of personal interest or of collective concern. Instead they may turn away from the idea of citizenship altogether, preferring their own constructed self-identities.

## Notes

1 Townsend, P. (1986) 'Ageism and social policy', in C. Phillipson and A. Walker (eds), *Ageing and Social Policy: a Critical Assessment*, Gower, Aldershot, p. 21.
2 Townsend, P. (1986) *op. cit.*, p. 29.
3 *Ibid.*, p. 32.
4 *Ibid.*, p. 41.
5 *Ibid.*, p. 43.
6 See Chand, S. and Jaeger, A. (1996) 'Aging populations and public pension schemes', *IMF Occasional Papers* No. 147, IMF, New York, for a general overview.
7 'The total income of pensioners will rise in years to come fuelled mainly by rising levels of contributions to private funded schemes . . . currently about 60 per cent of total spending comes from the state and 40 per cent from the private sector. Over time we expect this balance to change so that 40 per cent will come from the state and 60 per cent from the private sector', in *A New Contract for Welfare: Partnership in Pensions*, http://www.dss.gov.uk/hq/pubs/pengp/main/chpt12.htm.
8 Tanner, S. (1998) 'The dynamics of male retirement behaviour', *Fiscal Studies*, 19, 175–96.
9 See Blackburn, R. (1999) 'Grey capitalism and pension reform', *New Left Review*, 233, p. 5.

10 See Kingson, E. and Quadagno, J. (1999) 'Social security: marketing radical reform', in M. Minkler and C. Estes (eds), *Critical Gerontology: Perspectives from Political and Moral Economy*, Baywood Publishing Co., New York, pp. 345–58.

11 'The Government wants to allow older people as much choice as possible over their lives' . . . 'We will create an environment that enables people to build up sufficient pension funds and allows them to make their own choices to suit their own circumstances', Chapter 11, paragraphs 26 and 34, *A New Contract for Welfare: Partnership in Pensions*, www.dss.gov.uk/hq/pubs/pengp/main/chpt11.htm.

12 *National Health Service and Community Care Act 1990*, HMSO, London.

13 Wertheimer, A. (1993) *Speaking out: advocacy and older people*, CPA Report 19, Centre for Policy on Ageing, London; Dunning, A. (1995) *Citizen Advocacy with Older People: A Code of Good Practice*, Centre for Policy on Ageing, London.

14 See Cox, R.H. (1998) 'The consequences of welfare reform: how conceptions of social rights are changing', *Journal of Social Policy*, 27: 1–16.

15 From Table 1.4 in Diane Gibson's book *Aged Care*; the proportion of people aged 65 and over in receipt of home care services in OECD countries ranges from 17 per cent (Denmark) to less than 1 per cent (Spain, Italy). Gibson, D. (1998) *Aged Care: Old Policies, New Problems*, Cambridge University Press, Melbourne, p. 11.

16 Spence, J. (1996) 'Italy', in A. Wall (ed.), *Health Care Systems in Liberal Democracies*, Routledge, London, pp. 47–75.

17 Maarssen, A-M. and Janssen, R. (1994) 'Reforming healthcare in the Netherlands', *Health Services Management*, 90: 19–21.

18 Oberlander, J. (1999) 'Vouchers for Medicare: A critical reappraisal', in M. Minkler and C. Estes (eds), *Critical Gerontology: Perspectives from Political and Moral Economy*, Baywood Publishing Company, Amityville, NY, pp. 203–20.

19 See Lakdawalla, D. and Philipson, T. (1999) 'Aging and the growth of long-term care', *NBER Working Paper 6980*, http:www.nber.org/papers/w6980.

20 See Baldwin, S. and Corden, A. (1987) 'Public money and private care: paradoxes and problems', in S. di Gregario (ed.), *Social Gerontology: New Directions*, Croom Helm, London, pp. 90–103, for a contemporary discussion of the 1983–5 changes in British policy.

21 Gibson, D. (1998) *op. cit.*, p. 10.

22 It might be argued that the *lifetime chances* of entering a nursing home are by no means insignificant. However, the majority of people who enter a nursing home at least in the USA do so for periods of less than one year, where such entry is determined by a terminal illness. Less than a quarter of all the people who live past their 65th birthday can expect to spend a year or more 'in care' (Kemper, P. and Murtaugh, C.M. (1991) 'Lifetime use of nursing home care', *New England Journal of Medicine*, 324: 595–600).

23 See Gibson, D. (1998) *op. cit.*, Chapter 2, for more details.

24 See Harrington, C.A., Curtis, M., Carrillo, H., Bedney, B., Swan, J.H. and Nyman, J.A. (1997) 'State regulation of the supply of long-term care providers', *Journal of Applied Gerontology*, 16: 5–30.

25 The German government introduced long-term care insurance as a mandatory form of insurance that is levied on employees and pensioners alike. See *Journal of Human Aging* (1999).

26 See Mead, L. (1997) 'Citizenship and social policy: T.H. Marshall and poverty', *Social Philosophy and Policy*, 14: 187–230, especially pp. 225–30 for a discussion concerning the 'new' poverty and its alleged lack of any radical thrust.

27 Several US studies have pointed to the significant barriers facing the long-term care insurance market – e.g. Cohen, M.A. and Kumar, N. (1997) 'The changing face of long-term care insurance in 1994: profiles and innovations in a dynamic market', *Inquiry*, 34: 50–61; Marlowe, J.F. (1996) 'Long-term care insurance: a private sector challenge', *Employee Benefits Journal*, 21: 8–12; Granza, L., Madamba, A. and Warshawsky, M. (1998) 'Financing long-term care: employee needs and attitudes and the employer's role', *Benefits Quarterly*, 14: 60–72; nevertheless there is a process of slow and continued growth, over the last decade – see Snider, S. (1995) 'Long-term care and the private insurance market', *EBRI Issue Brief*, 163: 1–23.

# CHAPTER 7

# Ageing and its embodiment

Over the last century, social policy has contributed significantly to the social construction of old age. Underpinning much of that policy has been a view of old age characterized by the notion of progressive enfeeblement. The 'physiological neediness' of the ageing body has been seen as justifying many of the policies concerning retirement, social security, health and welfare that have evolved over the first half of the last century. Any 'marginalization' of older people by these policies, it can be argued, largely reflects the debilitating impact of physical ageing. In the following chapters, we shall explore some of the underlying assumptions about the ageing body and its status as the 'bottom line' that not only determines the agenda of social policy but also limits the cultural expression of ageing.

While social gerontologists have been critical of the 'biomedicalization' of ageing, they have made relatively little attempt to challenge the foundations from which studies of bio-ageing come. Within sociology and social theory, however, there has been a growing interest in the reciprocal relationship between our existence as bodies and as social agents. In order to better discuss the relationships between social and physical ageing, it is helpful, first, to consider in a little more detail what lies behind this new interest in 'theorizing the body'.

## Embodiment and social theory

The Cartesian tradition in Western intellectual thought has fostered a persistent division between the body and the mind. Until relatively recently, in the social sciences, the focal interest has been on relationships between individuals as rational actors. Their physicality – their bodily identity – had remained the legitimate subject principally and largely unquestioningly of the natural sciences.

One of the first sociologists to question this division of intellectual labour, Bryan Turner, has written:

> sociological theory has effectively neglected the importance of the human body in understanding social action and social interaction. The nature of human embodiment has . . . not been important in either social research or social theory.[1]

There has since been an outpouring of academic writing on the 'sociology of the body'. Over the last decade numerous books have appeared, conferences have been held and a new journal has been published – all concerned with the theme of the 'social' body.[2] Amongst the various reasons put forward for this interest is the privileged position the body has acquired within contemporary consumer culture. Sulkunen makes the point:

> The issue of the social constitution of the body is important in consumer society not only because everything we consume is taken in enjoyed and processed by the body, whether through the tactile senses of touch taste and smell, or through the distant senses of the eye and the ear. The body is important also because in its social and historical constitution the nature of the social bond is at issue.
>
> Consumer society is individualistic by definition. Consumption reflects and embodies our relationships not only to objects but also to others as choice and pleasure through the exploitation of goods and services usually produced by others but also through our own judgements as free decision makers. This has brought the body into focus for it is as embodied beings that we experience our separateness from others.[3]

The growing importance given to ageing has been a factor too. As we have already noted in Chapter 4, fear of bodily ageing permeates much of contemporary culture, boosting the sales of a wide variety of products ranging from anti-ageing cosmetics to vitamin supplements.[4] But the significance of ageing is not confined to its expression in the commodification of individual fears and desires. Within the press and broadcasting media there are endless reports and ruminations over the 'greying' of the population and the threats posed by increasing numbers of people in their sixth, seventh, eighth and ninth decades. Age-related bodily impairments are highlighted in public debates not principally because of their 'anti-aesthetic qualities' but because they are thought to present a growing demand upon the state that, if unchecked, will overtax the public purse. These were noted in the previous chapter. However, these two issues are not unconnected. Health and the prevention of morbidity have become central elements in people's lives – as well as becoming central to the renegotiation of public and private responsibilities in contemporary society. Looking after one's body and preventing or putting off a costly old age are increasingly interwoven 'postmodern' virtues – in what Bauman has referred to as the aestheticization of everyday life.

A third factor contributing to the rise of sociological interest in the body is the contemporary uncertainty that renders problematic both our understanding of the body and its place in human/social life. Shilling describes the contradictions that emerge out of the modernist attempt to control/make safe our bodies thus:

> while rationalisation may have provided us with the potential to control our bodies more than ever before and have them controlled by others, its double edged nature has also reduced our certainty over what constitutes a body and where one body finishes and another starts. [5]

This uncertainty is expressed in various ways. On the one hand developments in medical technology enable far more to be done to the body – grafting skin, transplanting organs, unblocking arteries, introducing biomechanical prostheses, re-designing sexuality and so on. The 'cyborg' phenomenon has become a common theme for science fiction novelists and now for some postmodern social commentators. It 'embodies' the idea that biotechnology will gradually undermine many of the foundational properties of human nature, including characteristics such as age and sexuality.[6] Fashion itself plays an increasing role in determining bodily physique. The body has taken on a more plastic quality. Physical appearance is now manufactured out of individual consumer choice rather than fashioned by the necessary labour that a worker performs. The body has become the site for a new transgressive aesthetic.[7] Challenging 'wholesome tastes', the physical stereotypes of masculinity and femininity, and foundationalist ideas of beauty, a growing range of bodily types compete as aesthetic models for the human form. Despite the postmodern crisis in the visual arts, there is a burgeoning interest in the aesthetic possibilities of the human body. This is sustained by – and no doubt sustains – developments in 'creative' marketing where the human figure is endlessly deconstructed and reconstructed in the expanding interests of retail capital.

The potentially significant progress in molecular genetics also raises the serious possibility of turning ourselves inside out. This 'new technology' offers tantalizing prospects of reconstructing human natures through cloning, gene splicing, organ synthesis and cell repair nanotechnology systems.[8] The idea of the body as a vehicle that – aside from a few patches – must carry us through life in a largely predestined fashion is challenged on several fronts. Just as the social boundaries of the lifecourse have become blurred, so too have the physical determinants of our bodily identity. While many of the possibilities for reconstructing biological structures remain largely unrealized – and most probably are unrealizable – the existence of this science suggests that it is within its capabilities to rewrite the story that our bodies express. It is this potential for reconstruction that so much echoes the mood of our postmodern times.

For these reasons – the rise of consumerism, the growing salience of age and the increased uncertainty surrounding the nature of bodies – the topic of embodiment has become an important part of (post)modern sociology. The physicality of ageing has always been a central issue in gerontology. Rendered problematic by the shifts of postmodern culture, the body continues to play a critical but now increasingly confusing role in the various approaches to understanding and making sense of ageing expressed at the end of the twentieth century.

## The body as the 'true' foundation of ageing: confronting physicality

While public policies contribute much to the social construction of old age, there is a strong perception in people's minds that ageing is really a bodily affair. This viewpoint is evident in gerontology where the body has been a central reference point from which to study and understand 'the ageing process'. Perhaps the bulk of gerontologists would argue that ageing is, in the end, a matter of biology, best defined by an increasing risk of irremediable physical disability and death.[9] Most gerontologists – indeed most social gerontologists – accept ageing as an immutable fact, one that is fundamentally unaffected by how the productive processes are organized and how goods, services and capital are distributed. The only arena for human agency is in equalizing the quality of life for each age group and for each category of physical and mental frailty.

It seems incontestable that there are limits to every lifespan. The more social environments support and enable everyone to reach old age, the more evident are these limits.[10] In the process of constructing a more equitable old age, what becomes evident is that age itself is unfair; that, in the end, age impoverishes more than poverty ages. Removing the skeins of social disadvantage exposes the greater disadvantage that is woven into our own imperfect DNA.

This kind of foundationalist position raises several questions for social gerontologists particularly when they adopt a 'social constructionist' account of old age as a product of social policy. The biological finitude of ageing is taken as setting the limits to the social construction of old age. The physicality that is the essence of old age seems to wipe away the imprint of class, gender and race that is so salient in earlier life. This view is illustrated in a comment made by Kathleen Woodward in her book *Aging and Its Discontents*:

> As we approach the extremity of old age we approach in the West the limit of the pure cultural construction of aging.[11]

Faced with the physicality of old age – the changes in appearance and function that are seen socially as defining adult ageing – it seems impossible to argue that ageing can be understood as rooted not in the domain of biology but in social relations.[12] It is in the biological materiality of the body that the 'cultural' approach toward understanding ageing meets its greatest challenge.

Postmodernism has developed a fascination with the body – particularly its plastic potential to fashion identities out of a cultural rather than a biological reality. The new sociology of the body reflects this fascination – with its focus on sexuality, physical culture, the aestheticization of the body and its products and the 'disciplinary' regimes to which the bodies of late modernity are subject. At first sight it might seem that ageing and old age are excluded from this discourse of bodily signification. Body image preoccupies teenagers wrestling with the problems of puberty and popular culture; bodily aesthetics provide a site for young artists, including the young disabled and the young whose bodies have been shaped by the knife and the scalpel. Physical culture offers both active and passive means of reshaping the body, but its domain too is youth and the youthful middle aged, those who are not intimidated by tireless work on the treadmill and the weights bench. At some point, it seems, age draws a line, effectively disengaging individuals from such cultural practices.

But now, at the start of a new century and a new millennium, drenched in the hyperreal cyber-cultures that promise endless human possibilities, discernible elements of 'modern' culture can be identified that continue to shape the body across the lifecourse. It is to these current cultural and technological practices that influence both the external appearance and the inner mechanisms of 'ageing' that we wish to turn our attention.[13] Highlighting such considerations serves to challenge any straightforwardly foundationalist position that seeks to establish the body as the unquestionable 'bottom line' in the discourse on ageing, enabling an examination of how the ageing body might be, and we would argue, is culturally differentiated.

## Anti-ageing and the aesthetics of the body

Cosmetic surgery is available only to a limited number of people. It is not funded within either taxation-based or insurance-based health-care systems. There are still relatively few people whose lives create sufficient dissonance between their public and private selves that they would go so much out of their way to realize a wish to look younger. Anti-ageing medicine remains very much a private business. Nevertheless, the rising popularity of cosmetic surgery has more than merely iconic value in demonstrating the plasticity of the ageing body. That a significant minority of people – usually those with considerable material resources – do choose to have aesthetic surgery to rejuvenate their appearance shows what the many without those resources might also do had they similar opportunities.[14]

Much of the work of cosmetic surgeons concentrates primarily upon 'anti-ageing' procedures. These are becoming more various and more technically sophisticated year on year. Current practice includes chemical skin peels to rejuvenate the appearance of the skin, scleropathy (removing distended veins on the legs), hair transplantation, facelifts and tucks, forehead lifts and blepharoplasty (correction of drooping eyelids). New techniques are constantly being introduced such as laser hair transplanting and 'botox' injections to relax lined and wrinkled skin. These developments are driven by market forces originating largely from the baby-boomer generation.[15] What is surprising is that 'anti-ageing' cosmetic surgery is sought not only by the middle-aged/third-age population but also by significant numbers of people in their twenties and thirties. As we pointed out in Chapter 5, 'age concerns' have spread across significant sections of the adult population. Surveys conducted in 1998 and 1999 in the United States indicate that the majority of 20-year-olds, 30-year-olds, 40-year-olds, 50-year-olds and 60-year-olds 'approve' of cosmetic surgery. Only after age 65 do the approval ratings decline. Equally significant, though less surprising, is the finding that approval ratings are lower, the lower the individual's income.

It seems probable that these cohort effects will persist, and cosmetic surgery and related procedures will become part of everyday life, providing more and more people with the opportunity to mould their appearance to how they would like to be. Surgeons themselves see techniques improving as they become more widely used and the growth of computerized systems using photographs of patients that were taken in their youth in order to 'redesign' the face in advance of surgery offers further evidence of what Baudrillard termed the simulation and hyperreality of modern life.

People aged 65 and over currently make up a small sector of the market for cosmetic surgery (teenagers are the smallest) but figures from the American Society for Aesthetic Plastic Surgery indicate a steady rise in the numbers of retired people undertaking such procedures. Moreover, members of each new mid-life cohort who undergo anti-ageing pro-cedures face a further dilemma deciding when to 'get out of' the market. One recent study indicates considerable variation between individuals about deciding when and whether to stop.[16] The growing individual-ization of the ageing experience makes it likely that such decisions will create still further distinctions amongst third-agers, between those adopting 'managed ageing' strategies and those opting for a strategy of 'lifelong prolongevity'.

In the absence of an inner logic to ageing, the play of signification that is involved in choosing how and when to age offers a wide scope for the marketing of desire. Skin peels, tummy tucks, forehead lifts, hair transplants, botox injections and facial fat grafting do not 'restore' a youthful appearance so much as improve the 'aesthetic' appearance of the ageing face. To that extent cosmetic surgery is less about anti-ageing and more to do with a general desire felt by many people to improve on their 'natural' appearance. The public appearance of 'agedness' is no deep signifier of incipient disability or closeness to death.[17] It is in that sense exquisitely concerned with the surface plane of 'signification'. However, without this connectivity to the interior pathways of old age, the increasing lifestyle aestheticization exemplified by anti-ageing cosmetic surgery might seem a cultural epiphenomenon of the com-modification and marketing of health rather than posing a serious chal-lenge to the foundationalist position of bio-ageing. At the same time, dissatisfaction with ageing is highly predictive of mortality amongst older adults – even after taking account of chronological age, socioeco-nomic status, health and other risk factors.[18] If aesthetic surgery suc-ceeds in reducing such dissatisfaction it may contribute quite incidentally to distancing chronological agedness from both decline and death.

Other anti-ageing technologies offer a more direct route toward preventing or delaying bio-ageing. Continuing medical research into various steroids, steroid-like compounds, vitamins and related nutrients (dehydroepiandrosterone (DHEA); estrogens and phytoestrogens; coenzyme Q-10; vitamin E; superoxide dismutase (SOD); etc.) suggests small but measurable benefits in terms of later-life disease prevention. Cross-national and temporal variations in the age-specific rates of car-diovascular disease and various cancers also suggest that there is scope for further gains in 'healthy years of life' by modification of lifestyle and dietary habits.[19] More radical proposals exist.

Ronald Klatz, a major proponent of anti-ageing medicine, confidently predicts that in the near future:

> A minimum of 40 000 lifespans [will be] extended annually by eliminating heart failure by a combination of medical options: totally implantable artificial hearts, a modified heart assist device, xenograph transplant/repair or micro-transplanation of fetal heart cells in devitalized heart tissue . . . A 30 year reversal in the aging process will be achieved by means of an implantable hor-monal/pacemaker device to deliver a concentrated mixture of growth factors/ hormones in cyclic rhythm to improve basic cellular function resulting in main-tenance of bone density, muscle strength and overall cardiovascular fitness.[20]

133

The ageing body is rapidly becoming a key element in the postmodern uncertainty over what constitutes the natural. While cosmetic surgery exploits the possibilities of surgical technology to re-aestheticize the ageing body in one swift act, it remains a private and risky enterprise that currently possesses a rather limited social value. Consumption of over-the-counter medicines and all the various 'anti-ageing' cosmeceuticals and nutraceuticals offers a less risky strategy but requires sustained lifestyle changes with little obvious to show for them. Both practices nevertheless represent the active choices of consumers. Other aspects of anti-ageing medicine relate less to consumerism and the health market. Rather they seek to derive their status from their ability to represent themselves as a continuing part of medicine's modernist 'triumph over nature'. Prophylactic high-technology surgery is a small but significant component of a largely private health-care industry that actively promotes itself as 'anti-ageing medicine'. The evidence base for such practices is extremely limited and often rather tenuously linked to experimental gerontological research. In fact, much of the secular and cross-national variation in age-specific morbidity seems to derive not from variations in access to the latest technology but from variation in lifestyle and environment. The claims of anti-ageing medicine represent more an aspirational science which has flourished within postmodern culture than traditional 'modern medicine'. Indeed all three elements of 'anti-ageing' health care can be seen as deriving from and reinforcing that particular form of 'ageism' ushered in by modernity. In the next section we examine the impact of such 'ageism' on the experience of bio-ageing.

## Ageism: the personal and the public

Using cosmetic surgery to determine whether and how to 'age' is not just a matter of personal aesthetics. It reflects the public valuing of 'agedness'. Expenditure of over \$15 billion on anti-ageing nutritional compounds in the USA is not just a matter of consumer choice. It represents a massive social dread of old age. While negative attitudes toward old age have been in evidence for centuries, they have rarely played the role that they do in contemporary society. What is unique about the ageism of modernity is that it is represented in numerous institutional practices that treat 'agedness' as a proxy for poverty, neediness and proximity to death. Therefore, we shall argue, current ageist assumptions constitute more than mere cultural by-products of particular economic and biological power relations. They exercise a direct and proximal influence upon the processes of bio-ageing itself.

Three routes mediate the effects of ageism on bio-ageing. In the first place secular changes in the economy have resulted until relatively recently in older adults occupying positions of lowered socioeconomic status. This position of socioeconomic disadvantage enhances their risks of ill-health, disability and death. Secondly, the internalization of negative attitudes about ageing and old age undermines the confidence of older adults in their dealings with the physical and social world, leading them to entertain lower expectations of themselves as agents. Such self-imposed limitations lead in turn to poorer health and fitness, increased risk of disability and ultimately a reduced chance of survival. Finally, institutional ageism limits access to those facilities and resources that promote health and well-being, prevent disease and facilitate recovery. Although this is most obvious in relation to health-care practices, it applies to a much wider set of institutions including the workplace, personal finance institutions and the educational system.

In short, ageism has economic, psychological and social effects that potentially impact upon the physical well-being of retired people. We shall consider the evidence for each of these propositions in turn.

## Ageism and economic disadvantage

Cowgill and Holmes were amongst the first social gerontologists to argue that the status accorded to older people varies across cultures and over time, depending upon the organization of productive forces.[21] They argued that systematic shifts in the status of older adults arise as a function of the economic power which older adults control within society. The economic power of older adults in turn is determined by the extent to which the productive forces within a society support the accumulation and transfer of both cultural and material resources within the patrilineal family.[22] Within this perspective, ageism reflects the devalued status given to older people resulting from their lack of economic and cultural power *vis-à-vis* the younger members of society. This is most marked during periods of social and economic change. The transition from an agrarian/mercantile to an industrial economy alters the control of the domestic economy exercised by older men. With industrialization, the future economic well-being of adult children is less dependent upon what they might inherit. Manufacturing industry provides increasing opportunities to sell one's labour/earn one's living independently of the home, with the prospect of gaining access to a wider range of resources than could be obtained by patiently working the land while waiting to inherit. This aspect of modernization theory – the term used by Cowgill and Holmes to describe this doctrine – has received a surprising amount of empirical support.[23] There is also evidence now that with current trends towards a new affluence amongst the younger members of the retired community, at least, a reversal of this status decline is taking place.[24] The impact of this 'post-industrial' turn should lead to consequent improvements in health and well-being. Such trends of improving health and reductions in disability do seem to be emerging and we shall consider them in more detail in the next chapter. For now it is sufficient to note that there are consistent signs of a steady improvement in the overall economic status of older adults – both in the US[25] and in the UK[26] – which might well be seen as predictable from the basis of modernization theory and all that it implies concerning ageism and relative economic disadvantage. These trends in improved economic well-being are associated with increased longevity and reduced disability.

What remains is the impact of economic disadvantage on groups within the retired population who remain 'vulnerable' by still retaining the devalued status that modernization conferred upon 'the old' in general. People from racial/ethnic minorities, widows from working-class backgrounds and people whose working lives have been locked into welfare remain particularly vulnerable. Table 7.1 illustrates the relative economic position of black and white householders in the United States at the onset of working life and after retirement.

Between 1987 and 1997 the average income of white retired US householders rose by 17 per cent from 75 per cent to 84 per cent of that of white younger adults; in contrast black retired US householders' average income rose by only 9 per cent during the same period, and actually fell from 75 per cent to 72 per cent of the average income of younger black adults. The position of retired householders from hispanic backgrounds was intermediate to that of white and black householders. In

TABLE 7.1 Average income in US dollars for US white, black and hispanic householders at ages 25–34 and 65–74 years*

| Year | White householder mean income: 25–34 years | Black householder mean income: 25–34 years | Hispanic householder mean income: 25–34 years | White householder mean income: 65–74 years | Black householder mean income: 65–74 years | Hispanic householder mean income: 65–74 years |
|------|------|------|------|------|------|------|
| 1987 | $45 963 | $27 644 | $34 296 | $34 438 | $20 765 | $23 375 |
| 1997 | $48 082 | $31 646 | $35 464 | $40 194 | $22 637 | $26 883 |

*Data derived from US Census Bureau, *Historical Income Tables*, Tables H-10A to H-10C, http://www.census.gov/hhes/income/histinc/h10.html

1987, their average income was only 68 per cent of younger adult hispanic householders, but, by 1997, it had risen by 14 per cent to 75 per cent of the average income of younger adults.

Paralleling this selective economic disadvantage are indications of a similar health-related disadvantage. Data from Medicare files for this same period indicate that, amongst those aged 65 years and over, age-adjusted mortality rates were 19 per cent higher for black men and 16 per cent higher for black women compared with white men and women. Hospital discharges likewise were 14 per cent and 15 per cent higher amongst black men and women.[27] These and other studies we shall examine later indicate the potential costs to older people arising from remaining at a disadvantaged socioeconomic position. That a positive 'postmodern' transformation in socioeconomic status has occurred for the majority of older people in Western societies seems undeniable; but for those still occupying such disadvantaged statuses, there are clear consequences for their health and expectation of life.

### Ageism and the internalization of failure

Several writers have argued that the widespread negative attitudes toward old age evident in contemporary society lead to an internalization of these values by older people themselves. This internalized ageism erodes the self-confidence of older people, reducing expectations, leading to poorer physical and mental performance, which are then treated as 'objective' evidence of an age-related decline.[28]

Evidence to support this argument is less well established. Nevertheless, there is some direct empirical support. Two particular examples are used as illustration. The first is a study examining the relationship between age, memory performance and attitudes toward ageing conducted by two social psychologists, Levy and Langer.[29] They sought to test the hypothesis that cultures which held positive views of old age would lead older adult members of that culture to experience less 'internalized' ageism. Consequently they would have greater confidence in their personal competence and perform better on mental performance tests – in this case memory tests. Comparing groups of younger and older adults in three different cultural groups – Americans, American Sign Language using deaf Americans and Chinese – they observed that the Chinese showed least evidence of 'questionnaire-measured' ageism and least evidence of age differences in memory test performance. In stark contrast, the Americans reported considerable 'ageism' in both young and old samples and highly significant age differences on the memory tests in favour of the younger adults. Results from the American deaf sample were intermediate between the other two groups.

A second study examined the impact of subtly reinforcing positive messages about ageing on measures of gait. Two matched groups of older people were filmed walking before and after playing a computer game during which they 'subconsciously' received either positive or negative messages about old age and the ageing process. Significant improvements in the speed and 'spring' of walking were observed in those receiving the positive message while those receiving the negative message showed no change.[30] The implications of both these 'experimental' studies are that at least part of the so-called age-related decline in physical and mental performance can be attributed to social and cultural forces rather than chronological age *per se*.

Bytheway has argued that all categorizations of old age are inherently ageist since such language first reifies then sets apart a group of people whose differences from others are a matter of degree rather than indicative of a fundamental discontinuity.[31] For Bytheway, the very act of distinguishing a period within the lifespan called old age carries with it connotations of 'otherness' that ignore the very real continuities across adult life. Certainly there is evidence that self-definitions of being 'old' or 'elderly' are associated with poorer health, reduced well-being and greater mortality. Just as self-rated health predicts future life expectancy, self-defined old age reflects a similar relationship[32] – suggesting either that the act of defining one's status as 'aged' influences how 'aged' one becomes or that self-defined agedness serves as an experiential marker of biological fitness. Whatever the mechanism, individual and cultural variation in the exposure to and acceptance of messages concerning fitness or 'agedness' does appear to be related to variations in late-life outcomes. Older people's pessimistic beliefs about their agedness, their health and their ability to 'control' these characteristics contribute to functional decline and death in later life.[33] These effects appear constant across quite disparate cultures.[34] More assertive attitudes amongst future generations of older people are likely. Asked whether they would be willing, as 'older' patients, to stand aside in waiting list queues for surgery in favour of younger patients, the majority of those not yet 'old' replied that when their turn came they definitely would not 'step aside' – in marked contrast to the willingness to do so evidenced amongst contemporary older adults.[35]

## Ageism and its institutionalization

Alongside the economic and cultural devaluing of age, there are other structurally embedded forms of ageism still evident in many of the institutions operating within the modern state. Numerous reports have found evidence of institutionalized ageism in health-care systems, in educational institutions, in the workplace and in the financial services sector.[36] Institutionalized ageism involves selective exclusion from, or reduction in access to, particular societal resources on the explicit basis of people's adult age. Within health-care systems this includes inadequate access to health care; inadequate investigation of health problems; and inadequate and/or inappropriate treatment of identified health problems.[37] Specific examples include failure to provide routine breast screening for women aged over 65; limited investigations performed on older patients following admission to hospital after a heart attack; denial of access to cardiac rehabilitation programmes; a more limited range of investigations and treatments offered to older people with various types of cancer; refusal to make available certain types of day surgery to patients aged over 70; excess use of neuroleptics (anti-psychotics) in nursing homes; widespread polypharmacy associated with a raised incidence of hospital admissions of older adults – the list is extensive and exhausting in its cumulative potential to demote the health of older people.[38] Although it is not possible currently to determine how much age-related restrictions on access to health care contribute to the excess morbidity and mortality of older people, it seems likely that there is a significant and measurable impact on the health and physical function of older people, which goes well beyond that which can be accounted for by the clinical 'risk' of being a certain age.[39]

The impact of age discrimination in the provision and range of financial services offered by the various private investment, insurance and pension schemes has not been subject to the same kind of research scrutiny as that conducted in the health field. Nevertheless, numerous examples have been reported to organizations such as Age Concern England. These complaints range from unwarranted restrictions on insurance covers to lack of access to some types of pension schemes, limited credit facilities and investment opportunities, and so on. The general conclusion to be drawn from these and other related reports is that older people are less able to invest in ways that can maximally improve their material conditions in comparison with younger adults.[40]

Ageism is not just a problem of cultural representation – the lack of representation or lack of respect given to older people. It has material consequences in the lives of older people, in their access to material resources, in their capacity to benefit from health care and in their own expectations of themselves. The power of cultural representations to influence the physical experience of later life may not be easily demonstrated, but there are plenty of reasons to believe that it can and does do so. The nonchalant acceptance of difference and the infinite potential to work and rework regimes of signification that are meant to be the hallmarks of postmodern life have yet to fully penetrate the lives of older people. Age and ageing remain largely, though by no means completely, outside the play of the more extreme transgressions of postmodern culture. However, while it may be possible to ridicule some of the naivety of postmodern writings, the fact remains that it is the institutions of modernity that have oppressed older people. The institutions that were built up in the nineteenth and early twentieth centuries – the foundations both of our industrial economy and of our welfare state – are the principal sites where the exclusion and the marginalization of older people have taken place. The embodiment of ageing that takes place in the institutional practices of geriatrics and gerontology reinforces the idea that ageing is at bottom a physiological affair and that the resolution of the ageism that exists in society requires primarily the moral exhortation of the state and other welfare institutions to stop it. Such an approach fails to engage with the nature of the dilemma – that cultures of ageing are also primarily cultures of resistance to age, not ways of embracing old age. They express the same antipathy to old age that has been present throughout recorded history. Anti-ageing surgical practices and anti-ageing medicines are not designed to counteract or to challenge ageism. They represent an aesthetic preference not to look like an old person; not to appear elderly. If resistance to ageism also requires opposition to such surgery (much in the same way that the advocates of deaf culture oppose cochlear implants) it is likely to collapse under the weight of contradictions that reside within conceptualizations of a 'positive' old age.[41]

## Ageing: appearance, reality and then some

If sex reassignment surgery is poised to be incorporated into the British National Health Service's 'free at the point of delivery' services, establishing a place for itself alongside sexual dysfunction clinics for people wanting a better sex life and infertility clinics for couples wanting to have a better family life, then why should not NHS surgeons be permitted to lift and abrade the skin, replace and re-position the fatty tissue and musculature of the face in order to restore a more youthful look to older men and women who feel they need an improved appearance? Why should health insurance programmes not include such procedures amongst their list of approved medical services? Why should general practitioners not be permitted to prescribe Viagra to all those older men who wish to have more regular and reliable erections? Why should peri- and postmenopausal women not be able to get a choice of estrogen-replacing prescriptions? Moreover, why should people approaching retirement not be entitled to the prophylactic benefits of grafts, transplants and other 'rejuvenating' forms of surgery? Why are limits drawn round those practices that could prevent aspects of bodily ageing which, in turn, put at risk the viability and opportunity for post-work lifestyles that aim at staying young?

Is it ageism, in short, that causes people to undergo cosmetic surgery – or is it ageism that prevents or restricts the accessibility of such surgery; is it ageism that seeks to set limits on how old a woman can be to receive fertility treatments; that asserts that death should be the appropriate fate of 'old' people but not 'young' people? Resolutions of these dilemmas will not arise from the shrinking postmodern state. Creating viable cultures of ageing depends upon establishing a sufficient economic base to sustain a level of consumption that will enable them to be expressed through the strength of individual demand. For most older people, the body is still too dangerous to serve such ends and after all consumer culture is not really about instilling physical self-confidence. Its success comes from achieving the very opposite. Our bodies are still too little our own. Retired people are establishing an increasing variety of post-work lifestyles, yet the body remains problematic, occupying a complex and contradictory position in relation to ageing and its cultural possibilities. Should one exercise it, dress it and decorate it or simply ignore it? Should it be tinkered with, tarted up or is it best left alone? Should the signs of age – grey hair, wrinkled and lined skin – be the basis of a new form of identity politics: should we be glad to be grey? And what features of bodily ageing should be selected as positive sources of significance and what features should be excluded?

Ensuring that people have access to effective health care, sound financial advice and savings systems, and a wide range of opportunities to develop their skills and knowledge, is an agenda that can be supported by adults irrespective of their working status. While access to the social material and cultural resources might be expected to yield benefits in terms of health, well-being and fitness, the principle of ensuring an age-irrelevant equity of access might garner more popular support than the principle of ensuring equalization of the lifespan. The body clearly is not without a material reality, but that reality can only be expressed through social means. There can be no pure human 'ageing'; no ageing under glass. Advice exists in many forms about how the body can be treated to reduce its significance as a marker of personal ageing and proximity to death. The aim of such advice is more or less the same as that of anti-ageing medicine – to reduce the negative markers of old age. What remains after the success of such an enterprise may well never be known – indeed it may not be knowable. Making clear the reasonableness of a position that states that people do not want to look old and unattractive, do not want to feel fatigue, pain and sickness, do not want to be incapable of carrying out those everyday acts that confer adult status and adult competence, in short that people are happy to age but not be aged, is a necessary step in establishing a cultural and political agenda to combat ageism. That agenda must be to resist those practices which seek to thwart such desires and support those practices which render them more likely to be expressed, legitimated and embodied in practice. It is a policy to reduce inequalities amongst adults as adults, and not to improve the treatment of old age.

Such a platform seems in keeping with the personal aesthetic that characterizes postmodern culture – including the inherent contradiction that lies at the heart of this message, namely that one day we must fail. The failure that is old age cannot be translated into a rallying cry. Seeking collective redress about the social revaluing of old age cannot ignite the kind of identity politics that exists around skin colour, gender or sexual orientation. Realizing virtue despite the handicap of age is clearly one widespread form of recognition that is often claimed – praise for doing something 'despite' one's age. But it privileges exception and requires that most people of that age remain unable. Resisting and challenging the structured inequalities within society may provide a firmer platform in that it promises to improve both the quality and length of life while offering a programme whose support is not determined by an age-based constituency. The extent to which such inequalities can and do structure bio-ageing is addressed in the next chapter.

## Notes

1 Turner, B.S. (1991) *Regulating Bodies*, Routledge, London, p. 34.
2 See for example Turner, B.S. (1984) *The Body and Society*, Sage Publications, London; Featherstone, M., Hepworth, M. and Turner, B.S. (eds), *The Body: Social Processes and Cultural Theory*, Sage Publications, London; Falk, P. (1994) *The Consuming Body*, Sage Publications, London; Shilling, C. (1996) *The Body and Social Theory*, Sage Publications, London, as well as the new academic journal *Body and Society* (from 1997).
3 Sulkunen, P. (1997) Introduction, in P. Sulkunen, J. Holmwood, H. Radner and G. Schulze (eds), *Constructing the New Consumer Society*, Macmillan, London, pp. 6–7.
4 It has been estimated that around 50 per cent of the adult population of the United States are taking vitamin supplements.

5 Shilling, C. (1996) *op. cit.*, p. 38.
6 See Featherstone, M. and Hepworth, M. (1998) 'Ageing, the lifecourse and the sociology of embodiment', in G. Scambler and P. Higgs, *Modernity, Medicine and Health*, Routledge, London, pp. 147–75; Haraway, D. (1991) *Simians, Cyborgs and Women: the Reinvention of Nature*, Routledge, London.
7 Postmodern challenges to fixed ideas of beauty can be traced back to the rise of photography as an art form, converting the marginal and the ugly into objects of aesthetic reflection (see Sontag, S. (1979) *On Photography*, Penguin, Harmondsworth, especially her essay entitled 'The heroism of vision', pp. 85–112: 'Photographs create the beautiful and . . . use it up' (p. 85) ). See also Mellor and Shilling's discussion of the 'baroque modern body' in Mellor, P.A. and Shilling, C. (1997) *Reforming the Body: Religion, Community and Modernity*, Sage, London.
8 See Markle, R.C. (1997) 'Nanotechnology and medicine', in R.M. Klatz (ed.), *Advances in Anti-Aging Medicine*, vol. 1, Mary Ann Liebert Inc., New York, pp. 277–86.
9 Maier and Smith, in their paper on predictors of mortality in the Berlin Longitudinal Study of Ageing, suggest that, with increasing age, genetically determined processes take over increasingly in shaping old age morbidity and mortality. See Maier, H. and Smith, J. (1999) 'Psychological predictors of mortality in old age', *Journal of Gerontology*, 54B: P44–54.
10 This viewpoint is clearly expressed in Fries' 1980 paper on the rectangularization of the lifespan in which he proposed a 'natural' lifespan of 85 years and argued that progress in health and social care would lead to an accumulation of deaths around this maximal point (Fries, J.F. (1980) 'Aging, natural death and the compression of morbidity', *New England Journal of Medicine*, 303: 130–5).
11 Woodward, K. (1991) *Aging and Its Discontents: Freud and Other Fictions*, Indiana University Press, Bloomington, IN, p. 194.
12 In Andrew Blaikie's recent book, with much of which we have considerable sympathy, still there is this sense of an unwavering 'bottom line', as when he writes: 'increased longevity also means more incontinence, more dementia, more bodily betrayals and breakdowns in communication' (Blaikie, A. (1999) *Ageing and Popular Culture*, Cambridge University Press, Cambridge, p. 109).
13 As one example, scientists in the research and development laboratories of L'Oreal are reportedly researching the mechanisms of age-related changes in human hair with the intent of delivering products that will reverse hair loss and prevent hair greying – see *Business Week*, June 28 1999, p. 28.
14 Figures from the American Society for Aesthetic Plastic Surgery state that nearly 2.8 million cosmetic operations were performed in 1998; figures from the American Academy of Cosmetic Surgery are much higher – they report 2.65 million operations performed in 1994 rising to 3.35 million operations in 1996.
15 Botulinum toxin is a major source of food poisoning. However, it also has antispasmodic properties which led to its use in the treatment of various neuromuscular disorders. Since the early 1990s it has been used as a means of reducing lines and wrinkles, through repeated injections spread out over several months.
16 See Ancheta, R.W. (1998) 'Masking mid-life: cosmetic surgery and women's experiences of ageing', *British Sociological Association Meeting, Making Sense of the Body*, Edinburgh, Scotland.

17 Peter Schnohr and his colleagues found in a study of 13 000 men and women that greying hair, baldness, skin wrinkles and changes in the appearance of the eye were unrelated to mortality (Schnohr, P., Nyboe, J., Lange, P. and Jensen, G. (1998) 'Longevity and gray hair, baldness, facial wrinkles and arcus senilis in 13 000 men and women: the Copenhagen City Heart Study', *Journal of Gerontology*, 53A, M347–50).

18 See Maier, H. and Smith, J. (1999) *op. cit.*, Table 2.

19 See for example Khaw, K-T. (1997) 'Healthy aging', *British Medical Journal*, 315: 1090–6.

20 Klatz, R.M. (1996) *op. cit.*, p. xiv.

21 Cowgill, D. and Holmes, C. (1972) *Aging and Modernization*, Appleton Century Crofts, New York.

22 See also Lee, G.R. (1984) 'Status of the elderly, economic and family antecedents', *Journal of Marriage and the Family*, 46: 267–75.

23 Clark, R. (1992) 'Modernization and status change among aged men and women', *International Journal of Aging and Human Development*, 36: 171–86. Cohn, R.M. (1982) 'Economic development and status change of the aged', *American Journal of Sociology*, 87: 1150–61. Gilleard, C.J. and Gurkan, A.A. (1987) 'Socioeconomic development and the status of elderly men in Turkey: a critical evaluation of modernization theory', *Journal of Gerontology*, 42: 353–7. Lee, G.R. (1984) *op. cit.*

24 Pampel, F.C. (1981) *Social Change and the Aged*, Lexington Books, Lexington, MA. Harris, R.J. (1986) 'Recent trends in the relative economic status of older adults', *Journal of Gerontology*, 41: 401–7; Smolensky, E., Danziger, S. and Gottschalk, P. (1988) 'The declining significance of age in the United States: trends in the well-being of children and the elderly since 1939', in J.L. Palmer, T.M. Smeeding and B.B. Torrey (eds), *The Vulnerable*, Urban Institute Press, Washington, DC, pp. 29–54.

25 Hurd, M.D. (1989) 'The economic status of the elderly', *Science*, 244: 659–64.

26 Johnson, P. and Falkingham, J. (1992) *Ageing and Economic Welfare*, Sage Publications, London.

27 Gornick, M.E., Eggers, P.W., Reilly, T.W., Mentnech, R.M., Fitterman, L.K., Kucken, L.E. and Vladeck, B.C. (1996) 'Effects of race and income on mortality and use of services among medicare beneficiaries', *New England Journal of Medicine*, 335: 791–9.

28 One of the earliest expositions of the malignant impact of cultural ageism was expressed by Robert Butler in his paper, 'Age-ism: another form of bigotry' (Butler, R. (1969) *The Gerontologist*, 9: 243–6).

29 Levy, B. and Langer, E. (1994) 'Aging free from negative stereotypes: successful memory in China and among the American deaf', *Journal of Personality and Social Psychology*, 66: 989–97.

30 Hausdorff, J.M., Levy, B.R. and Wei, J.Y. (1999) 'The power of ageism on physical function of older persons: reversibility of age-related gait changes', *Journal of the American Geriatrics Society*, 47: 1346–9.

31 Bytheway, B. (1995) *Ageism*, Open University Books, Milton Keynes.

32 One of the first studies to demonstrate the links between self-perceptions of being 'old' or 'elderly' and morbidity was conducted by Bultena, G.L. and Powers, E.A. (1978) 'Denial of aging: age identification and reference group orientations', *Journal of Gerontology*, 33: 748–54.

33  See for example Boult *et al.*'s study which indicated that older people's lack of belief in their control over their health accounted for more late life transitions to the status of having 'functional limitations' than did either arthritis, cancer, confusion, coronary disease or diabetes (Boult, C., Altmann, M., Gilbertson, D., Yu, C. and Kane, R.L. (1996) 'Decreasing disability in the 21ˢᵗ century', *American Journal of Public Health*, 86: 1388–93, Table 1).

34  Yu, E.S.H., Kean, Y.M., Slymen, D.J., Liu, W.T., Zhang, M. and Katzman, R. (1998) 'Self perceived health and five year mortality risks among the elderly in Shanghai, China', *Journal of Epidemiology*, 147: 880–90.

35  Mariotto, A., De Leo, D., Buono, M.D., Favaretti, C., Austin, P. and Naylor, C.D. (1999) 'Will elderly patients stand aside for younger patients in the queue for cardiac services?', *The Lancet*, 354: 467–70.

36  Age Concern (1998) *Age Discrimination: Make it a Thing of the Past*, Age Concern England, London.

37  Age Concern (1997) 'Healthcare rights for older people – the ageism issue', *Age Concern and Nursing Times Briefing Paper*, Age Concern England Policy Unit, London. Gilleard, C.J., Askham, J., Biggs, S., Gibson, H.B. and Woods, R.T. (1995) 'Psychology, ageism and healthcare', *Clinical Psychology Forum*, 85: 14–16.

38  The role of ageism in health care systems was clearly outlined in a *JAMA* editorial published in 1987 (Wetle, T. (1987) 'Age as a risk factor for inadequate treatment', *Journal of the American Medical Association*, 258: 516). Since then there has been a steady stream of papers providing specific examples of ageism in relation to the treatment and investigation of particular medical conditions. For an overview of ageism operating in health screening programmes, see Sutton, G.C. (1997) 'Will you still need me, will you still screen me, when I'm past 64?', *British Medical Journal*, 315: 1032–3. Evidence of inadequate investigation and treatment of various cancers has been documented by Turner *et al.* (Turner, N.J., Haward, R.A., Mulley, G.P. and Selby, P.J. (1999) 'Cancer in old age – is it inadequately investigated and treated?', *British Medical Journal*, 319: 309–12). Similar observations have been made about the treatment of cardiovascular disease – see, for example, Reynen, K. and Bachmann, K. (1997) 'Coronary arteriography in elderly patients: risk, therapeutic consequences and long term follow up', *Coronary Arterial Disease*, 8: 657–66; and Naylor, C.D., Levinton, C.M., Baigrie, R.S. and Goldman, B.S. (1992) 'Placing patients in the queue for coronary surgery: do age and work status alter Canadian specialists' decisions?', *Journal of General Internal Medicine*, 7: 492–8. There is consistent evidence of inadequate investigation and intervention of older patients with coronary heart disease (Bearden, D., Allman, R., McDonald, R., Miller, S., Pressel, S. and Petrovitch, H. (1994) 'Age, race and gender variation in the utilization of coronary artery bypass surgery and angioplasty in SHEP', *Journal of the American Geriatrics Society*, 42: 1143–9) and after a heart attack (Udvarhelyi, I.S., Gatsonis, C., Epstein, A.M. (1992) 'Acute myocardial infarction in the Medicare population: process of care and clinical outcomes', *Journal of the American Medical Association*, 268: 2530–6). The role of polypharmacy in contributing to older people's admission to hospital has been documented by Williamson, J. and Chopin, J.M. (1980) 'Adverse reaction to prescribed drugs in the elderly', *Age and Ageing*, 9: 73–80; while the health risks attending older people after hospitalization may be five times those of younger adults (Gillick, M.R., Serrell, N.A. and Gillick, L.S. (1982) 'Adverse consequences of hospitalisation in the elderly', *Social Science and Medicine*, 16: 1033–8).

39 There is evidence, for example, that although late survival after coronary artery bypass grafting is similar in young and older patients, it is offered to younger adult patients more commonly than older ones (Rohrer-Gubler, I., Niederhauser, U. and Turina, M.I. (1998) 'Late outcome of coronary artery bypass grafting in young versus older patients', *Annals of Thoracic Surgery*, 65: 377–82). Likewise evidence from the Heart Center, Dresden, indicates that although bypass surgery and balloon angioplasty confer significant advantages over standard medical treatment for over-75-year-old patients with symptomatic coronary heart disease, such patients less often received this type of surgery than younger patients (Reynen, K. and Bachmann, K. (1997) *op. cit.*).

40 Age Concern (1998) *op. cit.*

41 If bio-ageing represents an increased risk of developing disability and dying, then all bio-markers of age are also associated with such enhanced risks. It is only by not accumulating such markers – i.e. a relative absence of markers of bio-ageing – that one can consider a person to be 'successful' in resisting what otherwise seems the fate of those living for an increasing number of years.

# CHAPTER 8

# Bio-ageing and the reproduction of the social

In the previous chapter we raised the general question of how the biological nature of ageing might place limits on the social and cultural expression of ageing. We particularly addressed the way the appearance and idea of physical ageing disadvantaged individuals, both materially and socially, and how the negative value associated with physical ageing created in its wake the contradictory position of age resistance, manifested in various aspects of contemporary health consumerism. In this chapter we turn our attention to examine the impact of social factors on the processes of bio-ageing – on age-associated functional decline and death. In particular we address the question of whether with increasing age we witness the 'death of the social' and the growing dominance of a biomedical discourse of ageing and old age.[1]

Physical ageing seems to occur autonomously, whatever roles and resources society does or does not provide for later life. As such, it imposes its own constraints on how later life can be lived and experienced. It implies a pattern, a sequence and a direction that have to be adapted to, that cannot be fashioned. At the same time, evidence shows that access to the social and material resources of a society affects people's chances of survival and their likelihood of developing potentially disabling illnesses.[2] There is a large and growing body of research which shows that income level, income inequality and social deprivation contribute significantly to adult morbidity and mortality.[3] Nor can the effects of these structural inequalities be explained simply by class-mediated variations in individual health-promoting or health-damaging practices.[4] They operate cumulatively over the whole lifespan, involving complex interactions between the individual and those social and communal supports that maintain health. Such findings, however, are derived from studies of morbidity and mortality amongst adults of working age. Secular changes in adult mortality mean that deaths amongst adults of working age are less frequent. No longer represented as the 'forces of mortality', the steadily declining number of 'adult' deaths are now treated as 'premature' and by implication 'preventable'. Explanations are sought not only within the domain of the 'natural sciences' but increasingly within that of the social sciences. Representing health and disease as features of a broader socially structured inequality has proved a fertile ground for much recent research in the fields of public health and medical sociology. Socially based explanations in turn serve as the first steps toward addressing and overcoming what are viewed as mortal injustices, inviting and often demanding a governmental response.[5] The discourse and practice of health promotion and disease prevention have made death an event that is (or at least ought to be) confined to the margins of later life, which by implication are largely unaffected by social processes. Increasingly, mortality has become the defining element of old age. Unlike these earlier, premature deaths, death in old age is not to be explained, nor do particular causes need to be sought for it. Rather old age is constructed as the natural site where death is to be found. In these circumstances what reason is there to look for the 'social causation' of death in old age?

Even within the paradigm that makes death an event constitutive of old age, determining the point when death ceases to be 'premature' and, by implication, no longer in need of explanation remains an unresolved problem. Even if old age is death's natural site – a site placed as it were beyond the social – the problem remains of deciding when old age has arrived and when research should stop looking for explanations. Pursuing the social mediation of morbidity and mortality in later life challenges the unquestioning 'naturalness' of old age and by implication of death itself. Indeed it could be argued that pursuing any aetiological explanation of death in later life challenges its naturalness.

That challenge is at last being taken up by both biomedical and social scientists. In the last decade, several investigators working largely within the empirical traditions of public health and medical sociology have begun extending the examination of health inequalities into later life. Although the findings from research examining the role of social factors in accounting for variability in morbidity and mortality in later life remain ambiguous, the new focus is welcome. This recent research paradigm needs to be distinguished from earlier research paradigms investigating predictors of longevity. The latter field of research has a long and well-represented history within gerontology. The latter tradition (of longevity research) sought explanations for why some people didn't die, not why they did.[6] Death was natural – a given. The challenge was to find explanations for when it did not happen – typified by those research adventurers who went in search of the privileged 'secrets' of long-lived elites who invariably seemed to reside in remote corners of the developing world.[7] In a sense the aim of this research was little different from that pre-scientific tradition of looking for the elixir of life. The assumption was that some biological or lifestyle-related factor(s) could be identified and 'brought back' to the developed world, to be passed on as 'scientifically proven' methods of life extension. Even where the emphasis was upon social rather than bio-environmental factors, the focus was upon social–psychological factors such as attitudes toward life, sexual activity, hobbies and interests and so on rather than upon structural factors.

The stimulus for the new direction has been the growing body of evidence indicating universal, secular improvements in late-life mortality. These secular changes, now well documented, have encouraged researchers to search for the social processes that might account for them. Are there social, structural changes acting contemporaneously within the lives of older people which directly or indirectly influence bio-ageing? Or are these effects social products derived wholly from the past, accumulated from childhood onwards, which are now enabling more adults simply to realize old age? While the former suggests a continuing dialectic between the material and social construction of ageing and old age, the latter implies that old age must remain a residual social category, determined and dominated by the stochastic necessity of infirmity and death. To address these questions we shall examine two principal areas of research. The first concerns secular changes in late-life morbidity and mortality, the second the influence of structured inequalities on these parameters of bio-ageing.

## Secular changes in late-life mortality and morbidity

In most developed countries the mean age of dying has risen steadily over the last three decades. Mortality from some chronic diseases also has declined. More controversially, there is evidence that later-life mortality and morbidity are both on the decline. The United States Census Bureau has conducted regular surveys of chronic impairments in activities of daily living amongst nationally representative samples of both community and institutionalized persons aged 65 and over. Data from the surveys conducted in 1982, 1984, 1989 and 1994 have been analyzed by Manton and his colleagues at the Centre for Demographic Studies at Duke University. They found a marked decrease in the proportions of older people who are disabled in ADL during this 12-year period.[8]

As a result of these trends, Manton suggested that by 1996 there were 1.4 million fewer disabled older Americans than would have been anticipated on the basis of the first National Long Term Care Survey – a considerable reduction in misery as well as in costs. One question raised by this survey is whether the very real improvement in the standard of living of America's older citizens noted over the last two or three decades is yielding tangible effects upon the limiting conditions of old age. One might add, if so, is this an indication of the enablement of older people or rather the deconstruction of disability?

Using data drawn from the National Health Interview Survey, Timothy Waidmann and his colleagues at the University of Michigan have shown similar improvements in self-reported health throughout the 1980s and early 1990s.[9] Their analyses indicate that the proportion of older Americans who view themselves in poor or fair health – both men and women – has been declining for at least the last decade. Other recent US data confirm 'significant declines in the level of onset of disability'.[10] Adequate explanations of such secular changes may be difficult to specify, but they do suggest that the ills of ageing are neither invariant nor inevitable.

Is this evidence of improved well-being in later life a product of improvements in the specific circumstances of older Americans or are similar secular trends evident in other countries? International mortality trends suggest they are. Declining mortality rates in later life – particularly in those aged over 80 years – are being observed in many other countries. Most of these changes have occurred in the second half of this century. In a recent review, Kannisto and his colleagues commented that:

developed countries have achieved progress in reducing death rates even at the highest ages . . . [and] furthermore the pace of this progress has accelerated over the course of the twentieth century.[11]

Linking these findings with research conducted on non-human species, they argue that established views concerning the 'limits of life' need revising, that there is no single universal process of ageing,[12] that this process does not need to lead to an exponential increase in mortality with age, that human beings are not built like clocks constructed to run for a certain time before stopping and, basically, that no species have determinate lifespans.[13]

Kannisto and his colleagues point out that the clearest gains in later-life longevity have been found in Scandinavian countries – Denmark, Finland, Norway and Sweden – where the accuracy of reporting dates of birth and death is greatest. These gains appear to be widespread and cross all social strata.[14] In a recent Swiss study a 25-year linear rise in the median and modal ages at death was observed amongst those aged 50 and over.[15] If this trend were extrapolated, the authors suggest that early in the twenty-first century the modal age of dying in Switzerland will be 90 years, well beyond the maximal age of death proposed by Fries in his 'rectangularization of the lifespan' thesis.[16] Evidence that this 'life extension' is reaching some natural limit is weak and contradictory. Life expectancies continue to grow with no limit yet in sight.

Accompanying this increase in longevity in Europe is an improvement in health status amongst older people[17] which suggests that US trends form part of a wider demographic shift toward delaying and narrowing the period of old age. This improvement seems most evident in the reduction in serious and severe disabilities amongst the older population. As example, the last 20 years have seen a substantial reduction in the proportion of older (80 years and above) British men and women reporting major impairments in activities of daily living. This change is illustrated in Figure 8.1.

It would be disingenuous to present only findings that support the view that life is getting longer and better than ever before. While few would question the data on late-life mortality, evidence of secular improvements in age-related morbidity – rates of disease and disability – has been challenged by many researchers. Some surveys of secular trends in

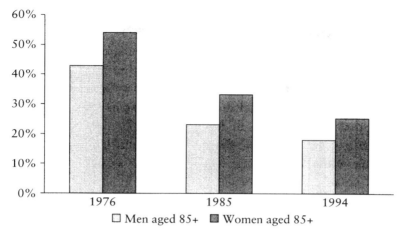

FIGURE 8.1 Changes in the percentage of older men and women unable to perform selected ADL activities, 1976–94[18]

disability and disease suggest that people may be experiencing worsening health and increasing disease in later life. Rather than applauding the gain in years of life, some researchers argue that society needs to consider the costs that arise as a result of such progress. Our next section examines these arguments and evidence around 'life extending beyond the limits of health'.

## Natural lifespan and the prolongation of life

The steady extension of human life evident in the twentieth century has caused several academic commentators to chafe against the 'unnatural practices' of modern science. Medical ethicists such as Daniel Callahan argue that forcing people to live longer than they should – i.e. than nature decrees – can only end in unplanned disaster – individually in terms of prolonged personal suffering and socially in terms of ever-increasing costs of care.[19] The disaster scenario that is outlined conjures up images of a vast expansion of nursing homes spreading relentlessly across the developed world, eating up 'our' surplus wealth and leading eventually to economic and cultural implosion in the greying dusk of modern civilization. Advocates of this neo-romantic position imply that there is an exponentially increasing personal and social cost arising with

153

each additional year of life won beyond the natural span. At the same time, the natural span of life is a boundary never quite settled (variously 70, 80 or 85) in a manner that is strongly reminiscent of those ageist practices in health care which established 'geriatrics' as a chronologically bound, yet never fully delineated, late addition to modern medicine.

Defining the point at which we stop caring is not easy. Nor is it so daunting that several writers and would-be policy makers have not had a fair stab at it. Fries' 'natural limit' was 85. Callahan implies 75 but is ambivalent. Whatever the actual age chosen, he argues:

> we can have and must have a notion of a 'natural lifespan' that is based on some deeper understanding of human needs and possibilities not on the state of medical technology . . . [it is] one in which life's possibilities have on the whole been achieved and after which death may be understood as a sad but nonetheless relatively acceptable event.[20]

Central to Callahan's argument is that the ideology of 'a natural lifespan' needs to be retained whether or not the actual lifespan is extended beyond that limit. Those cultural values embedded in past notions about the fixed 'structure' or 'stages' of life, he maintains, continue to serve a purpose in today's 'postmodern' world. By offering a socially reconstructed version of a prior foundationalist position concerning the natural limits of human life, Callahan seeks to establish a recovered meaning that will help ensure the dignity of both living and dying.

To criticize Callahan by making reference to data indicating secular improvements in age-related levels of disability and disease is to some extent to miss his point. He does not claim that there cannot be any extension of life or indeed any improvement in the quality of life even at the extreme edges of longevity. He argues rather that such efforts are undignified and merely serve to equate disability and death with failure – whether personal social or technological. This search to 'recover the life-world', as Moody has termed it, is somewhat disingenuous. There is increasing evidence that the limits of human life are less clear than ever before. Numerous, distinctly 'unpostmodern' biomedical articles challenge any ideas about the 'naturalness' of ageing, its status as an integrated biological process and its determinant nature.[21] Evidence of an ever-increasing number of disabled and dependent citizens remains equivocal. Recent US trends noted in Chapter 6 point to a *decline* in rates of nursing-home admissions despite the growth in the over-75 to 85-year-old sector of the US population.[22] Reports of increasing rates of self-reported disability may reflect changing expectations about health and functioning rather than any underlying increase in physical impairment. Trends showing increases in self-reported health problems alongside declines in clinical indices of ill-health suggest that the various discourses of health and ageing are complex and conflictual.[23] What seems most evident is that, as more and more people live to be 70, 80, 90 and 100, the 'nature' of that age becomes open to a wider variety of meanings from which a variety of cultures of ageing can emerge. In some ways the desire to set limits reflects the anxieties raised by the rapidity and by the fundamental openness of contemporary social change. At present, any attempt to set limits to the human lifespan seems as likely as setting limits to the world wide web.

Although collectively agreed limits to the lifespan may not be realizable, less determined social processes may contribute quite significantly to those limits. The average lot of retired people may be quantitatively better than ever before, but the beneficiaries of these secular trends are to be found disproportionately amongst the better off. The length, breadth and depth of the third age appear greatest for those who can afford it. If this is indeed the case, it implies very clearly that social factors can and do exercise a continuing influence deep into old age.

## Ageing and impoverishment

Do differences in access to and control over social and material resources contribute to the disability and dependency that is old age? Are the arguments for 'limits' to ageing really attempts to cover up existing age inequalities that ensure that the rich remain well looked after while the poor are denied access to sufficient health and welfare resources to guarantee them 'equality' of opportunity for a longer and healthier life?

As we have already noted, there is considerable research evidence that income differentials in adulthood account for significant variation in mortality[24] and that these income-related differentials may be increasing.[25] Research also suggests that income effects on mortality are more pronounced amongst those under rather than those over 65 years.[26] Several studies of health and disability in later life have found that socioeconomic differences do tend to lessen in later old age. In one study conducted in 1980 by the MRC Medical Sociology Unit at Aberdeen University Rex Taylor and Graham Ford examined various parameters of physical and personal well-being in a representative sample of over 600 men and women aged over 60 in the city of Aberdeen.[27] They observed that 'with increasing age, [the middle classes'] financial advantage remains relatively unaffected but they entirely lose their earlier health advantage'. Whether indexed by the presence of chronic health problems or functional limitations their figures suggest that amongst the 'oldest' old (those aged over 75 years) there is a waning social influence on bio-ageing, in contrast to clear 'social class' differentials in 'early' old age.

Further evidence minimizing the impact of socioeconomic factors on human ageing and disability comes from a study conducted in Marin County, California. Elderly residents of this county, who are amongst the most well off in the United States, reported rates of impairment and disability that differed little if at all from those of less advantaged populations. The authors of this report were suitably cautious in making any generalizations, but commented that their findings:

> suggest the possibility that the relative lack of poverty and ignorance in the Marin elderly has not greatly altered the burden of disease common in old age.[28]

Several other studies imply a declining impact of social class on the extent and progression of disability in later life. House and his colleagues in their analysis of chronic disability across the lifecourse found that while middle-aged Americans (45–54) in the lowest socioeconomic strata had as many chronic conditions affecting them as 'aged' Americans (75+) in the uppermost strata, the most marked decline in functional ability from ages 65–74 to age 75+ was observed amongst the most privileged strata.[29]

In a 12-year follow-up of over 3500 elderly Manitobans, Roos and Havens examined those features that predicted what they operationally defined as 'successful ageing' – people who rated their health 'good' or 'excellent', who reported no ADL impairment, who were not living in a residential or nursing home, who were not using walking aids and who were mentally alert. They found that

> none of the measures of socioeconomic status were significant . . . even though the measures available . . . were extensive.[30]

These and related studies[31] suggest that, if we are to address socially determined inequalities in health and length of life, such efforts should prioritize the task of redistribution within the period of adulthood and during working life. Reductions of socioeconomic inequality during the post-work life period would seem to be of little or no benefit in preventing the progress of bio-ageing. Since socioeconomic inequalities act cumulatively the benefits of reducing inequalities in childhood and early adulthood might well continue to have a positive impact upon the material circumstances of the newly retired. On the other hand promoting equality in later life may have little impact upon bio-ageing itself.

In short, there is a powerful relationship between access to and control over material and social resources and morbidity and mortality throughout most of adulthood. That relationship cannot be accounted for simply by arguing that the poor lead unhealthy lifestyles.[32] Social-structural factors influence not only who gets to be old but also how well people are and how well their bodies function having reached retirement age.[33] The impact of these material and structural differences on the *future* morbidity and mortality of older populations (aged 75 and over), however, seems less evident.[34]

The rich of Marin County appear as vulnerable to the disabilities of ageing as those from much poorer areas of the United States. Rich Manitobans are no more likely to age successfully than poor Manitobans. Elderly working-class Aberdonian men and women are no more disabled than their middle-class age peers. Gains in extra years of life in deep old age occur as commonly for those who have retired from working-class occupations as they do for former business men and professionals. If the extent of disability is receding amongst the retired population of the developed world, as both Fries and Manton claim, the explanation may lie in a universal improvement in the conditions that touch all groups of older adults, rather than from any redistribution of economic and social power within the retired population. While the experience of ageing may be mediated by social, economic and cultural processes for much of adult life, at some point there is a death of the social, leaving us each to face a universal old age and the limits of human nature.

Like many contemporary endings, such conclusions are premature. Not every study has observed the 'erasure of the social' in the determination of 'successful ageing'. Some have found very large income-related

TABLE 8.1  Income differential and ADL impairment in US elderly*

| Income | <$6000 | $6000– 8500 | $8500– 10 000 | $10 000– 12 500 | $12 500– 15 000 |
|---|---|---|---|---|---|
| ADL | | | | | |
| No/minor impairment | 21.5% | 28% | 28.5% | 32% | 42% |
| Severe impairment | 32% | 18% | 17% | 14% | 12.5% |

| Income | $15 000– 25 000 | $25 000– 35 000 | $35 000– 50 000 | $50 000+ |
|---|---|---|---|---|
| ADL | | | | |
| No/minor impairment | 44% | 53.5% | 58% | 58.5% |
| Severe impairment | 11.5% | 5% | 5% | 4% |

* Derived from Berkman and Gurland, 1998

differentials in functional disability amongst an over-65 population. Berkman and Gurland, for example, reported a straightforward linear relationship between income in later life and level of disability – as Table 8.1 shows.[35]

In another US study, Palmore and Burchett examined the development of disability in the years before death in a sample of older Americans all of whom were 'fit' at the beginning of the study. Over a six-year period, they observed that income status remained a significant and important predictor of incident disability (i.e. becoming disabled) prior to death even after controlling for age and other factors.[36] Grundy and Glaser in the UK have reported similar findings. They found that both the prevalence and the incidence of disability were greater amongst those 'living as a local authority tenant, having no qualifications and being of manual social class'[37] compared with less disadvantaged groups. Income itself, however, was not so strong an influence.

Marked effects of socioeconomic position were also found in the American Asset and Health Dynamics Amongst the Oldest Old (AHEAD) study. The first wave of this longitudinal study began in 1994 and examined the health and wealth characteristics of 7300 persons aged 70 or over living in independent households. Vast differences in the wealth of 'healthy' and 'unhealthy' older people were observed. For example, the median net worth of those couples who described their health as 'excellent' was US$285 000, while couples who described their health as poor had a median net worth of only US$41 000.[38]

Significant social class influences on mortality in retirement also have been reported.[39] In their study of British civil servants, Marmot and Shipley reported that:

> among men aged 40–69 years at entry to the [...] study, socioeconomic measures continued to be associated with differences in death rates over a 25 year follow up period to age 89 ... Even after retirement there was still an 86% increase in mortality among men in the lowest grade compared with the highest.[40]

Further complexity comes from studies that have tried to examine the impact of social and economic differentials at different stages of life and their influence on late life mortality. Hart and her colleagues in Glasgow found that indicators of social class based upon occupation in middle age exerted a stronger impact upon subsequent mortality than childhood social class. She found that those who retained a working-class status from childhood through to middle age fared worse than those whose social position shifted from working class to middle class as well as those who retained a 'middle-class' status throughout their lives.[41] Given the changing social class composition of post-war society these figures imply a slow and progressive attenuation of the impact of historical class differentials on mortality and, by implication, morbidity.

The attenuation of earlier social influences may arise from less benign processes. Social class differentials in morbidity and mortality in the post-retirement phase (e.g. 75 plus) may be less easily detected because earlier class differentials have lead to greater mortality at earlier ages (in middle and early old age). The 'fitness' of persons who have grown old in disadvantaged social and economic circumstances may be greater than that of their ageing peers who come from more advantaged backgrounds. This pattern of differential mortality pre-retirement might account for a lack of social class differentials in functional disability observed in studies such as the Aberdeen survey as well as helping explain the steeper increase in disability amongst more socially advantaged men in House's study.

Continuing income-related differentials in the development of disability even after taking account of initial health status differences suggest that social factors can continue to exert an influence on the kind, quantity and quality of later life that people experience irrespective of earlier selective mortality effects. Whether this remains true in deepest old age – the post-85-year-old lifespan that Fries argues exists largely as a residuum after the maximal guaranteed lifespan has been reached – is more difficult to answer. No studies have pursued morbidity and mortality data deeply enough into old age to determine whether the distal or proximal effects of class and social status operate throughout the whole of the realized lifespan.

## Bodily ageing: emergence or submergence of elites?

That there has been a widespread secular improvement in life expectancy in old age and in late-life healthiness seems incontestable. These trends appear linear and show no obvious signs of decreasing. There is also evidence that socioeconomic status derived from a person's adult working life and background matters rather less in shaping the kind and quantity of deep old age that people in the West can look forward to compared with the influence such factors have in determining who gets to be 'old' and the state of their health at retirement. Nevertheless, differential levels of social and material resources cannot be ignored in determining entry into deep old age and may continue to exercise an influence on the rate and consequences of disability right up to the point of death. A distinction must be borne in mind between the onset and impact of disability in later life and mortality risk. While there is evidence that the onset of disability – and by implication transition from a third- to a fourth-age status – is influenced by an individual's social and economic resources, with increasing age the impact upon mortality *per se* does seem to be lessened.

Several explanations may be put forward to accommodate these findings. It may be that SES impacts most harshly on the rate of those environmentally driven deaths that make up a small but still significant fraction of all deaths that occur deep in old age. Such deaths may be less common now compared with the kinds of death recorded earlier this century. Age-associated, or rather age-related, mortality might be less affected by secular trends particularly in late and very late old age. In other words social factors may play only a minimal role in structuring the underlying physiological processes through which the clinical outcomes of bio-ageing are expressed and it may be the latter processes which increasingly determine mortality at the oldest ages.[42] As the proportion of 'environmentally' induced deaths in the population is reduced, increasing numbers of people will reach a 'universal' old age. Entering this period of 'socially uninsured old age' (whose precise delineation remains hard to pinpoint), individuals may become subject to mortality risks that are determined in good part by stochastic processes of misrepair and replicative error within the cells of our body. Because of the stochastic nature of this process, there may be only a limited overdetermination of the lifespan arising from genetic processes.[43]

As a result the probability of dying very late in life may no longer be determined by underlying disease. There is, for example, good evidence that, in very old age, the relationship between disease and disability is masked, suggesting that factors associated with great age are more significant determinants of disability than the presence or absence of disease.[44] At the same time there is very little evidence that age mediates the relationship between disability and death, even in very old age. At every age, people with the greater levels of disability seem more likely to die. Even if age does 'take over' as the most powerful predictor of death and disability at some point along the lifecourse, it remains to be seen when exactly that is and whether it has to be so.

## Seeking, not setting, limits

Does the apparent decline in the significance of social forces in bio-ageing in very late life render irrelevant the approach to 'ageing' that characterizes the third age? If factors unrelated to social position and social identity provide the mechanisms by which bio-ageing is ultimately expressed, if luck and random breakdown rather than wealth, planning and personal resilience determine a very long life, what incentive is there to invest in this period of life? How relevant will personal long-term-care insurance plans be? How important is it to cultivate health promoting lifestyles deep into old age? Seventy-five-year-olds who become centenarians may simply be 'luckier' than their peers who die earlier. If reducing social inequality offers no solution to reducing the inequalities of deep old age and if social advantage cannot be converted into health gains later in life, does this undermine the rationale of both the political left and right? Does the disappearance of the social in deep old age mean that redistributive politics should focus only on those of working age? Should old age remain a matter either of social welfare or personal choice? Does this apparent decline of the social render the moral economy of the third age irrelevant, inducing those retiring to become even more consumer focused, spending now and spending down with no reason to plan for a deep old age for which they appear to have no individual responsibility?

While the third age is emerging as an increasingly important arena where power, status and citizenship can be played out, those in the fourth age or deep old age seem excluded from such a role. They are left to occupy the position of being nature's, not society's, casualties. If death and infirmity in later life are explicable in terms of age alone, the passage through old age cannot be easily represented as the result of personal and/or collective choices in the way that it can be during the third age. The naturalness of disability and death in old age implies a lack of social and/or personal responsibility, which denies old age a position of agency within society. The old aged person becomes simply the subject of natural justice, their old agedness unrelated to the social structuring of the life-world. The decline and death of class and culture in late old age lead then to the greatest impoverishment of all – exclusion from the processes that establish and give meaning to everyday life. No longer touched by the effects of economic oppression and exploitation, left with a disinvested existence, the very old survive within the interpretive structures of others, increasingly caught in the webs of significance spun by the functionaries of health and welfare systems.

Such a position forecloses prematurely a debate that has hardly begun. The study of health inequalities and health variations is both polarized and inconclusive. In part this may reflect the inadequacies of both the methodologies utilized and the theoretical assumptions behind this research.[45] Equally it may reflect the tremendous changes that have occurred to the occupational structure and the nature of wealth formation in the late twentieth century, rendering class analysis difficult if not impossible.[46] The research evidence is inconsistent. That there can be any period of life unaffected by either historically or currently determined differentials in social resources is implausible. An individual's social position and related access to social and material resources may determine not only who has access to a deep old age, but also the length, depth and quality of that old age. At the basic level of choosing between life and death within old age, people from 'resourceful' backgrounds may be more able and more likely to avail themselves of that choice, before they are lost in the indignities of a painful and powerless terminal decline. At the same time a range of potentially individualized options may be extended to reduce risk, improve fitness and promote longevity at every age of life, for those with the command of resources and access to choices to realize such goals.[47] While the evident benefits arising from health-promotional lifestyles are based upon research whose subjects have been largely in their sixties and seventies,[48] there are some later-life exceptions.[49] In the future there may well be more.

This very uncertainty about the power of people either as individuals or as members of social collectivities to prevent their decline into deep old age/fourth age is itself one more facet of what has been described as 'risk society'. Despite the increase in information available to people, perceptions of risk and uncertainty rather than diminishing grow.[50] As assured knowledge expands it reveals in its wake increasing areas of uncertainty. Such uncertainty and the evident indeterminacy of both nature and society act as stimuli for those in the third age to buy more heavily into the infinite desires of postmodern culture. If old age is uncertain, if death has no 'natural causes', what limits need one draw? The very openness of ageing can become an openness to endless spending on the promotion of a healthy appearance and a fit body. At the same time such openness challenges the state either to draw boundaries around its own constructions of old age or to withdraw even further from participation in such structured dependency, leaving ageing open to those who consume it.

## Notes

1 See Estes, C. and Binney, E. (1989) 'The biomedicalisation of aging', *The Gerontologist*, 29: 587–8.
2 Marmot, M.G., Kogevinas, M. and Elston, M.A. (1987) 'Social/economic status and disease', *Annual Review of Public Health*, 8: 111–35.

3  See Pappas, G., Queen, S., Hadden, W., Fisher, G. (1993) 'The increasing disparity in mortality between socioeconomic groups in the United States', *New England Journal of Medicine*, 329: 103–9; McDonaugh, P., Duncan, G.J., Williams, D. and House, J. (1997) 'Income dynamics and adult mortality in the United States, 1972 through 1989', *American Journal of Public Health*, 87: 1476–83; Lynch, J.W., Kaplan, G.A., Pamuk, E.R., Cohen, R.D., Heck, K.E., Balfour, J.L. and Yen, I.H. (1998) 'Income inequality and mortality in metropolitan areas of the United States', *American Journal of Public Health*, 88: 1073–80.

4  Lantz, P.M., House, J.S., Lepkowski, J.M., Williams, D.R., Mero, R.P. and Chen, J. (1998) 'Socioeconomic factors, health behaviors, and mortality: results from a nationally representative prospective study of US adults', JAMA, 279: 1703–8.

5  The current British government has made increasing the length of life and narrowing health inequalities its two main aims in health policy (Department of Health (1998) *Our Healthier Nation: a Contract for Health*, The Stationery Office, London).

6  'Long life may be looked upon as the result of the failure to die' (Simms, H.S. and Berg, B.N. (1955) 'Factors controlling longevity', *Geriatrics*, May: p. 229).

7  See, for example, Hayflick's discussion of 'superlongevous people' (Hayflick, L. (1996) *How and Why We Age*, Ballantine Books, New York, pp. 196–202).

8  Manton, K.G., Corder, I. and Stallard, E. (1997) 'Chronic disability trends in elderly United States populations: 1982–1994', *Proceedings of the National Academy of Sciences of the USA*, 94: 2593–8.

9  Prior to 1982 a rather different method of rating health was used, so earlier data cannot easily be compared with the more recent trends, but these recent figures do point to a slow but steady increase in the numbers reporting good or excellent health (see Waidmann, T., Bound, J. and Schoenbaum, M. (1995) 'The illusion of failure: trends in self reported health of the US elderly', *The Milbank Quarterly*, 73: 253–85).

10  Crimmins, E.M., Saito, Y. and Reynolds, S.L. (1997) 'Further evidence on recent trends in the prevalence and incidence of disability among older Americans from two sources: the LSOA and the NHIS', *Journal of Gerontology*, 52B, S59–71.

11  Kannisto, V., Lauristen, J., Thatcher, A.R. and Vaupel, J.W. (1994) 'Reductions in mortality at advanced ages: several decades of evidence from 27 countries', *Population and Development Review*, 20: p. 794.

12  A recent review on longevity genes and ageing makes a similar point – i.e. the absence of any single 'longevity' mechanism or clock (Jazwinski, S.M. (1996) 'Longevity, genes and aging', *Science*, 273: 54–8).

13  Kannisto, V., *et al.* (1994) *op. cit.*, p. 804.

14  Martelin, T., *et al.* have shown a steady gain of one year in life expectancy from the early 1970s to the late 1980s among cohorts of Finnish 80-year-olds. This gain of almost 20 per cent in life expectancy was experienced as much by ex-farmers and ex-manual-workers as by those retiring from 'upper non-manual occupations' (Marterlin, T., Koskinen, S. and Valkonen, T. (1998) 'Sociodemographic mortality differences amongst the oldest old in Finland', *Journal of Gerontology*, 53B, S83–90).

15  Paccaud, F., Pinto, C.S., Marazzi, A. and Mili, J. (1998) 'Age at death and rectangularization of the survival curve: trends in Switzerland, 1969–1994', *Journal of Epidemiology and Community Health*, 52: 412–15.

16  Fries' hypothesis is that there is a genetically fixed 'length of life' and that social and medical progress will lead to fewer and fewer deaths prior to that age, with deaths

increasingly occurring around a narrower and narrower age range, causing 'survival' or 'life' tables to shift from showing a gradual curve of declining mortality to a steeper 'rectangular' form, when just about everyone survives to 80 years of age and just about everyone is dead by age 90 (Fries, J. (1980) 'Aging, natural death and the compression of morbidity', *New England Journal of Medicine*, 303: 130–6).

17  Boshaizen, H.C. and van de Water, H.P.A. (1994) *An International Comparison of Health Expectancies*, TNO Health Research, Leiden. See also Synak, B. (1987) 'The elderly in Poland: an overview of selected problems and changes', *Ageing and Society*, 7: 19–36; Robine, J.N., Mormiche, P. and Cambois, E. (1996) 'Evolution des courbes de survie totale, sans maladie chronique et sans incapacité en France de 1981 à 1991: application d'un modèle de l'OMS', *Annales de Démographie Historique*, 31: 99–115.

18  Data from Grundy, E. (1997) 'The health and health care of older adults in England and Wales, 1841–1994', in *The Health of Adult Britain, 1841–1994*, Department of Health, London, pp. 182–205, Table 26.16.

19  See Callahan, D. (1987) *Setting Limits: Medical Goals in an Aging Society*, Simon and Schuster, New York.

20  Callahan, D. (1987) *op. cit.*, p. 26.

21  'Recently there has been a conceptual shift in our understanding of aging. The possibility of extending the maximum human lifespan has gone from legend to laboratory. This change has been prompted by a growing academic literature that suggests that the aging process itself . . . is modifiable' (Banks, D.A. and Fossel, M. (1997) 'Telomeres, cancer and aging: altering the human life span', *Journal of the American Medical Association*, 278: 1345–8); '[T]echnological advances have also revealed an untapped potential of the human genome to support major increases in life expectancy at all ages' (Finch, C.E. and Tanzi, R. (1997) 'Genetics of aging', *Science*, 278: 407–11).

22  Lakdawalla, D. and Philipson, T. (1999) 'Aging and the growth of long-term care', *NBER Working Paper 6980*, Washington, DC.

23  Waidman, T., *et al.* (1995) *op. cit.*, esp. pp. 276–9.

24  Wilkinson, R. (1992) 'Income distribution and life expectancy', *British Medical Journal*, 304: 165–8.

25  Pappas, G., *et al.* (1993) *op. cit.*

26  House, J., Kessler, R., Herzog, A.R., Mero, R., Kinney, A. and Breslow, M. (1990) 'Age, socioeconomic status and health', *Milbank Memorial Quarterly*, 68: 383–411; McDonough, P., *et al.* (1997) *op. cit.*; Lynch, J.W., *et al.* (1998), *op. cit.*

27  Taylor, R. and Ford, G. (1983) 'Inequalities in old age: an examination of age, sex and class differences in a sample of community elderly', *Ageing and Society*, 3: 183–208.

28  Reed, D., Satariano, W.A., Gildengorim, G., McMahon, K., Fleshman, R. and Schneider, E. (1995) 'Health and functioning among the elderly of Marin County, California: a glimpse of the future', *Journal of Gerontology*, 50A, p. M69.

29  House, J., *et al.* (1990) *op. cit.*, p. 407.

30  Roos, N.P. and Havens, B. (1991) 'Predictors of successful aging: a twelve year study of Manitoba elderly', *American Journal of Public Health*, 81, p. 66.

31  For example, Schwartz *et al.* (1995) reported no effects of childhood 'socioeconomic status' on longevity in an 80-year follow-up of the Terman 'Studies of genius' sample (Schwartz, J.E., Friedman, H.S., Tucker, J.S., Tomlinson-Keasey, C., Wingard, D.L.

and Criqui, M.H. (1995) 'Childhood factors and mortality', *American Journal of Public Health*, 85: 1237–45); Waitzman and Smith (1998) found no effects of 'social deprivation' on mortality amongst older adults in contrast to a marked effect in younger adults and Goldberg *et al.* (1996) found no effects of education or occupational status on longevity (reaching age 75 years) in the well-known Framingham heart study (Waitzman, N.J. and Smith, K.R. (1998) 'Phantom of the area: poverty area residence and mortality in the United States', *American Journal of Public Health*, 88: 973–6. Goldberg, R.J., Larson, M. and Levy, D. (1996) 'Factors associated with survival to 75 years of age in middle-aged men and women', *Archives of Internal Medicine*, 156: 505–9).

32 Lantz, P.M. *et al.*, *op. cit.*

33 See Lynch *et al.* (1997) for a powerful demonstration of the impact of sustained hardship during adulthood on functioning at retirement (Lynch, J.W., Kaplan, G.A. and Shema, S.J. (1997) 'Cumulative impact of sustained economic hardship on physical, cognitive, psychological and social functioning', *New England Journal of Medicine*, 337: 1889–95).

34 There is a large literature on socioeconomic influences on morbidity and mortality in both childhood and adulthood – e.g. Wilkinson, R. (1992) *op. cit.*; Feinstein, J. (1993) 'The relationship between socioeconomic status and health: a review of the literature', *Milbank Memorial Quarterly*, 71: 279–322; Duncan, G.J. (1996) 'Income dynamics and health', *International Journal of Health Services*, 26: 419–44.

35 Berkman, C.S. and Gurland, B.J. (1998) 'The relationship among income, other socioeconomic indicators and functional level in older persons', *Journal of Aging and Health*, 10: 81–98.

36 Palmore, E. and Burchett, B.M. (1997) 'Predictors of disability in the final year of life', *Journal of Aging and Health*, 9: 283–97.

37 Grundy, E. and Glaser, K. (2000) 'Socio-demographic differences in the onset and progression of disability in early old age: a longitudinal study', *Age and Ageing*, in press.

38 Smith, J.P. (1997) 'Wealth inequality among older Americans', *Journal of Gerontology*, 52B (special issue): 74–81.

39 Fox, A.J., Goldblatt, P.O. and Jones, D.R. (1985) 'Social class mortality differentials: artefact, selection or life circumstances?', *Journal of Epidemiology*, 39: 1–8; Marmot, M.G. and Shipley, M.J. (1996) 'Do socioeconomic differences in mortality persist after retirement? 25-year follow up of civil servants from the first Whitehall study', *British Medical Journal*, 313: 1177–80.

40 Marmot, M.G. and Shipley, M.J. (1996) *op. cit.*, p. 1179.

41 Hart, C.L. Davey-Smith, G. and Blane, D. (1998) 'Inequalities in mortality by social class measured at 3 stages of the lifecourse', *American Journal of Public Health*, 88: 471–4.

42 'It is possible that health outcomes in very old age are increasingly dependent on genetically determined processes which are relatively independent of socioeconomic conditions' (Maier, H. and Smith, J. (1999) 'Psychological predictors of mortality in old age', *Journal of Gerontology*, 548: 51.

43 Christensen and Vaupel suggest that at most 'one-quarter of the variation in lifespan in developed countries can be attributed to genetic factors' (Christensen, K. and Vaupel, J.W. (1996) 'Determinants of longevity: genetic, environmental and medical factors', *Journal of Internal Medicine*, 240: 333–41, p. 333).

44 Hogan, D.B., Ebly, E.M. and Fung, T.S. (1999) 'Disease, disability and age in cognitively intact seniors: results from the Canadian study of health and aging', *Journal of Gerontology*, 54A: M77–82. See also the observation by Boult and his colleagues regarding the overall significance of non-fatal conditions such as arthritis – compared with fatal conditions such as cancer or coronary heart disease – on the incidence of disability within an ageing population (Boult, C., Altmann, M., Gilbertson, D., Yu, C. and Kane, R.L. (1996) 'Decreasing disability in the 21$^{st}$ century: the future effects of controlling six fatal and nonfatal conditions', *American Journal of Public Health*, 86: 1388–93).

45 Scambler, G. and Higgs, P. (1999) 'Stratification, class and health: class relations and health inequalities in high modernity', *Sociology*, 33: 275–96.

46 Pakulski, J. and Waters, M. (1996) *The Death of Class*, Sage, London.

47 In one important study, Rudman *et al.* (1990) demonstrated the benefits to older men's fitness and physique arising from six months' injections of human growth hormone – but at a cost (US$14,000 per year) which would render the intervention beyond the reach of most but the well off (Rudman, D., Feller, A.G., Nagtraj, H.S., Gergans, G.D., Lalitha, P.Y., Goldberg, A.F., Schlenker, R.A., Cohn, L., Rudman, I.W. and Mattson, D. (1990) 'Effects of human growth hormone in men over 60 years old', *New England Journal of Medicine*, 323: 1–6; see also comments by Vance, M.L. (1990) 'Growth hormone for the elderly?', *New England Journal of Medicine*, 323: 52–4).

48 Stewart, A.L., King, A.C. and Haskell, W.L. (1993) 'Endurance exercise and health related quality of life in 50–65 year old adults', *The Gerontologist*, 33: 782–9; Fries, J.F., Singh, G., Morfield, D., Hubert, H.B., Lane, N.E. and Brown, B.W., Jr, (1994) 'Running and the development of disability with age', *Annals of Internal Medicine*, 121: 502–9; Lee, I.M., Hsieh, C.C. and Paffenberger, R.S., Jr (1995) 'Exercise intensity and longevity in men: the Harvard alumni health study', *Journal of the American Medical Association*, 272: 1179–84; Goldberg, R.J., Larson, M. and Levy, D. (1996) 'Factors associated with survival to 75 years of age in middle aged men and women', *Archives of Internal Medicine*, 156: 505–9; Vita, A.J., Terry, R.B., Hubert, H.B. and Fries, J.F. (1998) 'Aging, health risks and cumulative disability', *New England Journal of Medicine*, 338: 1035–41).

49 For example Fiatrone, M.A., Marks, E.C., Meredith, L.A., Lipstitz, L.A. and Evans, W.J. (1990) 'High intensity strength training in nonagenarians', *Journal of the American Medical Association*, 263: 3029–34; Suzman, R.M. (1992) 'The robust oldest old: optimistic perspectives for increasing healthy life expectancy', in R.M. Suzman, D.P. Willis and K.G. Manton (eds), *The Oldest Old*, Oxford University Press, Oxford.

50 This thesis has been outlined in Beck's book on 'risk society' and elaborated in Giddens' work on the concept of 'manufactured uncertainty' (see Beck, U. (1992) *Risk Society: Toward a New Modernity*, Sage Publications, London; Giddens, A. (1995) 'Replies', in U. Beck, A. Giddens and S. Lash (eds), *Reflexive Modernisation*, Polity Press, Cambridge).

# CHAPTER 9

# Ageing, Alzheimer's and the uncivilized body

In the previous two chapters we discussed ageing as it is expressed in the appearance and the functioning of the body. Here we address ageing expressed in 'the decline of self-care' and the loss of control of the self that is associated with dementia. Loss of bodily control is a key distinction between the third and the fourth ages. While it would be possible to examine this loss of control in relation to other 'fourth-age' transitions, falls and incontinence are examples that come readily to mind, none has quite the same impact as dementia for none embodies so completely that loss of social agency that lies at the heart of the fourth age.

While most people become resigned to the 'inevitability' of some aspects of bodily ageing, of changes in appearance and changes in the efficiency of bodily functioning, few can contemplate with equanimity that the mind too is mortal. More than the 'unconscious' irrationalities of physical need and desire, the embodied irrationality of dementia challenges the notion of a disembodied rationality that has been such a central tenet of classical social theory. In this sense 'senility', to revert to the use of this premodern term, represents the ultimate failure of the modernist project, the failure of what Elias terms 'the civilized body'. The body rendered mindless by senility can no longer sustain its claim to an identity based on personal and social agency. Those behaviours most associated with self-care – looking after oneself, keeping oneself clean, controlling bodily functions and modulating the expression of emotions, controls which Elias described as central to the civilizing process, become eroded. A body the mind has lost control of becomes instead the *de-civilized* body.[1]

## Elias and the civilized body

Shilling identifies three key aspects to the civilizing process as described by Elias: socialization, rationalization and individualization of the body.[2] Bringing bodily functions under social control, emphasizing the importance of poise and self-discipline, and locating identity specifically within the body were, for Elias, key developments in the emergence of modern ideas about people's relationships with each other and the development of separate public and private selves. The public failure of the individual to exercise control and the evident inability to effectively exercise such control exclude the person from participation as an agent within the civilized (social) world.

The process of civilization, in this formulation, is the slow but steady extension that the modern state has made over the regulation and control of social life. Increasing state control, in turn, demands greater 'self-control' on the part of the individual in public. Expressed in Foucauldian terms, the development of governmentality created the conditions for an increasing emphasis upon 'technologies of the self' or socially mediated 'self-care'. The modern state expects its members to regulate their conduct as a result of a 'growing reflexive understanding of their own actions, those of others, their interrelationships and their consequences'.[3] Failure to maintain such a system of self-regulation is always possible and a descent into barbarism remains an option for all societies, hence the importance in modern societies of monitoring signs of breakdown in civilized behaviour and the growing public discourse over crime and mental disorder.

Dementia, in this sense, is the public failure of an individual's claim to self-mastery and self-control. It is, however, an unwitting failure, for it is not the case that the person with dementia has chosen to transgress or that he or she has deliberately sought to exclude him- or herself from the civilizing processes of society. The progressive loss of agency, of socialized intent, in dementia is represented culturally as an 'internal' failure, a failure of control that presupposes a bodily not a social or personal failing. Traditionally the inability to look after oneself has been accepted as a not uncommon way through which old age begins, or ends. In the late twentieth century, a transformation of the relationship

169

between the state and its citizens has introduced a concomitant change in the way frailty and disability are regarded. No longer is it viewed as appropriate (or civilized) to consider the needs of the frail and disabled in terms of the local provision of charity – via poor houses, infirmaries and asylums or their late-modern equivalents. Instead everyone is to be regarded as a self-regulating citizen with his or her own individual needs. Representing citizens thus, not as the recipients of welfare but as consumers of health and social care products, requires framing 'welfare citizenship' in terms of individual choice and agency within a quasi-market. In such a market, there is no longer a place for asylum or charity. Instead health and social care function as potential consumables – as commodities.

Continuing to locate the failure of self-control within the discourses of the civilized body, and more particularly within the revealed truths of neuroscience, poses a dilemma for this new form of welfare capitalism. When government systems of health and welfare are treated as if they were part of a 'social market' presaged upon choice and agency, the state's response to the loss of self-control that is evident in dementia risks becoming increasingly contradictory.[4] The traditions of planning and intervention in individual lives that developed as part of the 'civilizing' modernist state and which tolerated, and perhaps even eased, the loss of agency ascribed to the mad, the frail and the disabled sit uncomfortably alongside the emerging forms of governmentality associated with the new politics.

For many centuries, the term 'dementia' was used as a way of acknowledging that some individuals cannot comport themselves in a civilized fashion – and that society is unable to compel them to do so.[5] Society rather than the individual was expected to do something about such public manifestations of personal loss of self-control, however meagre that response might be. Aside from the steady centralization of the response, this continued to be the dominant model of welfare provision throughout much of the twentieth century. Civilization could best be measured by the improvements in the comprehensiveness, regularity and reliability of that response as well as the number of hospital beds provided. In recent times this model of civilized charity has come under increasing criticism. The new paradigm seeks to represent all forms of disability as a particular demand for services. Such demand is considered best met by allowing the free play of market forces to determine the appropriate supply of services. The former recipients of a universal welfare system are redefined. They have become 'active' participants in market-like relationships: clients, consumers, customers or, rather more ambiguously, 'users'. By so continuing to support a discourse of social agency for disabled people, the 'liberal' argument goes, the unhealthy dependency that is structured by state administered charity is avoided. Whenever possible, people's own choices are to shape the kinds of service they receive, not the paternalistic welfare state. To enshrine the legitimacy of this position, such 'liberal' discourse has had to be applied to all disabled groups. Exceptions made for one group weaken the coherence of the argument as a universal principle of government. Reconstructing 'senility' becomes a necessary goal toward establishing the hegemony of this new form of welfare capitalism.

Tracing the reconstruction of dementia from its representation as a natural if tragic fate befalling those reaching 'old age' to its reframing as a distinct neurological condition affecting certain 'at-risk' individuals, we aim to show how the 'progressive' developments in the area of dementia care mirror this wider shift in social policy. But this *re-civilizing* of 'senility' is not solely the result of changing social policy and the associated commodification of welfare. It reflects upon other aspects of postmodern culture and particularly the changing way that modern medicine is beginning to approach and interpret 'old age'.

Over the course of the last century modern medicine has undergone three distinct shifts in its approach to ageing and old age. It began with the studious avoidance of old age that was enshrined in the practice of late-nineteenth-century hospital medicine.[6] The next phase coincided with the mid-century professionalization of medicine, when hospital doctors offered 'benign' support for and surveillance of 'old people' through the emergence in post-war Britain of 'geriatric medicine'. Now, at the turn of the century, a new approach is jostling for position, one that can best be described as 'anti-ageing medicine'.[7] This latest form of aspirational medicine approaches ageing and old age as things to be 'deconstructed'. Any totalizing quality that they once seemed to possess is dismissed or brushed aside and old age is reconstructed more as a compendium of risky but potentially avoidable medical conditions.[8] Ageing and Alzheimer's are treated as understandable, remediable and preventable.

To understand more clearly the significance of the civilized body in the cultural representation of ageing we must look first at how medicine, psychiatry and psychology began to separate *civilized* normal ageing from *uncivilized* abnormal ageing. The distinction between these two processes played a central role in the new scientific gerontology of the mid-century. Determining what constituted 'normal' age changes and what were 'abnormal' age changes formed a powerful and unifying research agenda for the various disciplines that were seen as constituting the new 'meta-discipline' of gerontology. However, the benefits of this division are being re-appraised now that the social and material costs arising from it have become more evident. Separating the 'normal' civilized aspects of ageing from the unacceptable, uncivilized aspects of old age has served to reinforce the rising expectations individuals have started to have about ageing. While such expectations were sustained and encouraged during much of the post-war period, the fiscal crisis that occurred in the mid-1970s altered governments' ideas about the capacity they had to ensure steadily improving welfare for all the 'uncivilized' needs that were being unearthed.

That process of re-appraisal is especially evident in the new 'Alzheimerization' of ageing. It illustrates the contradictory nature of much postmodern governmentality. On the one hand a discourse has been created that attributes and promotes the recognition of personhood and agency amongst many who for much of the last century had been constrained by their position as hapless recipients of enlightened civic charity. On the other hand it confounds the collective potential of social agency by promoting the idea that such agency is reducible to the individual selection of particular goods, services and 'experiences'. Moreover, behind many of these attempts to re-civilize the uncivilized body lie other more material goals, not least to shift the public cost of a fourth-age identity towards the private choices of less costly third-age ones. This re-appraisal of senility, this particular programme of re-civilizing the fourth age, involves three key elements. First and probably the easiest to chart is the conversion of the post-war problem of senility into the postmodern problem of Alzheimer's disease. Second, and consequentially related to the former, is the transformation of the public health focus upon dementia from one that was based on an epidemiology of need to one that is based on an epidemiology of risk. The third element is the wider shift in social policy referred to above, namely the reframing of health and welfare from a social right given to needy but helpless citizens to a choice of goods and services offered to individual citizen-clients, who have acquired this new status through the concomitant re-inscription of their 'personhood' within the discourses servicing Alzheimer's disease.

## The post-war transformation of senility

Age-related mental decline was one of the central topics in the newly founded gerontological research programmes of the 1940s and 1950s. Much of that research effort sought to establish what constituted normal mental decline and how if at all it contrasted with abnormal deterioration. Noting the parallels between the age-associated reduction in human brain weight and decrements in adult intelligence test performance, the US psychologist David Wechsler concluded that human intellectual ability underwent a natural involution as a result of an age-related decline in brain size and loss of neuronal populations.[9] While he assumed that intellectual decline was normal and inevitable, Wechsler was not so sure whether such decline amounted to senility. Was there, he speculated, a general involutionary process that affected some individuals more than others, or was there in addition an overlay of disease?

In the following years, research interest around this question pursued two very separate paths. One that dominated American research for most of the 1950s, 1960s and 1970s was concerned primarily with establishing just how normal age-associated decline in intelligence test performance was. This research has had few immediate or practical implications, but it did serve to reassure older Americans that their newly emerging retirement lifestyle was unlikely to be blighted by mental decrepitude. The message of most researchers was upbeat and they generally sought to disabuse the public of Wechsler's rather more negative opinions about the fate of intellectual ability with age.[10]

The other route began largely in British mental hospitals and was conducted with scant reference to the concerns and expectations of Britain's old age pensioners. It focused initially on the older residents of the infirmaries and asylums that had just been incorporated into the new National Health Service. The newly legitimized professions of psychiatry and psychology began to address the problem of mental infirmity in later life, seeking to make sense and order out of the charitable chaos that reigned in the nation's long-stay institutions. While the post-war, largely unregulated growth of the American private nursing-home industry meant that the transfer of old people into private nursing homes was enacted with little regard to medical classifications or indeed any form of medical control,[11] in Britain the integration of mental hospitals, local authority infirmaries and the regional acute hospital system achieved by the 1948 National Health Service Act provided the most important impetus for the gradual 'medicalization' of dementia – the precursor to the later 'Alzheimerization' of ageing.

This process began with the work of the British psychiatrist Martin Roth in the 1950s and 1960s. Roth's pioneering work laid the foundations for a new subdiscipline, 'psychogeriatrics', and he continued to influence much of British mental health care policy for older people for the next two decades. He began his work by concentrating on the problems of assessment, measurement and classification. Mental problems arising for the first time late in life, Roth argued, could be attributed to either functional causes – problems of psychopathology rather than brain pathology – or organic causes, where the reverse applied. The former were treatable, reversible (with or without treatment) and unlikely to lead toward progressive debility. The latter, in contrast, were untreatable, irreversible and highly likely to progress toward debility and eventually death. A portion of 'organic disorders' were, however, regarded as potentially reversible. These could be detected by identifying a range of 'masked' clinical conditions that exercised an acute but potentially transient effect upon the brain. These 'reversible' dementias held a particular iconic value by demonstrating the importance of biomedical investigation and diagnosis in the face of what otherwise might have been regarded as conditions impregnable to and hence best avoided by modern medicine.[12]

Funding from the British government's Department of Health supported the extension of this institution-based research into the community, enabling Roth and his colleagues to conduct some of the first population-based studies of the epidemiology of dementia. These surveys, conducted in the city of Newcastle, gathered information about the size and nature of the problem of dementia (senility) and the likely health-care resources needed to address it.[13] Several key findings emerged. In the first place they found that only a small minority of retired people suffered from 'senile' dementia; secondly they showed that the prevalence of these mental disorders became more common at later ages; and thirdly they pointed out that most people with dementia were living in the community and not in mental hospitals or nursing homes.

This research established a 'base' against which levels of services could be planned, and a framework developed for the work of a 'psychogeriatrician'. The late 1960s and early 1970s saw the further consolidation and institutionalization of psychogeriatrics within the British health-care system.[14] New psychogeriatric units opened, modelled on the geriatric assessment units where the geriatricians had first established their claims to be a modern hospital speciality. Rehabilitation units were set up, often by the simple act of renaming a couple of wards in the local mental hospital. Discharge of psychogeriatric patients into newly built local authority homes for the elderly mentally infirm demonstrated that rehabilitation was indeed taking place. Senility was derided as a term and fragmented as a concept. In its place came senile dementia and arteriosclerotic dementia, illnesses to be carefully distinguished from conditions which merely masqueraded as senility, such as 'acute confusional states', 'depression' and 'paraphrenia'. This 'modern' approach toward senile dementia was celebrated in a review article published in 1972 and entitled 'Senile dementia: a changing perspective'.[15]

This 'new perspective' was to last little more than a decade. By the 1980s another new agenda had begun to take over, one that saw 'a rising tide' of dementia threatening to swamp the health services.[16] This rhetoric was quick to cross the Atlantic, where it surfaced as a concern for the scourge that was becoming known as 'Alzheimer's disease'.[17] In the process, senility was finally abandoned, first transformed into senile dementia, and then, when the very remnants of senility were cast aside, re-emerging as a new public health hazard – Alzheimer's disease. It was at this junction that US interest resurfaced in this 'new' disease.

## The branding of Alzheimer's and the scientific approach

For David Wechsler, 'senility' could not easily be set apart from normal ageing. By the 1980s, senility had been almost completely set aside as both a lay and a medical term. Consigned to history, its place was being taken over by Alzheimer's, scourge of the third age. Optimization of cognitive functioning became the goal for the vast majority of retired people, a prospect made more practicable now that it was unencumbered by earlier associations of decline and impairment. The uncivilized body remained, but it was to be located in a more carefully delineated set of illnesses that were to be called 'Alzheimer's disease' or 'related disorders'.

Why did the rebranding and copyrighting of Alzheimer's disease prove so singularly successful? Up until the 1960s, neuropathological investigations into the ageing brain had been a research backwater, filled with technical difficulties in separating out the proteins involved in plaque and tangle formation in the brain, with little new development since the diagnostic staining techniques introduced at the turn of the last century. Alzheimer's disease had been considered a rare condition affecting a small minority of people in late middle age, modelled upon the original account of the eponymous disease published at the beginning of the twentieth century. In the original paper, Alzheimer described neuropathological changes in the brain of a middle-aged woman who had become progressively more forgetful, confused and 'senile'. Using recently developed silver staining techniques to study the pathology of the brain, he identified numerous abnormal structures in the nerve cells of the woman's cortex. He described these fibrous abnormalities in the nerve cells as 'tangles' on account of their appearance under the light microscope. In the following decades, many neuropathologists observed similar pathology in a wide variety of 'clinical' conditions. They were not seen as having major diagnostic significance, being considered common features of neuropathology observed in the brains of many older people who showed no signs of senility.[18] The real 'cause' of senile dementia was sought elsewhere and there was little interest in linking up the 'rare' pre-senile dementias that affected the middle-aged with the mental infirmity commonly associated with senility.

In the early 1960s, Roth was keen to build a stronger foundation for the classificatory system he had established for the mental disorders he observed in his elderly patients. Working with the neuropathologist Bernard Tomlinson, Roth and his colleagues developed a method of quantifying the neuropathological examination of the brain which could then be correlated with quantitative measures of mental decline that had originated out of his earlier classificatory research. Roth and his colleagues were able to establish for the first time an apparently clear link between the degree of mental decline in life and the degree of cerebral pathology at death.[19] But even this finding, while recognized as important at the time (1968–9) did not lead to any marked expansion of research activity in the field of dementia. The decade that followed saw a concentration in Britain and elsewhere in Europe upon service development issues. Dementia/senility was pinned down and split into two, one form seeming to arise internally from the nerve cells themselves and the other from peripheral atherosclerotic changes within the circulatory system. Neither formulation seemed to offer much hope for a therapeutic strategy – especially as the latter seemed specifically to exclude cerebral atherosclerosis as a causal factor.[20] Planning bed numbers and day places seemed a more sensible strategy for the immediate future.

A key change took place in 1979. At that point, a Conservative government came to power in Britain, favourably disposed to the 'new right' economics which had a distaste for central planning, seeking to promote individual choice and individual responsibility.[21] Coincidentally, reports began to emerge outlining a potential treatment strategy based on evidence[22] of a specific deficiency in the cholinergic system of the brain in patients with dementia.[23] Studies of the cholinergic system conducted on the brains of people variously described as suffering from 'Alzheimer's disease', 'senile dementia' 'senile dementia and other abiotrophies' or simply 'elderly people' suggested a selective loss of those nerve cells that used acetylcholine as the chemical transmitter of impulses in the brain – but with no apparent loss of the receptor sites to which the acetycholine molecules would bind. This latter finding was important because it meant that if one could somehow increase the production of acetylcholine, receptor sites still existed in the brain to 'receive' the neurotransmitter and thus restore mental functioning. The treatment trials that followed sought to draw direct parallels between the treatment of senile dementia, Alzheimer type and the 'successful' treatment of Parkinson's disease.[24] The argument was as follows. Parkinson's disease is an age-associated disorder of the central nervous system – so is senile dementia. Parkinson's disease is associated with lesions in a particular area of the brain, the substantia nigra, which contains cells that use the neurotransmitter dopamine to communicate. Senile dementia is associated with lesions in particular areas of the brain, the hippocampus and nucleus basalis, which contain cells that communicate via the neurotransmitter acetylcholine. The former disorder was named after the clinician who provided its first modern clinical description. So, let senile dementia be renamed Alzheimer's disease after the clinician who was now credited with providing its first complete clinicopathological description – albeit in a 53-year-old woman.

The impact of the 'cholinergic hypothesis',[25] the flurry of drug trials and the concomitant interest in 'reframing' senility as 'Alzheimer's disease' led to a mushrooming of Alzheimer's disease societies in Europe, America and Australia. From 1980 on all references to senility began to fade. A new terminology appeared, variously senile dementia – Alzheimer's type (SDAT); dementia, Alzheimer's type (DAT); and primary degenerative dementia (PDD). Spurred on by the pharmaceutical industry's desire to conduct treatment studies of dementia, national bodies were set up to rationalize and legitimize the diagnosis of Alzheimer's dementia, placing an official stamp on the term and finally and completely severing any remaining connection with senility. The initiative moved from Britain to the USA, home of the giant pharmaceutical companies.

A working group was set up under the auspices of the US Department of Health to lay the foundations of this new set of operationalized criteria for 'probable Alzheimer's disease'. It was made up of two bodies – the National Institute of Neurological and Communicative Disorders and Stroke (NINCDS) and the Alzheimer's and Related Disorders Association (ADRDA). Both represented the views of neurologists rather than psychiatrists. In the process, senile dementia was forever transformed, taken out of the asylum and re-inserted in the neurology clinics as Alzheimer's disease. This confirmed it as an issue soon to exercise the minds of a third-age audience – both as potential carers and as potential clients.

Subsequent drug research pursued the cholinergic hypothesis with considerable determination through a heavily financed programme of research and development and lobbying. This finally came to fruition in 1995 in the endorsement by the American Food and Drugs Agency (FDA) of the compound tacrine, traded under the name 'Cognex', as the first 'anti-dementia' treatment authorized and licensed for sale in the USA. Although the Committee for the Safety of Medicines (CSM) – the UK version of the USA's FDA – initially refused to grant a licence to tacrine, a successor product, donepezil, traded under the name 'Aricept', achieved recognition in Britain in 1997. Numerous other compounds are queuing up to be registered and drug research is actively and heavily exploring these and other avenues, particularly those linked with the amyloid hypothesis and the role of the fat-transporting protein apolipoprotein E in the pathogenesis of the senile plaque. National and international regulatory processes have integrated the operationalized definitions of Alzheimer's with the systematization of drug research paradigms. Reinforced by these very material pay-offs, Alzheimer's has now acquired a virtual monopoly on the 'problem of senility'.[26]

## Alzheimer's and the state

The reframing of dementia as a neurological disorder, the introduction of the cholinergic hypothesis, the widespread growth in drug trials and the proliferation of Alzheimer's disease societies have helped reconstitute dementia as a 'third-age' issue. Those who had once been excluded from the processes of normal 'civilized' ageing, under the category 'the demented elderly', are being reintroduced and re-civilized as the victims of Alzheimer's disease. However, the retired people who are entering anti-dementia drug trials are recruited from populations that are comparatively young, rich, healthy, socially integrated, male and ethnically very white – attributes that characterize the successfully retired.[27] While older people are typically 'recruited' into anti-dementia drug trials by their 'significant other', attempts are now being made to obtain 'real' volunteer patients, with an increasing interest in people showing the least degree of impairment consonant with the terms and conditions required for them to be judged to suffer from Alzheimer's.[28]

But senility has not vanished. It survives and indeed grows in the midst of other debates concerning a very fourth-age issue – the provision of long-term care. Despite the arrival of FDA- and CSM-approved anti-dementia drugs, the fate of large numbers of people suffering from dementia is to spend some part of their lives within an institution. In contrast to the participants in Alzheimer treatment trials, the residents

179

of these nursing home are typically old, widowed, female, poor and most notably senile.[29] With the demise of the asylum, the state hospital and other vestiges of public charity, the provision of long-term care has moved increasingly into private hands. But despite the privatization of provision, the financing of long-term care remains predominantly in the hands of the state – via Medicaid and Medicare in the Unites States, via local government departments of social security in Britain and via federal government funding in Australia. As we noted in Chapter 6, anxieties over escalating costs have led governments around the world to seek ways of providing less expensive supportive services that might keep the needy and the frail at home, via the policies of community care. Increased rationing and targeting of services have been employed so the state can more tightly define those who amongst the retired population might form the core of a fourth-age, state-dependent constituency – a constituency, as it were, of *uncivilized* bodies, unable to care for their selves. Those who are so targeted are at the same time those whose ageing most alienates them from others. Their 'uncivilized' loss of control makes social relationships difficult and social action impossible. Though the family has long been seen as the source of shelter and support for failed identities, families are increasingly ill-equipped to want or be able to sustain such dependency. The absence of living partners, the geographical distance between parents and their offspring, the individualization of the lifecourse and senility's own lack of exchange value leave those whose mental powers have failed them with few alternatives outside the state upon which to depend.

As long as it was believed that this fate was confined to an identifiable minority of the retired population, and as long as it was believed appropriate to redistribute some of the economic growth of a society to improving the welfare of those unable to contribute to that growth, it was possible for the state to conceive of long-term care as a necessary and containable cost. As dementia became increasingly acknowledged as an age-dependent state, as the epidemiological evidence clearly predicted an exponential growth in its future prevalence as a direct function of population ageing and as the fiscal crisis of the mid-1970s reoriented the politics of welfare in the subsequent decade, governments began to view long-term care as an escalating claim on public expenditure.

By redefining senility as Alzheimer's, it seemed as if the problem could be more precisely pinned down and rendered more manageable. The Alzheimerization of 'uncivilized' ageing ought then to free up the third age to concentrate upon smart drugs and 'staying young' mental activity programmes. But the copyrighting of Alzheimer's effectively excluded, through its scientistic criteria, a large number of 'uncivilized' bodies who remained recalcitrantly senile, to whom no anti-dementia drug prescription could or would be offered. In response, another new paradigm began to emerge – one that frames the problem of Alzheimer's not as an inevitable responsibility for the state but as an avoidable risk for the individual. The final decade of the twentieth century has seen one more twist in the relentless process of renegotiating ageing identities – one that re-presents the contradiction at the heart of the Alzheimer's/senility debate under a new guise. This is the shift from an epidemiology of need to an epidemiology of risk.

## Alzheimer's – from need to risk

The early epidemiological research into dementia was conducted within the established paradigms of the post-war public health system. It was largely an enterprise conducted in the social democracies of North Western Europe. The aim was to obtain reasonable estimates of need for services. Following the work of Roth, Kay and Bergmann in Newcastle, a number of similar epidemiological surveys were carried out during the 1960s and 1970s in countries influenced by this social democratic tradition of matching needs with resources through central planning.[30] The results of these studies showed a clear consensus. Every prevalence study showed that the longer people live the more likely they are to experience failing intellectual powers and a growing inability to manage themselves. The consequence seemed to be an inevitable need for greater and greater 'long-term care' provision as the population aged.

In the Reagan–Thatcher years of the 1980s the emerging Alzheimerization of ageing research[31] led to a dissatisfaction with these 'old' studies. The committee-based operationalization of Alzheimer's required that surveys more clearly delineate 'Alzheimer's disease' from 'dementia'. Dementia was treated as an unsatisfactory category, undifferentiated and redolent of the earlier term 'senility'. It had to be subordinated to

TABLE 9.1  Recent estimates of the prevalence of dementia and Alzheimer's disease in later life

| Age range | DSM III Dementia | DSM III Alzheimer's |
|-----------|------------------|---------------------|
| 65–69 | 1.6% | 0.9% |
| 70–74 | 3.2% | 2.1% |
| 75–79 | 5.5% | 4.3% |
| 80–84 | 12.4% | 8.5% |
| 85–89 | 19.8% | 16.0% |
| 90–94 | 38.7% | 34.8% |
| 95+ | 57.8% | 47.8% |

the more precise delineation attributed to the nosology of Alzheimer's disease. As a result a number of studies were conducted in the 1980s which provided separate prevalence estimates of dementia and of Alzheimer's. Unsurprisingly, both sets of figures closely parallelled each other. As shown in Table 9.1, dementia/Alzheimer's was rare amongst 60- and 70-year-olds. It was, however, commonly and usually observed amongst 90-year-olds.

By the mid-1980s, an interest in identifying the 'risk' factors associated with Alzheimer's disease appeared. Initially these were case control studies, comparisons of patients with a diagnosis of Alzheimer's disease with people who did not differ in terms of age, sex, background and so on but who were judged 'free' of Alzheimer's disease. The most significant outcome of these studies was to identify the raised prevalence of Alzheimer's amongst first-degree relatives – i.e. indicating that Alzheimer's had a familial component. This provided the beginnings of a notion that there were indeed people 'at risk' of developing Alzheimer's (and by implication many others not at risk).

As research began to suggest an understandable aetiology for Alzheimer's disease, first through the cholinergic hypothesis and later through the amyloid cascade hypothesis,[32] growing evidence that genetic factors were involved in 'disease expression' strengthened support for a specific biological aetiology.[33] From this point, epidemiological research changed track and by the late 1980s it had began to focus almost exclusively on the question of individual risk.

In order best to answer the question of who is at most risk, the ideal design is to follow people up as they grow older and 'pick up' the cases who develop dementia/Alzheimer's. Such large-scale population-based incidence studies of Alzheimer's disease emerged in the late 1980s, and from 1990 onwards they have focused upon the study of 'risk.' By now a large and growing number of studies has been published. Researchers have demonstrated familial risk factors, risks associated with exposure to various industrial hazards, risks associated with habits such as smoking, lack of exercise and the presence of atherosclerosis. A number of 'protective factors' also have been observed – for post-menopausal women, taking oestrogen; for both men and women taking non-steroidal anti-inflammatory medication and anti-oxidants such as vitamins C and E and, at least for people in the West, a good education.[34] Numerous reports world-wide have confirmed that the presence of a particular version of a gene coding for a protein involved in lipid transport increases the risk of Alzheimer's by a factor of 5 or even 10.[35] The cumulative impact of such risk factor research suggests that a primary prevention strategy for Alzheimer's disease is realizable – one that offers a role for individual lifestyle management as well as one that means opportunities for clinical trials.[36]

Of course incidence studies do more than simply suggest risk factors – they also indicate something about our lifetime chances of developing Alzheimer's/dementia. Although not always made salient, what incidence studies indicate most clearly is that the greatest risk that can be conferred arises from living a very long life. Thus the risk of developing dementia rises inexorably with each passing year and shows no sign of 'plateauing' even at the very oldest ages.[37] As a result of nothing but the passage of time, a condition initially representing a very small risk for 'third-agers' becomes a very large risk for the majority of 'fourth-agers'. The parallel with the risk of death is obvious. Age-independent risk factors, such as the apolipoprotein E ε4 allele, may help determine when but they do not determine whether a person develops Alzheimer's.[38]

Alzheimer's is remarkably democratic, affecting people in developed countries as much as those in the third world, affecting men and women, white-collar and blue-collar workers, rich and poor with apparent total disregard for status. Despite the ubiquitous finitude that Alzheimer's seems to express, research continues to seek potential 'risk groups' who may need special treatment or who may need to adapt a 'health-promoting' lifestyle. Even when the 'inevitability' factor of senility is recognized, the aspirational Alzheimer's scientists merely shift the argument towards an emphasis on a reduced period of 'dementia-related disability' – a kind of rectangularization of the mindspan – if a dementia-free existence cannot be delivered.[39]

There are of course enough hints and clues to awaken some interest in those third-agers of a mind to reduce their own risk of becoming senile. The recipe is mostly familiar – stay fit, don't smoke, exercise, take ibuprofen (better than aspirin), high doses of vitamins C and E, maybe add extract of *Ginkgo biloba*[40] and, for post-menopausal women, take HRT or a phytoestrogenic equivalent. Alzheimer prevention strategies[41] follow the prolongevity strategies typical of much recent self-help literature targeting the third age. They reinforce the message of personal responsibility that matches current health and social care policies. Even writers whose own research suggests that physical and mental fitness are pretty much unrelated cannot refrain from perpetuating the message that it is still in our hands to keep our minds active – to use it so that we do not lose it.[42]

Given the likelihood that most people will reach their 85th birthday neither senile nor needing to be placed in an institution, acting upon a concern to keep one's mind active is unlikely to make much difference. But by making Alzheimer's something that you might develop rather than a matter of fate and the length of life, it becomes possible to present it not as an uncivilized status deserving pity and charity but as a risk against which to be insured. The significance of the shift in epidemiological research from need to risk lies in its underlying relationship to the rise of 'governmentality' more generally and 'governmentality' of old age in particular. If senility is not simply one of the misfortunes of later life, for which governments need to provide and individuals need to be prepared, but an illness that affects some individuals rather than others, both the individual and the state should try as well as they can to protect themselves against that risk.

## Alzheimer's, personhood and the re-civilizing of senility

We began this chapter with a consideration of dementia as a problem of loss of self-control and the unwelcome re-emergence of the ***uncivilized*** body. If even postmodern identities are presaged upon the existence of a knowing, if not always rational, agent, one who chooses to express a particular identity and pursue a particular lifestyle, the failure of rationality and insight poses a serious problem for the development of new paradigms and cultures within which to age/stay young. Equally, the failings of the civilized body pose serious problems for the 'postmodern' state. If dementia is not 'someone's fault' – if it is a common and sadly inevitable way in which the majority of people will pass their final years should they live long enough – then the state is faced with either reinstating a 'back to basics' policy of inducing families to care more or taking up the theme of more recent times, having to plan for those who cannot plan for themselves. As we have seen, both options have been found wanting. Instead the emphasis has been upon treating all citizens as customers seeking health and social care services within the framework of contract law. The copyrighting of Alzheimer's seems to offer one way of maintaining this view, by treating the sufferer as a person legitimately seeking treatment for a disabling neurological condition. Despite this approach toward re-civilizing senility, the aspirations of Alzheimer science have so far outstripped their realization. One might even argue that they have served merely to exclude more completely all those uncivilized bodies who cannot pass muster as true third-age clients in need of better treatment. Likewise the tangible benefits of a second and some might say supplementary route, namely treating Alzheimer's as a risk to be protected against rather than a fate to which to be resigned, are as yet extremely limited. While the consumption of self-help literature and the various nutraceuticals associated with prevention strategies has risen in consequence, there has been little increase in the uptake of personal long-term-care insurance, even amongst those able to afford it.

A third approach has emerged, one that seeks to re-civilize the ageing body without specific recourse to the limiting discourse of biomedicine. Importantly it is one that promises to all those 'fourth-agers' excluded by such discourse new, socially inclusive identities. This promise is framed under the general rubric of 'discovering the person in dementia'.[43] Emerging within the health and welfare professions toward the end of the 1980s, this new approach to 're-civilizing' the aged body has been described specifically as the 'new culture of dementia care'.[44] According to this approach, the social exclusion of the person with dementia is seen as the consequence of an oppressive and malignant psychology, effectively preventing the person from remaining a member of civilized society. It is an approach most closely associated with the work of Tom Kitwood in Britain and somewhat less explicitly of Naomi Feil in the United States.[45] In its focus upon the role of a malign social system or structure it shares and indeed draws upon some of the tenets of structured dependency theory.

Without going through all the details that make up this approach, the broad thesis is that 'malignant social psychologies' take away from people 'their last remaining traces of competence and self-respect' leading to a deterioration in 'personhood'. The goal of the 'new culture' is to replace this malignant social psychology with a 'benign' version which 'might over a period even provoke some structural regeneration among the neurones that remain'.[46] Inevitably responsibility for both the malignant and the benign social psychologies lies with other people – families, friends, carers – who are credited with the power/responsibility to re-civilize (Kitwood uses the term 'rement') the dementing person.

A small but significant literature has appeared that pursues the process of re-civilizing senility by seeking to 'hear the voice of the person with dementia', treating people with dementia as 'users' or 'consumers' of services, seeking out ways of representing their views directly or through the use of advocates.[47] Various metaphorical terms have been coined to provide a system of signification from which these 'new cultures' can be devised. 'Inhabitants of a lost kingdom' is one recent example. Attempts to maintain/restore/preserve an identity for the person with dementia involve placing responsibility for his or her continued socialization in the hands of individual carers. Institutions and institutionalized care are represented as potentially if not actually malignant environments responsible in some way for the senility and dementia of those who have been placed there.

The task of these progressive forces is to act as re-interpreters of the language of Alzheimer's. New meanings are to be attributed to the actions and inaction of the victims of Alzheimer's and a new language taught to carers. Thus equipped with a new map and a new culture, they can discover the person within the disease and re-discover the disease within the person. The rhetoric of this new dementia culture seeks explicitly to re-civilize Alzheimer's. In the process, it seeks radically to alter the culture and civilization of the broader society, which is viewed as giving too much emphasis to 'individuality and autonomy'. By taking reason off its pedestal, Kitwood claimed, and re-civilizing Alzheimer's a new perspective will emerge that will see:

> a new and vibrant humanism . . . gaining ground: more strongly committed, more psychologically aware, more culturally sensitive, more practical and pragmatic than anything that has gone before.[48]

Such a strategy not only seeks to re-inscribe the person who suffers from dementia but also seeks to re-present the very nature of dementia as part of a much wider and less rational conceptualization of the individual both as social being and social agent. The cultural turn it seems comes full circle. Autonomy and rationality themselves need to be re-civilized through a new 'Alzheimerization' of society.

## Alzheimer's and sustainable ageing

In the 1970s few people had ever heard of Alzheimer's disease. At the end of the twentieth century it is probably one of the most widely known medical conditions in the developed world. It continues to spawn a vast research and clinical literature. People of a certain age now joke about developing Alzheimer's when embarrassed by a lapse of memory or attention. Regular Alzheimer's Disease Society 'awareness' weeks ensure that the subject does not get forgotten. Although research continues to refer to dementia as a broad umbrella term, studies of dementia and studies of Alzheimer's overlap to such an extent that dementia seems likely soon to be completely subsumed under the term 'Alzheimer's disease and related disorders'. The partner that accompanied Alzheimer's throughout the first half of the twentieth century, Pick's disease, has been virtually eclipsed. Senile dementia's clinical comrade-in-arms, atherosclerotic dementia or cerebral arteriosclerosis, has been sidelined and now lies in conceptual confusion roped haplessly into the rubric of 'Alzheimer's disease and related disorders'.[49]

But if Alzheimer's disease is something that sustains an importance and significance that gives it potential cultural capital within the context of aspirational medicine, and provides a name that helps dignify the disabilities of dementia in ways that senility and dementia do not, it is an achievement of 'civilization' that comes with a cost. That cost involves shunting dementia into a residual social category, a kind of antechamber where social death precedes biological death. Those excluded from the scientific civilizing category of Alzheimer's remain a potential or actual public burden. Other attempts at re-civilizing dementia have equally costly consequences. Whether the circumstances of those who become mentally frail are treated as the result of a personal flaw, arising from the individual's inappropriate or ineffective management of risk, or whether they are represented as the reproduction of a malignant social psychology embedded within the practices and institutions to which they are consigned, the consequence remains. The 'cost' of mental frailty in old age is transformed from a responsibility to be planned for and borne by any 'ageing' state to one that resides primarily with individuals – whether as victims or as carers.

Within late modern society, where lifestyle consumerism and the search for personal fulfilment and recognition play such an important role in the dynamic of social life, failure to embody the culture resulting from a loss in the capacity for self-care represents one of the most serious of identity flaws. Indeed, it challenges the sustainability of any 'culture of ageing'. If there should be limits to human ageing, the mortality of the mind may prove the most instrumental in setting those limits and, *pace* Kitwood, the most unyielding to any attempt to blur or redefine them. Redistributive policies do not guard against the impoverishment of dementia whilst gender politics address those who care, not those who suffer from dementia. Consumer choice and the technologies of the self seem of little account in preventing the occurrence of dementia or in transforming its meaning. Yet, despite all the contradictions, the modernist project remains undaunted. Over one hundred anti-dementia preparations are or have reached the stage of clinical testing. Not one of them is hemlock.

## Notes

1  Elias, N. (1978) *The History of Manners. The Civilising Process*, vol. I, Urizen Books, New York.
2  Shilling, C. (1996) *The Body and Social Theory*, Sage Publications, London. pp. 163–7.
3  van Krieken, R. (1998) *Norbert Elias*, Routledge, London, pp. 114–15.

4  See Gilleard, C. and Higgs, P. (1998) 'Old people as users and consumers of healthcare: a third age rhetoric for a fourth age reality', *Ageing and Society*, 18: 233–48.

5  See Jones, R. (1912) 'The varieties of dementia and the question of dementia in relation to responsibility', *Journal of Mental Science*, 58: 411–24.

6  For an account of those excluded from admission to the hospitals that opened during the course of the nineteenth century, see Smith, F.B. (1990) *The People's Health, 1830–1910*, Weidenfeld and Nicolson, London. They included significantly 'the dirty and unrespectable, the very poor, women burdened with small children and the aged' (p. 254).

7  See the introduction in Klatz, R.M. (ed.) (1996) *Advances in Anti-Aging Medicine*, Mary Ann Liebert, Inc., New York.

8  It might be argued that this view of 'aspirational medicine' is simply a dressed-up 'postmodern' version of the pre-modern adage *'senectutus morbus est'* – old age is a disease. Our position, however, is that aspirational medicine 're-interprets' that old adage, treating the 'natural' features of old age as a series of discrete conditions that accumulate in the later part of adult life, leaving open the question of what ontological status old age may possess.

9  Wechsler, D. (1955) *The Measurement and Appraisal of Adult Intelligence*, Williams and Wilkins, New York.

10  See as example Baltes, P.B. and Schaie, K.W. (1974) 'The myth of the twilight years', *Psychology Today*, 7: 35–40.

11  The first attempt at legislating for US nursing-home care began in the 1970s in response to growing concerns over the nature of care provided to residents. More directive legislation emerged within the Omnibus Budget Reconciliation Act, 1987.

12  Any quick scan through the 'psychiatry of old age' literature in the 1960s and 1970s would demonstrate the importance given to the biomedical investigation of dementia and the related search for treatable causes. In contrast, it is hard to identify any such studies in the 1990s research literature on Alzheimer's disease and its 'related' disorders.

13  The main epidemiological studies were reported in the recently renamed *British Journal of Psychiatry* in 1964 (Kay, D.W.K., Beamish, P. and Roth, M. (1964a,b,c) 'Old age mental disorders in Newcastle Upon Tyne. Part I. A study of prevalence', *British Journal of Psychiatry*, 110: 146–58; Part II. 'A study of possible social and medical causes', *British Journal of Psychiatry*, 110: 668–82; Part III. 'A factorial study of medical psychiatric and social characteristics', *British Journal of Psychiatry*, 111: 939–46).

14  Markers of the status of the 'subdiscipline' include the appearance, first of the World Psychiatric Association monograph, *Psychiatric Disorders of Old Age* (1966, Manchester, Geigy) followed by the edited volume *Recent Developments in Psychogeriatrics* (1971) (D.W.K. Kay and A. Walk (eds), Headley Brothers, Ashford, Kent).

15  Alexander, D.A. (1972) 'Senile dementia: a changing perspective', *British Journal of Psychiatry*, 121: 207–14.

16  The reference to a rising tide seems to have appeared as the title of a British Health Advisory Service document, published in 1983 (Health Advisory Service (1983) *The Rising Tide*, Department of Health, London). The spectre of Alzheimer's disease as a major public health hazard has gained rapid, global acceptance since.

17  One of the first researchers to draw attention to the public health problem of Alzheimer's in the United States was Robert Katzman who in a series of articles in the late 1970s and early 1980s wrote of 'the prevalence and malignancy of Alzheimer's disease' (Katzman, R. (1976) 'The prevalence and malignancy of Alzheimer's disease',

*Archives of Neurology*, 33: 217–18) and later helped define the final rebranding of senility/senile dementia as 'Alzheimer's' in a 1980 paper (Katzman, R. (1981) 'Senile dementia of the Alzheimer type – defining a disease', in G. Maddox and E. Auld (eds), *Proceedings of Seminars 1976–1980*, Duke University Council on Aging, Durham, NC, pp. 19–40).

18 See, for example, Grunthal, E. (1926) 'Über die Alzheimersche Krankheit', *Zeitschrift für die Gesellschaft Neurologie und Psychiatrie*, 101: 128–46; Gellerstedt, N. (1933) 'Zur keuntius altersinvolution', *Uppsala Läkareforenings Forhandlingar*, 38: 1–193; Rothschild, D. (1937) 'Pathologic changes in senile psychoses and their psychobiologic significance', *American Journal of Psychiatry*, 93: 757–84; Rothschild, D. and Sharp, M.L. (1941) 'The origin of senile psychoses: neuropathologic factors and factors of a more personal nature', *Diseases of the Nervous System*, 2: 49–54.

19 Roth, M., Tomlinson, B.E. and Blessed, G. (1966) 'Correlation between scores for dementia and counts of senile plaques in cerebral grey matter of elderly subjects', *Nature*, 209: 109–10; Blessed, G. Tomlinson, B.E. and Roth, M. (1968) 'The association between quantitative measures of dementia and of senile changes in the cerebral grey matter of elderly subjects', *British Journal of Psychiatry*, 114: 797–811.

20 Cerebrovascular dilators had been marketed for much of the 1950s and 1960s as potential therapeutic agents with claims that they dilated the cerebral arteries and 'improved circulation'. Roth and his colleagues' work found no association between the extent of cortical ischaemic damage and the severity of cerebral arteriosclerosis.

21 The Thatcher–Reagan years were marked by the ideological influence of 'liberal' political economists such as Hayak and Freedman who championed the argument that market forces alone form the 'best' means of ensuring freedom and justice (see, for example, Friedman, M. and Friedman, R. (1980) *Free to Choose*, Penguin, Harmondsworth; Hayek, F.A. (1944) *The Road to Serfdom*, Routledge and Kegan Paul, London).

22 Evidence of a specific deficiency in those enzyme systems involved in the metabolic pathway of the neurotransmitter acetylcholine was reported in three key papers: Davies, P. and Maloney, A.J.F. (1976) 'Selective loss of central cholinergic neurones in Alzheimer's disease', *The Lancet*, ii: 1403; Perry, E.K., Gibson, P.H., Blessed, G., Perry, R.H. and Tomlinson, B. (1977) 'Neurotransmitter enzyme abnormalities in senile dementia', *Journal of Neurological Sciences*, 334: 247–65; White, P. (1977) 'Neocortical cholinergic neurones in elderly people', *The Lancet*, ii: 680–1.

23 Etienne, P., Gauthier, S. and Johnson, G. (1978) 'Clinical effects of choline in Alzheimer's disease', *The Lancet*, I: 508–9; Peters, B.H. and Levin, H. (1979) 'Effects of physostigmine and lecithin on memory in Alzheimer's disease', *Annals of Neurology*, 6: 219–21.

24 William Summers, one of the early tacrine researchers, wrote: 'THA is no more a cure for Alzheimer's disease than levodopa is a cure for Parkinson's disease. Just as levodopa ceases to have effects in patients in the final stages of Parkinson's disease we anticipate that oral THA will cease to have effects as Alzheimer's disease progresses' (Summers, W.D., Majovski, L.V., Marsh, G.M., Tachiki, K. and Kling, A. (1986) 'Oral tetrahydroaminoacridine in long-term treatment of senile dementia, Alzheimer type', *New England Journal of Medicine*, 315: 1241–5).

25 The 'cholinergic hypothesis' became a shorthand way of describing those models of Alzheimer's/dementia which saw the loss of cholinergic neurones as the core

aetiological foundation of the mental decline in dementia and the restoration of that cholinergic deficit as the means of remedying Alzheimer/dementia. See Perry, E.K. (1986) 'The cholinergic hypothesis – ten years on', *British Medical Bulletin*, 42: 63–9.

26  Since the NINCDS and ADRDA criteria were established they soon became linked to the FDA's requirements for anti-dementia drug trials, so that all anti-dementia drug trials conducted since the late 1980s have become driven by the Alzheimer terminology. Studies using drug compounds which originated prior to the 'cholinergic hypothesis' – variously thought of as improving cerebral circulation or cerebral activation – have tended to stick to more old-fashioned terms, but these studies invariably appear in non-mainstream publications (typically Francophone research) and clearly exist outside the contemporary Alzheimer canon (e.g. Dartenue, J.Y., Belloussof, T., Meriaud, M., Clavel, M. and Chousasat, H. (1978) 'Etude en double-aveugle du Praxiline dans l'insuffisance circulatoire du veillard', *Geriatrie*, 6: 325–7).

27  See Schneider, L.S., Olin, J.T., Lyness, S.A. and Chui, H.C. (1997) 'Eligibility of Alzheimer's disease clinic patients for clinical trials', *Journal of the American Geriatric Society*, 445: 923–8.

28  Witness the direct advertising in recent issues of *Modern Maturity*, the American Association of Retired Person's monthly magazine, of *Aricept*, the trade name for donepezil, one of the few 'anti-dementia' drugs currently approved by government drug licensing bodies in both Britain and the United States.

29  See Rockwood, K., Stolee, P. and McDowell, I. (1996) 'Factors associated with institutionalisation of older people in Canada: testing a multifactorial definition of frailty', *Journal of the American Geriatrics Society*, 44: 578–82.

30  Akesson, H.O. (1969) 'A population study of senile and arteriosclerotic psychoses', *Human Heredity*, 19: 546–66; Broe, G.A., Akhtar, A.J., Andrews, G.R., Caird, F.I., Gilmore, A.J.J. and McLennan, W.J. (1976) 'Neurologic disorders in the elderly at home', *Journal of Neurology, Neurosurgery and Psychiatry*, 39: 362–6; Nielsen, J. (1962) 'Geronto-psychiatric period prevalence investigation in a geographically de-limited population', *Acta Psychiatrica Scandinavica*, 38: 307–30; Parsons, P.L. (1965) 'Mental health of Swansea's old folk', *British Journal of Preventive and Social Medicine*, 19: 43–58. The rationale for such studies was stated clearly in Roth's 1980 account of priorities for psychiatric research in later life: 'Epidemiological and socio-logical investigations are needed to define the character and size of the problem that are . . . emerging and so make possible the planning of future health and social services for the aged' (Roth, M. (1980) in M. Lader (ed.), *Priorities in Psychiatric Research*, Wiley & Sons, Chichester, p. 92).

31  The term the 'Alzheimerization of aging' was coined by Richard Adelman, professor of biological chemistry at the University of Michigan, in a critical editorial published in 1995 (Adelman, R.C. (1995) 'The Alzheimerization of aging', *The Gerontologist*, 35: 526–32).

32  Perry, E.V. (1986), *op. cit.*; Hardy, J. (1997) 'Amyloid, the presenilins and Alzheimer's disease', *Trends in Neuroscience*, 20: 154–9.

33  See for example Breitner, J.C.S. (1994) 'Genetic factors', in A. Burns and R. Levy (eds), *Dementia*, Chapman and Hall, London, pp. 281–93.

34  Several studies have reported the protective value of education. Katzman has suggested that the more well educated a person is, the greater their 'cerebral reserve' (Katzman, R. (1993) 'Education and the prevalence of dementia and Alzheimer's disease', *Neurology*, 43: 13–20).

35 Gilleard, C.J. 'Is Alzheimer's disease preventable?', *Aging & Mental Health*, 4:101–18.

36 Thal, L.J., Carta, A., Doody, R. *et al.* (1997) 'Prevention protocol for Alzheimer disease', Position paper·from the International Working Group on Harmonization of Dementia Drugs Guidelines, *Alzheimer's Disease and Associated Disorders*, 11 (Supplement 3): 6–7.

37 For illustrative incidence studies, see Letenneur, C., Commenges, D., Dartigues, J.F. and Barberger-Gateau, P. (1994) 'Incidence of dementia and Alzheimer's disease in elderly community residents of South-Western France', *International Journal of Epidemiology*, 23: 1256–64; Ott, A., Breteler, M.M.B., van Harskamp, F., Stijnen, T. and Hofman, A. (1998) 'Incidence and risk of dementia: the Rotterdam study', *American Journal of Epidemiology*, 147: 574–80; Rocca, W.A., Cha, R.H., Waring, S.C. and Kokmen, E. (1998) 'Incidence of dementia and Alzheimer's disease: a reanalysis of data from Rochester, Minnesota, 1975–1984', *American Journal of Epidemiology*, 148, 51–62.

38 Meyer, M.R., Tschanz, J.T., Norton, M.C., Welsh-Bohmer, K.A., Steffens, D.C., Wyse, B.W. and Breitner, J.C.S. (1998) 'APOE genotype predicts when – not whether – one is predisposed to develop Alzheimer disease', *Nature Genetics*, 19: 321–2.

39 Katchachurian, Z. (1997) 'The five–five, ten–ten plan for Alzheimer's disease', *Neurobiology of Aging*, 13: 197–8.

40 Rai, G.S., Shovlin, C. and Wesnes, K. (1991) 'A double blind, placebo-controlled study of *Ginkgo biloba* extract (Tanakan) in elderly outpatients with mild to moderate memory impairment', *Current Medical Research and Opinion*, 12, 350–5; Le Bars, P.L., Katz, M., Berman, M., Itil, T.M., Freedman, A.M. and Schatzberg, A.F. (1997) 'A placebo-controlled, double blind, randomized trial of an extract of *Ginkgo biloba* for dementia' (1997) *Journal of the American Medical Association*, 278 (16): 1327–32.

41 One recent example can be found in Mahoney, D. and Restak, R. (1998) *The Longevity Strategy: How to Live to 100 Using the Brain–Body Connection*, Wiley & Sons, New York, esp. pp. 102–7.

42 Cf. Powell (1998) *op. cit.*

43 Downs, M. (1997) 'The emergence of the person in dementia research', *Ageing and Society*, 17: 597–608.

44 Kitwood, T. and Benson, S. (eds) (1995) *The New Culture of Dementia Care*, Hawker Publications, London.

45 Kitwood, T. (1997) *Dementia Reconsidered: the Person Comes First*, Open University Books, Buckingham; Feil, N. (1993) *The Validation Breakthrough*, Health Professions Press, Ohio.

46 Kitwood, T. (1997) *op. cit.*, p. 280.

47 See Goldsmith, M. (1996) *Hearing the Voice of People with Dementia: Opportunities and Obstacles*, Jessica Kingsley Publishers, London.

48 Kitwood, T. (1997) *op. cit.*, p. 144.

49 For example the recent US 'consensus' statement is about the diagnosis and treatment of 'Alzheimer's disease and related disorders': cf. Small, G.W., Rabins, P., Barry, P.P., Buckholtz, N.S., DeKosky, S.T., Ferris, S.H., Finkel, S.I., Gwyther, L.P., Khachaturian, K.S., Lebowitz, B.D., McRae, T., Morris, J.C., Oakley, F., Schneider, L.S., Streim, J., Sunderland, T., Teri, L.A. and Tune, L.E. (1997) 'Diagnosis and treatment of Alzheimer disease and related disorders: consensus statement', *Journal of the American Medical Association*, 278: 1363–71.

# CHAPTER 10

# The inevitability of the cultural turn in ageing studies

By the year 2020, one-fifth of the population of Western Europe will be made up of people over retirement age. Households will consist largely of single people or couples. Multigenerational households will be unusual and few adults will have experience of living with individuals from an older or a younger generation. Single people and couples of working age will be no better off than similar 'pensioner' households.[1] Consumption – how one spends one's time, money and other material resources – will continue to be a dominant theme in most people's lives whether or not they are working.

Whatever heuristic value it once possessed, structured dependency theory and the 'political economy' approach no longer provide a satisfactory understanding of ageing and old age. Post-work lives have become richer and more complex. Not only has this approach failed to acknowledge the agency that individuals exercise in retirement but it has signally failed to recognize the diversity of the social processes and structures that shape the choices available to people in later life. Four key elements underpin this diversity. Firstly, more people are reaching retirement age and within this population is an increasing diversity of cohort, class and gendered relations that guarantees a demographic heterogeneity. Secondly, successive generations moving through time have gained increasing access to financial, cultural and social capital. Thirdly, the way in which citizenship is expressed and exercised has been transformed, changing the very rationale and nature of modern welfare states. Finally scientific and technological advances, particularly in the fields of biomedicine and information technology, have provided a renewed challenge to any notions of 'natural boundaries' or 'fixed limits'.

The first element makes ageing a demographically central issue, while the second has established lifestyle culture as central to the experience of each and every generation. Successive cohorts have been exposed to particular moments in popular culture as 'youth culture' has emerged and taken root within each group. Though the form in which this occurs may differ, the experience for each generation is inescapable. The third element, the decline of mass social citizenship, has re-oriented the way governments address the link between retirement and old age. The final element, the technological breakthroughs in biomedicine and information systems, has fostered an 'aspirational science' that plays such a significant part in postmodern culture.[2]

All four factors have contributed to a general destabilization of age-based identities undermining the traditional equation between age, lack and need that the modern state established, expressed and reinforced. We have argued that this destabilization has been played out within the realms of self-identity, citizenship and the body. Our argument is not that there are no poor old people, nor that retired people do not, in some cases, experience significant limitations in managing their daily lives. Nor do we claim that retired people are free from the fears of impoverishment and dependency traditionally associated with ageing. Rather we are arguing that through emphasizing the plight of the poor and disabled within the retired population, an academic and popular discourse has been perpetuated that makes these phenomena the very essence of ageing and ageing studies.

## The implications of our argument for ageing studies

What are the implications of our argument for the future direction of social gerontology and the social sciences generally? We believe that ageing is moving to centre stage in all of the social sciences. Recognizing that cultures continue to be formed after working life is over is a challenge to both sociology and social theory. Both have tended to treat ageing as a residual category that is best left as a problem for social policy and one primarily concerned with endings. Both have seen ageing as constructed out of 'other' processes – modernization, social policy or biological decline – and not as something that is constructed out of the lived experiences of men and women seeking a satisfying and satisfactory post-working life. Productivity, disability and death have been the reference points from which to construct its meaning. Conversely, phenomenological accounts have sought to rescue old age from its position as a residual category by seeking to valorize the aged state as conferring moral worth. Neither position engages with ageing as a central element of social life. Ageing can no longer be represented as either a residual or oppressed totality.

The increasing diversity represented within the various age cohorts poses an equally pressing challenge to those foundationalist positions that dominate psychology and medicine. Within these disciplines there has been an overwhelming desire to delimit the parameters of 'normal' and 'abnormal' ageing. Loss and decrement have been endlessly assigned to one or other of these dimensions. Decline in memory, decline in lung function, decline in psychomotor performance, decline in kidney function – each arena plays out the same message. Some aspects are identified as 'abnormal', functional decrements that are actually or potentially remediable, while others are assigned to the category of 'normal', the inherent manifestations of the true nature of ageing. Ageing cannot escape from the coda of decline. Defining ageing as that which is intrinsic, universal and deleterious, the goal of both disciplines remains bound to issues of loss and finitude. The shift toward self-construction sits badly with the ontological assumptions of beginning, middle and end that predominate within these disciplines. Faced with the evident instability of the category 'normal ageing', these scientist-practitioners increasingly turn to the identification and measurement of that which is diseased, abnormal or impaired.[3] Notable by its absence is any interest in or attempt at understanding the majority of men and women whose post-working lives are constructed out of more than the prophylaxis of mental and physical decline.

## Opening ageing out

For any fraction within the retired population a particular 'take' on ageing can be highlighted. In the case of the UK, for example, just as a minority of older people are poor, equally it can be argued that a minority of older people retire abroad. This latter group could justifiably be the focus for studies on ageing. Pre- and post-relocation lifestyles

195

could be measured and theories developed about 'successful' and 'unsuccessful' ageing. This particular minority of 'emigrant' retirees may have an equal claim to represent the essence of what later life is about. Likewise, retired people pursuing new relationships through personal advertisements and through introduction agencies might well be minorities. And should they not also be the subjects of gerontological scrutiny as well as those who frequent day centres for 'the elderly'?

Is the money spent on anti-ageing cosmetics or anti-ageing 'nutraceuticals' worth less attention than the money spent on domiciliary care or on hip replacements? Are the lives of ageing personalities in the arts and entertainment industries less interesting to gerontology than the conversations of 70-year-old people suffering from 'Alzheimer's'? Is the movement of 'grey' capital in the pensions and insurance industries of less relevance than the proportionate spend on the nursing-home industry? What is it that makes social gerontology pursue such a limited vision of ageing as that which dominates its textbooks and journals – what is it in fact if not precisely those state policies toward 'the elderly' that the 'political economy' approach has done so much to berate? Not ageing, but social gerontology itself, has been constructed by the state and its 'old age' policies.

Rather than assume that the only aspects of later life that illuminate our understanding of ageing are the relatively decommodified aspects of health and welfare, we are advocating a more culturally oriented gerontology. In place of the endless surveillance of disability and welfare service utilization, we envisage gerontological social science beginning to pay closer attention to patterns of consumption in later life and to the cohort-based 'ageing' of generational lifestyles.[4] It needs to make a distinction between those features that constitute the cultural strategies of 'staying young' and those that constitute 'third ageism' within post-working lives. Instead of research to map out the boundaries between 'normal' and 'abnormal' ageing, 'successful' and 'unsuccessful' ageing, we would wish to focus on the contrasts between consumption that is oriented toward 'self-construction' and that which is oriented toward 'self-maintenance'.

How for example should we distinguish between self-maintenance strategies which represent actively 'staying young' and those that represent the gradual 'crystallization' of a generational lifestyle? Is Greer's advocacy of the adoption of a post-menopausal identity as a 'virtuosa of the art of ageing'[5] a call to a third-age self-creation or simply a form of generationally-bound transgressive self-maintenance? The point in raising these various rhetorical questions is to emphasize that ageing studies need to be released from their social welfare straightjacket. They must open themselves out to the variety of ways that ageing is now experienced by successive generations entering post-working life.

## The cultural divide: third-age and fourth-age futures

Even within the social policy agenda, there is evidence of a fundamental division. A faultline has emerged along the axis between the third and the fourth ages. Government policies toward pensions and social insurance increasingly emphasize personal agency and responsibility. Throughout the world, governments see later life as a matter of individual responsibility. The task of the individual citizen is to invest appropriately to create a post-work income that will enable him or her to live well in later life. Rather than assuming that leisure time can be bought and consumed completely during working life, it is as if leisure time is now to be banked during working life and spent increasingly after work is over. The last 50 years have not seen a massive expansion in leisure time that commentators in the 1950s and 1960s believed would occur as a result of increased productivity. The predicted transformation of working life never occurred. What has occurred, certainly in the last 25 years, has been an expansion in leisure time, but this period of 'after-work' leisure is one that occurs 'in retirement'. This is now the really big holiday that we are all meant to be saving up for, the one that 'never has to end'.

While the state seeks to retire from its role as principal provider for people's post-working life, governments internationally are more occupied than ever with the problems of disability and ill-health that affect people toward the end of their lives. Retired citizens, their embodied selves made fit by a lifetime of personal investments in the culture of late modernity, remain vulnerable to unforeseen changes in the value of their personal stock. This remains true of both the successful and the unsuccessful investor. Both can be equally hard hit. Under such circumstances it has been customary to turn to the state to help out in a spirit of common humanity. While this morality still retains its resonance, the fiscal implications lead to demands for changes, creating a contradiction with the disengagement that characterizes the state's involvement with the third age. Health care, its costs and its distribution remain very much an issue for all governments, even for those most committed to 'free markets'.[6] These concerns largely relate to the needs of an older population. The ills that constitute 'old age' serve both to dominate much of the discourse and practice of gerontology and to maintain the connection between age, lack and need that retirement policies seek to unravel. The third-age/fourth-age dialectic makes ageing an impossible point around which a politics of identity can form. For many people life after work is to be enjoyed; the freedom from work and its attendant responsibilities and burdens is welcomed even if not universally looked forward to. Increasingly post-work life is a meaningful juncture for both sexes, and in some ways more meaningful than those junctures that are more biologically situated, e.g. the menopause. Irrespective of their chronological age, most people see health as both important and good. The worries they have about it are shared across the generations, as is their response.

Government concerns over rising health costs and particularly the rising costs associated with 'long-term care' are motivated by long-term fiscal consequences rather than representing the collective worries of a particular generation or age segment of the population. Few people, even in the United States where there is extensive private health insurance, are choosing to purchase 'long-term-care insurance' and most governments have to raise taxes from the working population to defray the public costs of long-term care.[7] Attempts are being made to make long-term-care insurance as mandatory as social insurance, but in some sense this amounts to no more than another form of direct taxation, in much the same way that governments demand vehicle tax to defray the state's expenditure on transport infrastructure.

Fourth-age agendas remain agendas for 'the other' in contrast to the self-interest of third-age ones which are personal. Books are written about retirement, about how to make financial provision for it and about how to enjoy it. They are addressed invariably to the reader – how 'you' can write years off your life; be fitter and live longer; be happier and more energetic; be better off, etc. In contrast the textbooks about social care address impersonal 'elders' or 'users'. Few books would find a mass audience by addressing issues such as how you could ensure your time in a nursing home is as pleasant and as comfortable as possible, or how you can determine that you end up being better nursed in your dotage. Even those well-intentioned documents designed to ensure good-quality care in residential and nursing homes are written not for the end consumer but for the intermediaries who regulate or who are being trained to take responsibility for long-term care. No collective representation of 'old people' can be brought to bear on these fourth-age policies. Inevitably 'the frail elderly' remain as the 'other' – a problem always framed in the third person, for and by every voting adult.

The third-age/fourth-age dialectic is an important feature within the cultures of ageing. It represents a disjuncture between 'modern' and 'postmodernized' forms of representing age. Moreover it allows a focus on the issue of ageing rather than upon the aged. While it may well be true that some third-agers become fourth-agers, seeing this as a necessarily contingent relationship engenders a failure to take seriously the specifics of what post-working life means. By separating out the third and the fourth ages, it becomes possible to examine both the vertical and the horizontal stratification of later life. The vertical stratification arises from the influence of class, gender and, increasingly, ethnicity, each of which shapes the transition into and passage through post working life. This has been well documented, to the relative detriment of horizontal stratification which occurs as a result of generational and cohort experiences as well as the personal awareness of time passing and the interweaving of social, personal and physical change. The major thrust of our book, indeed its central argument, is the need for a much more active examination of the experiences and practices that make up individuals' post-working cultural lives. Much more attention needs to be given to the social structuring originating in the vertical divisions of class, gender and ethnicity. Equally, more attention should be given to the horizontal structuring of cohort and generation which is set against the evolution of 'post-war' youth culture and the continuing technological developments fashioning our material being.

## Yes, but . . . addressing potential criticisms

We anticipate several criticisms of the position outlined in this book. Broadly, we would see them as likely to focus upon four main points:

(a) the continued existence of poverty, lack and need within the older population that is structured by gender class and ethnicity;
(b) the physical reality of ageing and the inevitable age determination of disability and frailty, undermining any cultural capital that contemporary retired people may have acquired;
(c) the periodization implied in our thesis and its short timeframe making contemporary trends matters of passing interest, with no fundamental need to revise the traditional view of ageing as a matter of progressive emiseration and loss;
(d) the failure to engage with policy and moral frameworks around issues of equity and entitlement.

### Age is still a time of poverty, lack and need

Significant disparities exist within the retired population in both wealth and income. These inequalities reflect, in large measure, differential access to full-time, well-paid employment. While post-work self-identities may not be shaped by work, the individual's working life history constrains the range of choices that are open to them in retirement. Hence those in semiskilled and unskilled occupations, women and members of ethnic minority communities are likely to have more limited access to the kind of assets and income that white males retiring from white-collar occupations have. Moreover, those who retired some decades ago are also less likely to have benefited from the level of occupational pensions that contemporary retirees have. This group is also unlikely to have acquired many of the consumer durables that have become widely available in recent decades (VCRs, home PCs, central heating, freezers, etc.).[8] Consequently amongst the poorest households in most OECD countries there will be an over-representation of older working-class women and persons from minority communities.

However, these are not unique social phenomena that 'emerge' in retirement. At all ages, adults from black and ethnic minority communities are poorer, in terms of both assets and income. Likewise, at all ages, single adult women are poorer than single adult men and of course white-collar households are better off throughout adult life compared with blue-collar households. While these inequalities persist in retirement and may in some circumstances increase, these are not the kinds of social facts that either define or distinguish ageing from other periods of adult life.[9] The diversity that is emerging within the ageing population, the different voices and different lifestyles that are beginning to fashion our contemporary cultures of ageing may well be thrown into sharper relief by the presence of such inequalities. But they are not constructed out of those inequalities. If anything they are created out of the growing continuities that now exist between income and wealth in adult working life and in post-working life.

The transition to retirement and retirement itself are experienced differently by men and women.[10] While this is no doubt true, increasingly retirement is becoming a normative transition in both men's and women's lives. As pointed out in Chapter 3, while there are evident inequalities between single men.and women before and after retirement, it is also important to note that for single people there are trends toward the reduction in gender-based inequalities in retirement income. For married women, the situation may be more complicated but the assets and household income potentially available to married men and women at retirement are nominally the same. It is by no means clear that after retirement the actual use of disposable income is significantly different between husbands and wives.

After the age of 75 women are in the majority, and widows make up the largest defined group in that section of the population. The experience of widowhood seems to result in a distinct loss of resources for many older women for which there is no comparable male experience. Gender roles clearly do contribute to the creation of poverty during the course of retirement. This exaggerates some of the aspects of inequality created by the gendered division of labour and the disadvantages many women suffer during their adult lives. At the same time, as Gibson has pointed out, gender differences in the experience of ageing do not always favour men. Women live longer, sustain stronger social networks and experience fewer discontinuities during the course of their later life.[11]

While for some women, and particularly those from ethnic minority backgrounds, poverty may remain the most defining feature of their old age, it would be mistaken to identify the position of older women purely from this economic perspective. As we have noted in Chapter 4, the negative experience of age is more salient for women throughout the whole of their adult lives rather than just at one point in them. As Greer has argued, it may be possible for women to experience a degree of liberation in later life from the oppressiveness that the threat of age has exercised over their identity in earlier adult life. In short, the gendered nature of ageing needs to be acknowledged as much for its cultural context as for its equating ageing with poverty.

## The physical reality that is ageing: biological fundamentalism revisited

We have discussed already in Chapter 8 the question of the social limits to ageing. However, our failure to resolve the question of limits may be seen as little more than sophistry, particularly by those who would claim that bodily ageing is an inescapable experience that has always and will always govern our understanding of what it means to grow old.

In response we would argue that the 'meaning' of growing old is no longer so simple or so singular. People retiring at the turn of the century at age 55 may well experience a 25-year period of post-working life much of which will be free from the discourses and practices that constitute disability and dependency. Saying this is not to deny that some will be unemployed and unemployable, retiring on medical grounds to spend their final years as invalids, eking out a semi-pensionerhood. Of course there are the physical changes that most people experience as ageing, but these do not need to serve as defining moments in individuals' post-work lives. Health is the major preoccupation for most of the adult population, a modern-day virtue almost without a serious competitor. But our health-conscious society, and our life-prolonging society, affects younger and older adults alike. Birthdays are as much or as little fun at 30 as they are at 70.

The treatment of balding is now a serious business. A recent reviewer of 'treatments for hair loss' in the very model of a modern medical journal, the *New England Journal of Medicine*, had to have her commercial links exposed in order that readers would be alerted to the potential bias that the company who funded her research might induce. Such scientific seriousness about balding is illustrative, not so much of how superficial topics have become areas of research (a claim more often made about cultural studies than biomedicine), but because of how there is a new questioning of what once was largely unquestioned and not taken seriously. Whatever the future may hold, there is widespread recognition that our biological heritage is a matter of deep uncertainty – what it is, what effect it has and what it will be in future. The uncertainty and the challenges that are mounted in order to determine what is or is not natural are a central feature of our postmodern times. When venerable biomedical researchers such as Richard Peto and Richard Doll can publish an article in the *British Medical Journal* entitled 'There is no such thing as ageing', clearly the naturalness of old age is up for grabs.[12]

## The 'periodization' of being 'an ageing society'

It may be said that our concerns arise out of the passing flirtation with 'postmodernism' now evident in all the social sciences. In a similar vein, the idea of a fragmentation in the experience of ageing may seem to give undue credibility to passing trends in the markets that have enabled a minority of retired people to indulge in the kind of lifestyle consumerism that has previously been confined to younger adults.[13] This group, it can be argued, will remain a small and relatively insignificant minority. The majority of older people's lives will continue to be spent as before in the shadow of potential poverty, isolation, ill-health and dependency.

Our answer to this criticism is to simply point out that the demographic future of most developed countries is one dominated by a continuing shift toward an older population. There is likely to be a longer period of retirement or 'post-working life' accompanied by rising levels of affluence – on average – amongst retired people and, if anything, a slight fall in the rates of severe disability at later ages. Expecting any of these trends to suddenly shift into reverse seems implausible and would itself require a specific explanation. Times are changing. The majority of people living in the various 'worlds of welfare capitalism' have experienced a rise in their inflation-adjusted income and are better off at the end of the twentieth century than they were 10, 20 and 30 years before. This improvement in standards of living is mirrored in the improvements in working conditions and in the opportunities for leisure and self-development that an increasing fragment of the population now enjoy.

The changes that have arisen from many countries moving out of an industrialized manufacturing economy into an economy dominated by retail and finance capital have altered the position of many people's relationship to 'the productive processes'. To quote one recent post-modern sociological account:

> postmodernization involves a shift in patterns of differentiation from the social to the cultural sphere, from life chances to life styles, from production to consumption. . . . status will not depend on one's location in the society, especially its system of production and reproduction but on one's status accomplishments in the sphere of consumption, one's access to codes . . . while they may give rise to well recognised and sometimes oppressive inequalities they will not give rise to divisive or enduring ones.[14]

It is not necessary to adopt a full-blown postmodernist account of these changes to recognize the significance of this shift toward consumption. The widespread engagement with understanding the nature and origin of this change has preoccupied a whole generation of social scientists. While there may be a 'post' postmodernism, what is evident is that there will be no straightforward return to issues that dominated the concerns of mid-century sociology and social theory.[15] Consumption and culture show no sign of being eclipsed by other processes. Age's ability to resist incorporation into the commodifications of culture will diminish as age itself becomes increasingly commodified as a risk that influences lifestyle choices for adults of all ages. Just as 'ageism' in birthday cards will not disappear, neither will sales of nutraceuticals and cosmeceuticals[16] suddenly drop. Geriatric medicine will eventually be exposed as a form of institutionalized ageism while a more aspirational anti-ageing medicine grows in confidence (if not in competence). No age boundaries will institutionalize premature death or premature disability. No Habermasian consensus will form around the limits of 'aged' welfare. And in the end it will be evident whether or not we are misreading the signs when in 10 years' time we either publish a second edition of this book or are forced to reconstruct our argument and, with a very different title, 'go back to basics'.

## The moral critique

The last critical point we must address is the potential charge that we have ignored the key issues concerning the entitlements of retired people, the need for equity between the generations and the need to offer a moral framework from which to make sense of ageing. In short that we have unfairly dismissed the position of those gerontologists who draw upon the idea of a moral economy in later life.

In some senses this criticism misses the point of the book. We are less concerned with what ageing should or should not be, or what constitutes a 'fair' deal for retired people. Our concern is to highlight those processes and structures that are destabilizing any essentialist biosocial categorization of ageing. The outcome of these processes is a more heterogeneous and fragmented experience for people reaching retirement age as well as more contradictory practices by which to live one's life as a retired person. There are many cultures of ageing in contemporary society, not simply one that is driven by biological processes and steered by social policy.

Does this position mean that we support a neo-liberal welfare regime, demanding minimal state intervention targeted at the margins of need and lack? Does it mean that we deny any possibility of understanding cause and effect in accounting for social relations in later life; or that we believe ageing has become a 'hyperrealized' category whose meaning has imploded?[17] Are we advocates or opponents of 'consumer society'? Do we care about the circumstances of the retired population who are frail, poor and more often than not female?

Treating the differentiation of ageing as a social process does not mean we either applaud or excoriate it. It is a phenomenon of our times, one that we believe has important implications for society and the disciplines that seek to understand and interpret society to itself. We do not believe it is possible to make sense of this process by setting it against some totalizing moral or ontological position regarding either the true nature or the destiny of ageing.

We do, however, think that this process of differentiation and individualization of ageing offers considerable benefits through the creation of richer and maybe more significant cultures within the retired population. This will be accelerated by the processes of generational change that consumer society fosters. In order to strengthen the power of those cultures to be 'a presence' it is desirable that there are as many players as possible and undesirable that there are individuals shut out from the processes involved in making those cultures.

But the principles involved in the reduction of poverty, the avoidance of social exclusion and the maximizing of social goods and their access are not the principles of ageing studies. They apply at all ages and demand political action because of their very age irrelevance. If older people's lives and experiences are better and richer than before it is largely because of improvements in the conditions of people's working lives. In the United States, contributions to social security reflect rising incomes; likewise improved cover and returns from occupational and other personal investment returns reflect rising earnings, rising productivity and greater economic development. In Britain too, the improved economic circumstances of older people reflect a rise in standards of living, with better coverage and returns from occupational pensions and an increased accumulation of capital assets. In Germany, France and elsewhere in Europe where income in later life is derived more from the returns on compulsory pension and social insurance contributions, the improved status of older people likewise reflects the benefits of increased earnings and rising productivity during their working lives.

In short, the task of ensuring a satisfactory income in later life demands both increased social product and a more effective redistribution of that wealth, in order that the disposable incomes that people earn during their working lives can establish personally satisfying post-working lives. If, as recent analyses suggest, social inequalities tend to wane over time, in all forms of welfare capitalism,[18] it seems reasonable to pursue policies that minimize long-term disadvantage arising from short-term exclusion from the productive processes.

That said, the aim of an increasingly commodified economy is to maximize people's ability and willingness to spend at each and every point in their lifecourse. Structured inequalities are inimical to the expansion of retail capital, even if in the process they stimulate their own forms of temporary and stylized inequalities. The restlessness of capitalism as an economic and social system has been remarked upon by Marx as well as others who have followed in his wake. Out of this restlessness a great deal of energy and fluidity has emerged. The 'development' of capitalism over the last century has led to an increasing differentiation of status and lifestyle. Later life is now incorporated into that flux. To borrow a model from the psychology of intelligence, individual and social 'fluidity' is necessary for creative engagement in a culture.[19] Social policy that seeks to crystallize the category of 'old' or 'aged' can only serve as a brake toward realizing the expansion of post-work lifestyles and post-work cultures. To use Baudrillard's terminology, old age is one aspect of the social that needs to be imploded, leaving free a space for progress to take place.[20]

# Notes

1 See Wallace, P. (1999) *Agequake*, Nicolas Brealey Publishing, London.

2 See Sokal, A. and Bricmont, J. (1998) *Intellectual Impostures*, Profile, London, for a critical view of the use made of scientific discourse in postmodern writing.

3 Discussion of the increasing research focus on pathology in biological and psychological gerontology can be found in Adelman, R. (1995) 'The Alzheimerization of aging', *The Gerontologist*, 35: 526–32.

4 By the 'cohort-based ageing of generational lifestyles' we mean the changes occurring to a generational lifestyle, e.g. 'the 60s' or 'the 80s' expressed by different cohorts as they grow older. This occurs in two ways: firstly through the changes that occur in the generational lifestyle itself and secondly through the ageing of each particular cohort who have been 'exposed to' and 'engaged with' that culture.

5 Greer, G. (1992) *The Change: Women, Ageing and the Menopause*, Penguin, Harmondsworth, p. 416.

6 By the end of the century it is expected that the government – through federal, state and local government – will account for half of the total health care expenditure in the USA. Commenting upon this, John Iglehart quotes leading health economist Victor Fuchs 'No matter how committed the country is to the idea of free markets and capitalism, government plays a substantial role in health care'. See Iglehart, J.K. (1999) 'The American healthcare system: expenditures', *New England Journal of Medicine*, 340, p. 70.

7 The most recent figures available (1997) indicate that the largest contribution to the costs of nursing-home care in the United States comes from government sources (62 per cent) with only a very small proportion coming from personal health insurance schemes (4.9 per cent) (National Center for Health Statistics (1999) *Health, United States, 1999, with Health and Aging Chartbook*, Hyattsville, MD, Table 120, p. 289).

8 See Table 1.2 in Vincent (1995) for illustrative figures regarding differential ownership of consumer durables in later life (Vincent, J.A. (1995) *Inequality and Old Age*, UCL Press, London, p. 27).

9 Estimates of 'poverty' amongst those aged 65 and older vary. Calculating poverty rates (incomes below 50 per cent of the national median disposable income) for the period 1985–94, Goodin *et al.* estimate that 25 per cent of US 'ageing' households are poor; 12 per cent in Germany and only 0.3 per cent in the Netherlands. By comparison poverty rates amongst households of working age are generally lower – 13 per cent in the US; 6 per cent in Germany but the same, 0.3 per cent in the Netherlands. Goodin, R.E., Headey, B., Muffels, R. and Dirven, H-J. (1999) *The Real Worlds of Welfare Capitalism*, Cambridge University Press, Cambridge, Tables Pov1C and Pov1D, pp. 277–8.

10  See Bernard, M., Itzin, C., Phillipson, C. and Skucha, J. (1995) 'Gendered work, gendered retirement', in S. Arber and J Ginn (eds), *Connecting Gender and Ageing: a Sociological Approach*, Open University Press, Buckingham, pp. 56–68.

11  See Gibson, D. (1998) *Aged Care*, Cambridge University Press, Melbourne, esp. pp. 134–45.

12  Doll, R. and Peto, R. (1997) 'There is no such thing as ageing', *British Medical Journal*, 315: 1030–2.

13  For example, in France, 'recently retired people now have a standard of living which is higher than the young economically active' (Ogg, J. (1999) 'The big French pension debate', *Generations Review*, 9: 4–5).

14  Crook, S., Pakulski, J. and Waters, M. (1992) *Postmodernization: Changes in Advanced Society*, Sage Publications, London, p. 133.

15  We recognize for example that as pensions increasingly move to relying upon capital markets, retirement income may well become less reliable. Nevertheless we do not expect that the vagaries of international capital markets will lead to any return to the dominant role played by government-led pay as you go pension schemes that has characterized most of the twentieth century.

16  See Wallace, P. (1999) *op. cit.*, pp. 84–9.

17  Baudrillard, in his essay 'In the shadow of the silent majorities, or, the end of the social', outlines several 'hypotheses' explaining how 'our society is perhaps in the process of putting an end to the social, of burying the social beneath the simulation of the social'. In one such 'hypothesis' he describes the social as residue, that which is left after progress has marched on. 'We are in a civilisation of the supersocial . . . with the social expanding . . . as a rational control of residues and a rational production of residues' (Baudrillard, J. (1983) *In the Shadow of the Silent Majorities*, Semiotext(e), New York, pp. 72–3). In that sense the meaning of ageing has already imploded as the real lives of older people are increasingly replaced by the discourses of disability, quality of life years, 'user empowerment' and so forth.

18  Goodin *et al.* (1999) *op. cit.*, pp. 262–3.

19  For an account of fluid and crystallized ability and ageing, see Botwinick, J. (1977) 'Intellectual abilities', in J.E. Birren and K.W. Schaie (eds), *Handbook of the Psychology of Aging*, Van Nostrand Reinhold, New York, and Horn, J.L. (1982) 'The theory of fluid and crystallised intelligence in relation to concepts of cognitive psychology and aging in adulthood', in F.J.M. Craik and S. Trehub (eds), *Aging and Cognitive Processes*, Plenum Press, New York.

20  Baudrillard, J. (1983), *op. cit.*

# CHAPTER 11

# Concluding comments

There is an inevitable temptation to exaggerate the radical possibilities of a historical period when everything seems to be changing. The mix of change and continuity that has to be unravelled by social science is equally present in the changing landscape of adult life. Have we, in this book, been guilty of succumbing to an impressionistic account of these changes? We would argue no. We have placed a considerable emphasis on the cultural because it is increasingly dominant to the lived experiences of older people in much the same way as state social security and state pension schemes created the conditions for 'old age' earlier in the twentieth century.

By emphasizing the shifting cultures of ageing, we have sought to demonstrate a coherence to the study of ageing that has been buried in its identification with old age as a problem for social policy. We see it as necessary to acknowledge what in some senses should be evident to everyone – namely that ageing as experienced by most people for most of their post-working lives is no longer, if it ever was, a unitary experience. Certainly, it is not one exclusively characterized by disabilities, dependencies or indeed impoverishment. Rather than viewing ageing as a process 'disengaged' from the main currents of social life, one 'constructed' out of welfare and lack, it is necessary to situate ageing as a central constituent in the cultures of our times. Age and the resistance to ageing form the real agendas for gerontology. This truism will become more evident as the twenty-first century unfolds.

Ageing, not old age, has been the focus for the book. If old age has an essentialist status, structured and determined by physical decline and social marginalization, ageing can be seen as a process of negotiation between that and the statuses of adulthood. Negotiating how to remain an adult, how to develop as an adult and how to avoid the loss of adult statuses is a task confronting more and more people as they enter post-working life. This extended period of life after work is one of the impressive achievements of the twentieth century. It forms a central part of the complex and evolving processes of postmodern culture. We have argued that the social and cultural structures that influence these various individual negotiations are multiple, complex and increasingly differentiated. For heuristic reasons we have separated those 'identity'-forming processes that constitute 'third-age' cultural strategies (outlined in Chapter 3) from those that exemplify 'staying-young' ones (outlined in Chapter 4). To temporarily borrow from Marxist terminology there is a necessary distinction to be made between base and superstructure. We argued that the third age is derived principally from the rising economic status that retirement and pension schemes conferred upon the working population during the post-war period. The latter idea of an identity formed from resisting age is, in contrast, derived from the development of a consumer culture that has permeated the lives and experiences of successive adult cohorts. Although these two lines of thought are not reducible to one another, they have been contingent in recent North American and European history.

As we have noted, the status and position of the third age is not unproblematic in terms of its connection to the wider circuits of capital. While old age itself may be resisted, becoming a third-ager means that the individual opts out of having to sell their labour, a choice that is both permitted and welcome to most who now anticipate a post-working life financed through pensions and/or investment income. Although this decommodification of one's time is desired as a stable position by many, it remains potentially troubling to global capitalism. Living off retirement income results in a subtraction from available surplus rather than making a contribution to it. Part of the argument regarding the potential for intergenerational conflict draws on the impact of one generation paying out dividends to another. What this draws attention to is that, while much of the framework for under-standing old age may have become anachronistic, the shift toward these new 'cultures of ageing' has by no means sorted out many of the con-tradictions associated with consumer society. Celebrating the end of the fixed periodization of adult life, as some advocates of positive welfare have done, carries the implication that there may be 'no holiday' from working life for future generations. The fluidity of boundaries that current retirees are benefiting from may disadvantage those who come later. As income in post-working life becomes more dependent upon the performance of capital markets and less upon government-set benefits so the stability of that income depends increasingly upon a steadily expanding global economy. The history of capitalism over the last 150 years has not been distinguished by stability and the nature of post-working life may change in ways that are difficult to forecast.[1]

Equally unstable are our current understandings of bodily ageing and its potential transformations. Social policy and social gerontology have both assumed a fixed quality to old age, presaged upon a socially accepted natural involution to life, with its inevitable descent into physical decline and helplessness. The centrality of social policy to ageing has been taken for granted. As we have argued throughout, this position can no longer be sustained. Within postmodern culture the body has become a site of contradiction rather than a defining context. Medicine itself has begun to move away from its supporting and surveying role to challenge the determinacy of ageing. Mid-life cultural practices have increased the care given to maintaining healthy (and thereby non-ageing) embodied selves. Social and economic changes have altered the material conditions of both domestic and productive labour. Old age has become a much narrower and much more selective category of need, and policies toward retirement have shifted from ensuring a level of state provision sufficient for a limited and limiting old age to ones that assume an expanding period of post-working leisure and an expanding range of choices in which that time is spent.

While the economic remains a major determinant of the possibilities through which post-working lives can be experienced, the cultural increasingly has become the lens through which it has expression, justification and, particularly, authenticity. Old age traditionally has been thought of as structured by policy and physiology. Ageing, however, derives from a more complex matrix of historical determinacies at both collective and individual levels. The task we set ourselves at the beginning was to show how ageing has become one of the key cultural phenomena of our times. We feel we have outlined this cultural turn and traced much of its origin. We have made our case for the social sciences to take a radically new look at ageing. We now hope that those interested in the future of ageing will take up the challenge we have thrown down.

## Note

1 Brenner, R. (1998) 'The economics of global turbulence', *New Left Review*, 229: 1–262.

# INDEX

Index

214

# Index